dancing
beyond
cancer

dancing
beyond
cancer

A True Sedona Synchronicity

Brandon Strabala

Self-Published

Dedicated to My Late Wife, Danielle Elise Claire, may her memory dance on through these words.

Contents

Introduction

I am honored to have known an individual as unique, extraordinary, and loving as Danielle Elise Claire. Even though our time was limited, we lived a full life together. To this day, I cannot fully express in words what Danielle meant to me. Through this story, I hope to convey most of those feelings and emotions to my audience. A story of finding genuine love with an engagement so short we barely had enough time to plan our wedding. A wedding date filled with fear and trepidation but overshadowed with hope. Gratefully we had each other as we navigated our magnificent journey while facing a mighty nemesis. A testimony of love conquering all.

Danielle and I shared a connection that I have never shared with another living being. We truly had something unique, and it would be that connection that would give us the strength to face the struggles that lay ahead. We discussed this book and our story extensively before her passing. It was important to her that she could help contribute to it with her lifetime of knowledge. Putting our experience on paper would be therapeutic for me while also serving an even greater purpose. The lessons we learned and the mistakes we made would have a profound impact on both of us. I, most of all, had to learn from my mistakes for the sake of my wife.

It is a beautiful story that goes into the depths of love, loss, and ultimately recovering that which was lost. Through the journey, I was shown many signs that the universe was conspiring to help us against all the odds. Despite the many different names people give to the energy all around us, I found that God or Spirit dwelled within our days. Even when it appeared, all hope was lost, we found the inner strength or the perfect answers to guide us. Danielle and I both faced dark nights of the soul on several occa-

1

sions only to have a miracle manifest enabling us to soldier on.

My wife's life gives purpose to why this story needs to be shared. A life of mystery and intrigue surrounded Danielle throughout her twenty years in Sedona, Arizona. Several closest to her said she was like a cat with nine lives. She had so many close calls throughout her life; it was a miracle she was with us in the first place. Danielle was a survivor to her core; it was likely the biggest shock to all who knew her. Especially all who wished to be there but weren't.

As a society, we are failing. We must start helping those who are in need. So many in our society are suffering because of sheer ignorance. I seek to stomp out this ignorance and help our society move in the right direction to provide a safe place for people to heal or pass peacefully. We can't allow people to suffer needlessly in our society if we can make the situation better. I agree with Gandhi when he said, "A nation's greatness is measured by how it treats its weakest members." We have a long way to go before we live up to that measure of greatness.

In expressing the many problems, we faced; I hope to share the magic and miracles that carried us through. Although Danielle and I may have faced one of our planets most fearsome adversaries, it was us together that made the best out of terrible circumstances. An ending that without our genuine love, might have been far more tragic.

For as much as this story might seem tragic on the surface, there is so much more beauty hidden in this life; and Death is never the end.

1
A Wife and More

Danielle was more than just my wife. Miss Danielle, as most would know her, was an inspiration, a leader, a protector, a survivor, and a best friend to so many who crossed her path. To say I had the pleasure of marrying one of the most incredible women I have ever met would still be an understatement. I cannot even in this book express the impact she had and continues to have in this world. I only hope to convey a small portion of that which made Miss Danielle great, to you.

Since our first meeting after having dropped her off at her house on Inspirational Dr., I knew she had inspired me. I was inspired to be a better version of myself. I even stopped a 6-year tobacco addiction, cold turkey. I found myself inspired to express myself through dance being encouraged in her Dance studio by not only my future wife's support but also the support from all her students. I had to be voted in to be in her elite class; it wasn't completely Danielle's decision. She only sparked the inspiration for me to try out.

Living on Inspirational Drive must have been destiny. Danielle would spend nearly twenty years inspiring little dancers from her small dance studio in Sedona, Arizona. It was amazing to witness her actively kindle dance in all her students. I was only witnessing a small portion of what made Danielle's career so special. Many of her students were able to find their expression through dance because of her guidance. Even in my dance, she mentored me to be a better dancer. The lessons she taught still follow me to this day, lessons that made me a more confident dancer. I gained power with my dance that I would never have had without her.

Danielle, in her teaching, had a true method of giving power back to her students. Traditional ballet is far from allowing people to express themselves freely; it is about form; it has a rigid structure. Danielle still found this to be the best way to build a solid foundation within her students. Danielle said it was the best way to start all of her students. Having a foundation was important for growth into dance, as she would put it.

As the years progressed, she would allow her students more freedom. With freedom also came more responsibility. I was impressed by how she was able to teach not only dance but healthy life lessons. She never treated children as children but as potentially equal individuals, individuals who could earn the right to talk at the table as equals. She respected all people and children for who they were and would also provide an environment to foster this in all her students.

This caring nature is what made Danielle special. She would see people for who they were, and it was something we both seemed to share. She would see the infinite potential in even the most challenging children. In our conversations, she even mentioned that at one point, she worked with problematic children in New York City. There was something about her ability to get children to express themselves that made her a true healer. I know that it was her caring nature, combined with the power of dance that made her truly effective. To this day, I know the world is missing out from the benefit of such an individual. Her actions set her apart, but the experience gave her the strength to take those actions.

I, on the one hand, tend to see the better side in people always. In my experience, people are rarely out to hurt or harm me, so I don't always see the worst in people. Danielle would see people in their entirety. Those lessons come from a life filled with people attacking, disrespecting, or projecting jealousy. Danielle's experience was far different than mine as a white male. I won't deny the disadvantages our society makes for people who don't fit into that mold. Danielle was particularly cautious in life, especially since she was a strong, beautiful woman. It shouldn't surprise anyone that being a beautiful woman, has both its advantages and huge disadvantages. The disadvantages are a topic I found more interesting.

It was no surprise to hear all the stories she had about jerk guys. Being a male, I never had to endure the problems women face from men. It didn't mean I wasn't aware of the problem; there is just a huge difference from witnessing a problem and being a repeated victim of the problem. I sympathized with her feelings about men, considering I observed the behavior as a guy my whole life. I even ended close relationships over that type of behavior. Danielle and I connected deeply and would talk extensively on this subject. Conversations that do not have much to do with this story, other than I think the lifelong trauma contributed to the issues she faced with her cancer. Trauma that we resolved too late to make a significant difference. We desired to heal this societal problem, which we did find by the end of our journey.

Throughout life, Danielle helped by being a good example for her students. An example which continues to inspire me to be a shining example. She was a leader in that she led through action. She taught most of all through her actions, to do what is right. Danielle would do what was right even if it made her the bad guy; she wouldn't stand for misdeeds. She held herself to these standards, she held her elite students to these standards, and she respected those who couldn't always meet those standards. Her mistakes taught me how we say something is more important than what we are saying. She recognized the power and risks of being a big voice in a small town.

Danielle taught me many lessons about living in a small town. Sedona was not just a small town, but it is also a rather wealthy town. It isn't cheap to live here, and those challenges were constant struggles. She recognized how important diplomacy was in a town where rumors could spread like wildfires. In a world where people will cause harm to others to feel better about themselves, I understood her plight. She couldn't always stand up for what was right without having to face sometimes bitter consequences. The lessons she learned controlled many of her actions. She shared these lessons with me.

We were able to learn together. In our time, we were able to form a bond that I have yet to cultivate with another person in my life. Danielle was someone who I admire for her ability to communicate. She was my greatest teacher. Teachers would come in all forms to help us. Teaching us how not to behave or being shining examples of hope, as Danielle and I tentatively navigated our way through this dark space called cancer. We learned many lessons that we could never have imagined.

We didn't realize how much a community could help or hurt a situation. Many people must grow if we are to be successful in administering to the sick, elderly, or dying. Many nurses expressed to us the same concerns we observed from our own experience. Our, encounters showed us most people act inappropriately, a true source of anger for Danielle. Since being caring and compassionate seemed to come naturally to her.

Danielle often spoke of the times she would confront people for acting unfittingly. She told me about throwing people off her property for behaving inappropriately or if they put her students in danger. She was practically the enforcing arm of our local neighborhood watch. While there is not technically a neighborhood watch, she was the known enforcer.

Dangerous Speeding has always been an issue with dancing children wandering into the street. She always radiated her protective spirit, and she made sure many speedsters stopped the behavior. She had no problem involving the authorities, although she always hoped to handle the situation without their involvement. First, she wasn't afraid to stand up for what was right.

Danielle would walk right up to someone's house and confront them directly. She wouldn't avoid a confrontation if she knew it was the right thing to do. She was fearless when it came to protecting others. There wasn't anyone that intimidated her, and even when it came to the dangerous types, she was even more ferocious. Several of her friends even expressed witnessing the fire that was always part of Danielle. Danielle would call it her inner Kali, which represented her rebellious mother goddess nature. This protective motherly energy was a power she even aimed to tame.

In one of her more entertaining stories, she had to put her next-door neighbor in his place. He showed up to her door in his underwear. She had to throw him off her property while also setting him straight, with all the anger she could muster. She couldn't believe that he would show up at her dance studio in such horrendous attire. It didn't stop there, because after this he tried to run her over with his car. She barely escaped the incident while also calling the police on him knowing; he was having drinking problems. She said his DUI put an end to everything. He moved shortly after that happened.

Standing up for what is right also can be a difficult path to walk. People don't enjoy being wrong much less are open to being corrected. Schools teach us being wrong means failure, so these days it can be a challenge to right wrongs. Sadly, wealthy people are even less likely to respond well to being wrong, leading to many unnecessary life struggles for Danielle. It is sad that rather than admit to their faults, people will attack another's character, to avoid owning up to their shortcomings. This problem, according to Danielle, is even more ruthless when it is a woman vs. a woman. I have witnessed, heard, or been a victim to some of the most callous behavior, and not from men but women. I feel lucky that I haven't been the repeated target of jealous or sociopathic women like Danielle had to endure.

I learned more about how difficult being a woman in this world is from Danielle. The reason I most loved my wife, within her studio of dance, was her dedication to creating a safe space for all girls. It brought me so much happiness to know that she wouldn't stand for rude or elitist attitudes. It didn't matter who was the star dancer; everyone had the same opportunities. It was amazing to be in love with someone capable of creating such a space for self-expression. The loving experience she provided was incredible.

The protective spirit that she embodied was nothing short of miraculous. A protector of those that couldn't speak for themselves. Danielle spoke up on behalf of those that she knew didn't have a strong voice. A protector of children and the meek. I have met many since her passing that has only further proven the kind of person she was.

It touched my heart to hear all the stories about Danielle standing up on behalf of others. So many people said she stood in your corner no matter the circumstances. The more difficult the circumstances faced, the more of a friend Danielle would prove to be. She wasn't someone who bailed at the first sign of trouble. She didn't with me either. It made me even more proud to know her when I found out that her support of local businesses also saved those businesses. She would show up for people in every way that she was capable of carrying out.

Danielle would pay for services far in advance because she knew businesses would need the payments. She would repeatedly drop off food or offer emotional support for people going through a tough time. Several people mentioned that she stood up to people who were attempting to take advantage of a situation. Danielle wouldn't stand for injustice, and her righteous anger would always create a solution. The most entertaining part of the stories was Dan-

7

ielle's power in her presence, the fear she seemed to instill in those she confronted. "A force to be reckoned with" as several people put it.

Many have considered her someone who was always there to help. She was supportive; she knew how to listen. She also was good at coming up with solutions and would always be working to move forward. Danielle wasn't there to listen to problems unless that was the answer to the problem. Danielle was always someone who was there to improve someone's situation. Being of service to others was her natural gift. I experienced this in our relationship, along with all the people we encountered along our journey. My wife taught me that lesson more times than I can remember, and in ways that I still am trying to comprehend. I still hear stories of her magnificence from this world and the next.

Living in Sedona spiritual experiences are almost common-place, especially for those people who cultivate that belief. In my observations, I have found that death is far from the end. While there is naturally a sadness that we can no longer be present and experience the physical form, I've found that people are much more than just their physical representation. We have so many layers, and in those layers, we continue to exist. So, when people started sharing about how Danielle would appear to them in Dreams or through animal appearances, it didn't surprise me. I had similar encounters.

After almost a dozen people told me of their encounters, combined with my own experiences, I saw a huge pattern. Danielle wasn't just visiting people in their dreams, but she was helping people in the dreams too. I feel that it was just part of who she was; to be of service to others. Since I've found we carry so much of who we are to the other side, it made sense that she would still be serving people she loved. I'm excited to continue to hear more about the mystery that was Danielle, in this life and about her actions in the next life too.

I knew the moment I met her that she was unshakeable, she was confident, and yet still a huge mystery to me. I had never met anyone like her, so I didn't know what to expect. I was captivated to know just a little more about this mysterious woman. I could tell she had so much more just sitting on the tip of her tongue perched to tell me. The constant discussions, sharing of experiences led to me unraveling a story that could have likely made a wonderful block-buster movie. It was a life filled with experience, joy, loss, bliss, anger, and every other emotion you could imagine. Despite all the hardship she had proven herself a survivor, and a fighter for life.

Due to family issues, Danielle spent time as a late teenager growing up on the streets. She was a bit of a rebel and lived as a rebellious youth in Philadelphia in the '80s. She learned quickly to read people and be hyper-aware of her surroundings. The risks she faced as a beautiful young girl were scary. She said she often used the AIDS scare to keep herself safe from potential attackers, which also led her to date top local thugs for the best protection. I laughed when she mentioned some of the less savory men from her past. Regardless she was a survivor, and her knowledge of the streets blessed her with invaluable wisdom. Danielle used that wisdom to do more with her life than most people can fathom.

I used to call her my Dancing James Bond since the penalty of death comes with sharing anything further. She would usually share details from less classified stories of adventure and often survival. Danielle's secret life remained a secret even to me. The stories she did share usually did not involve hunting down bad guys, even though I enjoyed those the most.

Danielle's crowning achievement was beating a virus deadlier than HIV, and the culprit's name still alludes me. She beat that nemesis using herbs and hyperbaric oxygen chamber treatments. It was three weeks of hell, but she overcame certain death. She also had the strength to recover from a nearly fatal amount of blood loss later in life. There was the neighbor who almost ran her over with a car or the time she was even kidnapped by a serial killer, which was classified, but interesting to know she survived it. Hearing people confirm the stories, told me that she was truly a survivor.

She even developed Lupus, an autoimmune disease, that she eventually put into remission. In addition to battling total adrenal failure that occurred almost simultaneously, nothing seemed to keep her down. She even used the lessons to offer support to others who suffer from similar issues. Several people mentioned the beneficial wisdom and ideas she shared about how she put her diseases into remission. She didn't do things the way most people do, but she did do things her way, a way that always seemed to work for her.

I heard tales from people that made me realize that Danielle had shared many important experiences with many people. Living in Sedona for over four years has brought more richness in my existence than I could have ever imagined. Only now do I realize that for twenty years, my wife was able to share that knowledge of those experiences daily with wonderful little dancers and amazing people across Sedona. I am grateful that she shared so many of her experiences with me, considering those were the ones that left the greatest impact on her life. It mainly is the stories of her kindness that have truly touched my heart.

Most of all, the parents who have told me the difference Danielle made in their children's lives. She showed a sense of love and passion for her craft that was indescribable. Parents were even telling me that their children showed improvements in all aspects of their lives after only a short time of taking her classes. Danielle even showed up as a second parent for many children. She was a rock and pillar for many who faced trouble at home. Her past gave her great insight and compassion.

I again wonder at the real number of stories that could be told about how amazing she was. I know I've only met a fraction of the people whose lives she touched, which leads me to conclude that there are so many other people out there who have had their lives changed by Danielle. It also means that many people are likely still receiving her help from the afterlife. Even in my life, it feels like I have a completely indescribable friendship since I have no other friendship to compare it to, she is still the Best friend I've ever had.

After her passing, I found out just how many people truly loved her and considered her to be one of their best friends. It touched my heart in so many ways to know that was just the person she was. It made me look again at what it means to be a good friend. I realized that I hadn't always been the best friend possible, and now I have an example. Danielle's example of friendship should be something we all strive towards achieving.

I love to admit where I fall short because it means that I can rise above. Danielle was one of the best teachers for me because she knew how to point out my shortcomings while doing it in a way that allowed me the opportunity to grow. I didn't realize it at the time, but as much as she was helping me to grow past my limitations, I was equally teaching her to accept hers. Our story together tells of this in so many ways. It was that mutual connection that we both needed to mirror our shortcomings so that we ultimately would be allowed to grow past them.

Friends of Danielle's still tell me about how they miss brainstorming with her. Since Danielle knew how to listen, she would often have the solution to the problem without having to tell the person a thing. People, when allowed to talk about their problems, are often freed from the energy they were holding on to in the first place. Danielle knew this better than anyone. There was no stewing in someone else's misery; it was about getting to the root of the problem. I think it is why psychiatry works so well; many people need a safe space to express their feelings. I like to express my feelings through dance; one thing my wife loved about me.

My wife loved her dance students more than anything else in the world; it could inspire jealousy if I were a jealous person. I only want to express how much she truly cared for her "children." They were one of the biggest reasons for many of the decisions she made with regards to the dance studio. She did things most people wouldn't do, to keep the dance going, even enduring great pain physically and emotionally.

Danielle projected an image that she was indestructible to anyone who knew her. It was something we both seemed to have in common. We were unbreakable; nothing could hold us down. Her students even joked about it regularly. Her students were constantly confirming the more outrageous stories that Danielle would tell. I didn't need the validation, but it was nice.

When it came to her students, they were the priority. She made sure that with all her communications and letters to the community, she was always thinking about the students. While I may not have always agreed with her methods, I knew I need to support the decisions she was making. She had the experience, and it was not in my place to recommend actions to issues I lacked experience. It was one of the lessons I had to learn the hard way. One of the many lessons I promised her I would share with the world. It is an honor to be of further service to someone who is still so important in my life.

Her students put her on a pedestal, and for that matter, I put her on a pedestal. The most interesting person I have ever encountered, combined with being stunningly beautiful inside and out. It was hard not to see the power she held just being herself. The

11

respect she almost demanded was hard to ignore. It wasn't a show either; it was a conscious effort on her part. While she was aware that she could behave another way, she wanted to hold herself to the standards as an example to others. The genuine kindness, concern, and love she showed to all people she encountered were impeccable. It made me nicer, kinder, and more loving just being around her. I'm sure our expressions of love made a few people nauseated.

We were truly inseparable, from the moment we first met. We were connected at the hips, hands, and feet. We showed that we could dance through life as a power couple; we didn't need anyone else. Both she and I had spent many years on our own, supporting ourselves, being productive members of society, and now we had each other. It was a miracle to have found someone who I could so easily mingle into my life. We were truly meant to be together.

I was able to meet her in her full power as a woman, and as a kindred soul looking for a connection. We shared so much in common. We both had a passion for dance that can't even be quantified. My mission continues because I know that I would have pursued my passion for dance sooner had I received the encouragement I saw Danielle give her students every day. I know that after many years of influence, people like Danielle continue to make a difference. If only we could have more Danielle's to inspire, lead, protect, and befriend all those who need us today.

2
A Life Unchained

I hold joy knowing that Danielle will live on through all the lessons that she taught and the example that she lived by. It is who she was that I find so incredible and that is who I want to introduce. It is more than just something she did; it is who she was that made her special. Everything exuded with such a level of grace and elegance. Her spirit was wild, and her life was beyond remarkable. Danielle was a lover of Dance as much as a lover of teaching the art form she loved so much. The lives she affected and changed will forever remember her and the legacy she instilled.

It is this legacy that has left so many who truly knew her with a huge hole in their hearts. I'm sad the world was robbed of such an incredible individual. Many lost a true friend, mentor, and mother. Her ability to be an authentic friend cannot be replaced. I too fall short of her greatness. Danielle was truly the best friend I have ever had, and she inspired me to be a better friend, a role model, and a better lover of all people.

She was truly a pure soul, a soul, which, through my experience, often becomes a target for people of unsavory character. I can't explain the male desire for a pure woman and the ability to tarnish that purity with basic desires. It didn't help that her physical beauty and dancer physique was something that rivaled the world's most beautiful models and actresses. She was a true beauty inside and out. She was something rare, and for many, a prize of conquest. Some even viewed her as the perfect art piece for their lives, nothing more than another thing to add to their treasures.

Danielle told me many stories of very arrogant men whose behavior was outrageous. The behavior that comes from men who don't get the concept of "No." Many times, I have witnessed as men pursue women in ways to win them over regardless of what the woman wants. Most times, these are men who are obsessed with stunningly beautiful women. Danielle is one of those stunningly

13

beautiful women and a perfect target for all those men who are constantly on the hunt.

Unfortunately, many women have expressed being overwhelmed by men and their displays of affection. Often women suffer from the extreme advances of men after repeatedly declining. The men see it as an obstacle to be overcome, simply needing the right coaxing. I've ended close personal friendships with guys who won't respect the boundaries of women. Many people seem to test boundaries; it must be in our nature, but some men think boundaries are challenges to be overcome. This pure intention to find ways around boundaries can reach truly dangerous proportions.

It blew my mind to hear even more horrific stories from Danielle. To this day, the one that still causes me to cringe is about one of her past serious relationships. From my understanding, this relationship lasted over seven years, having many ups and downs. She even helped to raise his two sons over that time. To the outside world, their relationship was perfect. It was behind closed doors that the extreme levels of disrespect occurred. While his general behavior and sociopathic tendencies aren't worth mentioning, there is one situation that bears mentioning.

Since Danielle was a Dance teacher, it meant that each dance semester would have a huge recital to display all the progress made by each student. Three times a year would be a time of high-stress overload for over a week leading up to each event. Danielle would put all her creativity, love, and care into each event. It would be special for everyone involved. I even lived with someone who worked for her during that time as a personal assistant and chef. He had nothing but the best things to say about working for her.

It was during one of these recitals that there must have been some tension in her relationship at home. A relationship she had nurtured for over seven years. She practically considered herself a mother to the children as was in her nature. Nothing could have prepared her for what was about to happen.

Danielle had gone in for the day to prepare for the recital. She would rent the local amphitheater for thousands of spectators to sit in attendance. There was a lot to do on the day of a show; it was the reason she would often hire help. She spent the day setting up and she expressed that everything was going perfectly as the show started. It was shortly into the show she realized that she left some-

14

thing at home. Thankfully she lived five minutes down the road and could quickly run home. During an intermission she ran home, to find one of the most horrible scenes she could have imagined.

Her lover, including his children, had packed up everything in the house that was theirs and left in one afternoon. Without warning and notice, they disappeared out of her life. They left only a note. I would never learn what was said in the note, but it honestly doesn't matter. It devastated her to have something like that occur on a day that was so important to her. Clearly, that man didn't understand just how important her recitals were to her and her students. It is this complete lack of compassion for others that pushes my buttons. People can't just do what they want at the expense of others. The behavior is unacceptable, and I believe most would agree.

Both Danielle and I had been victims to male predatory behavior throughout our lives. I would have to say that in my case the advances, while sometimes flattering, are completely unwelcome. I respect people, but I have had my fair share of men who don't respect the boundaries I will put up. It is this lack of concern for boundaries, that often causes much trauma in this country and all over our planet. Danielle understood this from the lifetime of teaching beautiful young women. Much of her experience like my own has come from listening to others and applying what I have learned in my own life. Danielle even taught me more about my traumas, some of which were quite revolutionary.

Danielle shared with me an experience of being violated by a massage therapist of the opposite sex. She had fallen asleep at the time and awoke to her sexual arousal, and it quickly turned more sinister as she became aware of what was occurring. Someone in a position of power had stepped across an unspoken boundary and violated her personal space. She awoke to his fingers inside of her, creating pleasure she never intended to have. It was a confusing experience to have the enjoyment be jaded by such a lewd act. It hurt me to hear this, but it also made me recount a similar experience I went through.

I too, had felt the power that someone had used over me to make me feel a certain way, that I didn't choose to feel. Through sensual touch, predators convince the victim that it is okay, that something that feels so good isn't wrong. It is abuse, it is wrong on every level, and it is occurring every day all around us. If only we would open our eyes to the behavior, then we might start addressing the problems.

My own experience was quite similar. I had needed some massage work on my legs as I had slightly injured myself playing soccer the previous week. I don't think I ever expected a simple leg massage from a qualified and licensed massage therapist would be anything other than that. It didn't go at all the way I expected as first he lightly grazed across my private parts. I was immediately alerted while also uncomfortable about the experience. I didn't stop the massage, thinking it truly might have been accidental. I knew better the second time it happened as it also included a far more sensual graze. I was appalled. I immediately jumped up and expressed my disapproval. I never expected the response I received.

This man decided to point out the fact that I had become aroused by his touches. He used my arousal to turn the scenario back on myself, telling me that I should explore my desires. Honestly, I couldn't explain how a man could have brought me to an excited state. I felt so violated not just physically but mentally too. I had never felt feelings towards men, ever. I had plenty of friends who even wished I was curious, but it never interested me. This violation hadn't inspired me to explore the experience; all I wanted to do was leave. I left as soon as I gathered my things.

I don't have the scars that many live with because I only experienced it once. I never had to endure extended abuse from family members or other predators. I am grateful for that, but I also didn't understand how differently she and I dealt with similar trauma. I was able to let it go rather easily because I found a silver lining in the experience.

If a man could make me feel that uncomfortable, then I probably didn't need to question my sexual orientation. I also didn't have to act like a man to be a man. I can embrace my more feminine attributes versus pretend they don't exist. Some men act manly to prove to others that they are straight. I wear more pink without worrying about what others might think. I grew in my experience, while Danielle faced far more psychological issues.

I hadn't realized just how violated I was until I talked to Danielle. It made me understand further the traumas she had endured her entire life. Traumas that she shared included the traumas she shared with no one. It would have been impossible for her to share all the traumas from her life with me; it wasn't our primary focus and won't be mine either. Our focus was on the joy we could find in every experience we were given, not to muddle in the sadness of the past.

Danielle told me about the two violent physical rapes that also happened to her. These were far more traumatic to her than the massage therapist. They aren't stories I can share much detail about since Danielle only shared bits and pieces. Suffice to say she was able to help capture and imprison one, and never told me about what happened to the other. Considering her top-secret past, I knew better than to ask questions she wouldn't answer. She always seemed to have a desire to make things right. The local Sedona Police Department attests to many arrests as a result of her efforts.

Danielle lived a traumatic life, despite the grace and beauty she actively cultivated in her life. Danielle had a difficult life as a woman, including over thirteen miscarriages throughout her lifetime. Despite all her efforts to be a mother, she could never make it very far through the pregnancy. Thankfully she was never short of children in her life. Despite her shortcomings, she lived in an abundance of glorious children. Dancing and her students helped keep her sanity through all the trauma.

It broke my heart to hear about the miscarriages. It was something that I never felt Danielle had fully healed from, especially one instance that stood above all the others. Many years before I met her, she was engaged, and she was planning on starting a family. Her fiancé traveled for work, and sadly on his trip suffered an accident that claimed his life. She found out shortly after that occurred that she was pregnant with his child. I couldn't imagine what she went through during that time even after she explained it to me. To end the story with losing the baby too, Danielle had to be mentally devastated.

Left alone, with insurmountable losses, Danielle told me of the struggles she faced. The sadness and depression were overwhelming. To cope, she slept on the red rocks under the stars. Being under the night sky brought her a sense of peace. Danielle told me how much she isolated herself from people during that period of her life. Often, she hid her traumas from her students. I can't completely explain why she did this, but I feel it was to protect them.

Only her senior students shared in the stories that were inappropriate for children.

I only pray that people aren't left to fend for themselves in those situations. I found that Danielle spent much time retreating from the world after the biggest traumas. This understanding helped me realize more and more that it takes time to come to terms with big traumas. Danielle was my greatest teacher to learn methods she used to grow past the pain. I have yet to find a way to stop suffering, but I have learned lessons on how to cope better.

My greatest lesson being the power of movement. I found the risks that arise when I'm not moving a lot, and I've seen the benefits of creating a lot of movement in my life. Life lessons that have gone back through decades, including my youth playing soccer. As someone who suffers from expressing anger and anxiety, it is important I have ways to move my energy. Dancing has become a powerful medicine in my life that brings healing in my body and my mind.

The dance was always a big part of Danielle's healing. She expressed her emotions as I do through dance. Depending on her mood, she could show such emotion in her dance that it would bring people to tears. Danielle knew the power of expressing those emotions and the power of expressing those feelings in the form of something she loved. She found through dance ways of transmuting her traumas. Her presence was even healing to those who watched her.

Danielle danced with a Passion that few people express in their lives. The passion she danced with could have sent her on to glorious heights of fame and glory. She told me of the many times people proposed that life to her. She decided every time to pass on that life, realizing fame was not something she wished to achieve. Her goals in life were far simpler. To do what she loved in a place that she loved. Sedona, while not the perfect place, was a place she wanted dancing to thrive.

Danielle was for eighteen years, "The" Dance teacher in Sedona, AZ. Several others had tried, but no other teachers had made the commitment she did. Danielle had brought big town experience to a small mountain town. In the New York Dance community, she was well known. Her talent had gained the attention of many aristocrats who lived in the city. She rarely name-dropped but on occasion would point out actors whose children she taught, but I honestly don't remember a single one.

Danielle taught and performed Dance for nine years in New York, including performing in Cats on Broadway. Despite her talent she chose to teach thousands of children over the years, most of those years taught out of a Studio connected to her house in Sedona. For much of the '90s and until the recession business was great. She was even awarded several women's achievement awards for running a successful business locally.

Danielle told me stories of how she exercised her independent spirit during her life, including choosing to leave home at an early age. She accomplished great things with little resources, including putting herself through an accredited dance academy in New York City. It is amazing to hear how she rose from practically nothing, to become the woman she was when I met her. The stories she told of her days in New York were fantastic, outrageous, and heartbreaking. It was the heartbreaks that weighed the heaviest on her heart.

Danielle witnessed eighty of her friends from the Dance community lose their lives to AIDS. She expressed the devastation it caused throughout the community. People were afraid of the disease. The disease held a horrible stigma, which caused many to reject the infected individual. Danielle didn't fear the people who had AIDS or HIV. She held space for compassion and sympathy. The incredible person inside her decided to show up for eight people who had been abandoned by everyone in their lives. She told me of the horrors of dying of AIDS when the outbreak first appeared. What the disease did to the body was frightening to witness. The fear caused many friends and family members to act irrationally. For all too many, it was a terrible and lonely way to die.

The stories she told of how people would treat the sick and dying were appalling. They would walk in and blame the person or lash out with cruel words. They are expressing all their anger and frustration to the one person who doesn't need that release. Danielle would not stand for inappropriate behavior and was not afraid to throw people out. I would have to say that people's behavior towards the sick and dying is, I guess you could call it, complicated. I have an entire chapter dedicated to this topic as it is something, I ended up going through extensively with Danielle.

I made many mistakes myself. I am far from perfect. However, there is very little that I regret because I always did everything I could to fix my mistakes. Some mistakes I still wish I never made, and this book will help, so others don't make the same mistakes. It isn't always easy to realize when people need help, especially ourselves. Danielle and I encountered many people who behaved poorly and some beautiful souls who acted admirably. We came across simple mistakes all people can make. Despite the blunders often time, people neglected to offer help in the first place. Fear cripples many into never taking proper action.

Danielle's life was full of taking proper action. Danielle tried to live a life of proper action. Living in a big city, she learned the power of presenting the right image. The transition to a small town taught her even more lessons about the power of projecting a positive image to the community. I don't know if Danielle would have moved to Sedona in the first place if she understood half the troubles she would face.

Sedona had captured her interest many years before she moved from her home in New York City to the desert southwest. It was another instance where life decided to tell her she must leave the big city. She expressed how healing Sedona always felt when she visited. This natural healing energy drew her to one of the most magnificent landscapes, in my opinion, only bested by the Grand Canyon. The beautiful views are unforgettable, and the people who live here are beautiful. Sedona is magical, and Danielle appreciated the beauty that is Sedona. Despite all the problems she faced with people during her 20 years in town, she never ended up moving.

I appreciated the insights she would share about living in a small town as I grew up in cities many times larger than Sedona. It isn't hard to hide from people in a huge city, however living in a small city comes with its own set of problems. Challenges we would come to realize in their entirety as we progressed together as a married couple. We would come to many realizations about why people behave in ways that defy common sense.

It was incredible the way that Danielle and I connected in our understanding of the problems of "normal" society. She and I both had zero tolerance for injustice or cruelty. Which we both agreed were plaguing society. We both chose to live by example to put an end injustice and cruelty. We each did it our way.

Danielle accomplished this in ways that I can't even convey.

She stood up against the male ego that pushes and manipulates its way to gain what they want. She endured much criticism and verbal abuse for simply doing the right thing. Today those who choose to do the right thing are rarely celebrated or applauded. Often, they become targets for gossip and rumors which are aimed to discredit those who are in the right. I can't hear one more guy complain about his girlfriend being mad at him, when I know that he is unfaithful, lies, or manipulates her. Despite her best efforts, she was still often a victim of the male ego.

Danielle Elise Claire was a beautiful example of the Divine Feminine, the energy of Lilith. The woman in the Bible who walked away from Adam in the Garden for she wished not to be his servant or object of desire. Danielle told me Lilith was banished to the sea for her slight. Then God created Eve to fill Adam's Desires. I found other versions of the story, but I always enjoyed Danielle's interpretation. A perfect representation of what she stood for. Danielle would not willingly be the servant or object of another person's desires. She stood up for herself almost as much as she stood up for others. A remarkable person in every way and that is how she lived her life.

We are all incredible people living incredible lives. Only by looking at the synchronicities in our lives can we hope to gain true meaning to what our existence is all about. Our lives each have more potential than most people realize. We each have so much to offer this planet and the other people in our lives when we accept the path life is trying to provide. Some call it being in the flow, others refer to it as the zone, while others may call it divine inspiration. It sounds great, but it is not an easy state to achieve. It seems the more you do the right thing and follow the right path, the more challenging the path seems to become. I guess I'm trying to tell you that through my experience and observation, the best things in life are never easy.

It is only by facing the challenges, heartache, and pain that can hope to achieve something bigger than ourselves, become greater than the sum of our parts. The universe has allowed each of us to follow a path that could change the world; few say yes. However, many today are following these ancient lessons. All the Prophet's, Savior's, and Enlightened individuals of our time have told us similar stories and spoke about the path that leads to infinite beauty. It takes understanding the ugliness in the world that people truly find the greatest appreciation for beauty. In facing the ugliness, Danielle and I found much-hidden beauty.

Our journey together, through the hardest part in Danielle's life, was a gift more than simply a curse. A gift I didn't fully understand but do now. I am thankful I could be there for such an incredible person through one of the most horrible Cancers existing on the planet. The importance of allowing someone to die on their terms is something that I cannot overstate. Danielle didn't want to go into an assisted home or a hospice center. She wanted to stay in her house, and it was one of her greatest desires.

However, we lacked the support that could have made it easier for both of us. It was heartbreaking to hear that many people never have the support we did. Like us, many families don't do what is necessary to help each other out, and economic conditions have made that even more of an issue. So many choices are boiled down to what the family can afford as opposed to what is best for the person in question.

Danielle didn't want to end up in some medical establishment because she knew she would die quicker. It doesn't surprise me when I hear about how people pass more quickly in nursing homes. It made more sense after I learned about the medical practices for people nearing the end of their lives. Hence the primary goal of those places is to medicate people to the point that they feel nothing. Something that I will say is the opposite of what we went through. Medications prescribed from most doctors were practically ineffective throughout the entire process. The resulting severe side effects being more problematic than the original issue.

Our journey is far different than your traditional Cancer patient. We didn't follow the traditional medical approach, and it brought many unforeseen consequences. Our attempts to work with the medical establishment were even disastrous or counterproductive. Danielle lived by her own constitution.

Danielle was not normal in the fact that she practically never drank alcohol, because the hang-over would last for days. She didn't even smoke marijuana as an adult. Although she eventually admitted that she did do it in her youth, stopping when it started making her paranoid. She was hypersensitive showing even legal medications were problematic. She couldn't take over the counter meds without nasty side effects. She was as pure a person as I have known.

Finding medications that would help with her health problems were far more challenging. This story will discuss the challenges Danielle and I encountered when facing a traditional medical industry that practically solely uses prescription medications to solve the health problems that arise. The irony of the situation is I was actively working in the counter industry, helping all the cancer patients the mainstream medical industry had already failed.

My first year in Sedona was nothing like what I would have expected. I had heard that Sedona is a place that can chew people up and spit them out. I have observed this repeatedly and heard from many other sources, strange and interesting stories. The many discussions revealed how the natural energy that exists in this town has a unique effect on people's lives. Many refer to it as a journey through the dark part of your soul. The energies that exist in Sedona seem to accelerate one to a higher level of one's purpose in life. It brings many struggles and yet to those who persevere great rewards await.

Rewards that may not always seem like rewards. I doubt many would see the rewards in the initial thought of my story. How there be a silver lining in such a tragedy? I hope this story will shed light on finding the good when all else seems lost. While Sedona affects everyone differently, those who are open to life and new experience will be in for the ride of their lives. Those who fight change are presented with a barrage of challenges until one either gives up and leaves town or faces those inner demons head-on.

In my experience, I found this to be true beyond words. To say life works out in mysterious ways is an understatement. The countless people who come through town and have mystical if not paranormal experiences are so numerous that there are bookshelves dedicated to the subject. It will take an entire book to fully convey the bizarre if not a synchronistic string of events that led me to write this book. It goes beyond words to tell you that the sorrow I feel at the loss of my wife has led me down a different path in my life; it has given my life more purpose. I am unchained from the limits I once had.

23

3
The Meeting

It was August 11th, 2015, and it was a day like no other because it was the only day every year that was also my birthday. Like any other summer day in Sedona, AZ, it was blistering hot. Occasionally we would be blessed with evening monsoon showers, but temperatures hovered around 100 degrees in the sun. However, I was still greatly enjoying my first summer in Sedona.

I had moved about four months prior from Tucson, Arizona, which is about 3.5 hours south of Sedona. The State Capital, Phoenix, our largest city, was directly in the middle. Thankfully the weather in Sedona is about 10 degrees cooler than Tucson and 20 degrees cooler than Phoenix. After 16 years of unbearable heat, I was thrilled that the thermometer rarely broke 100 degrees. Meaning I could go out hiking and biking to my heart's content. Throw in an unlimited monthly Yoga pass, and I was in heaven.

Sedona was the perfect place for me and on my birthday. I was starting with yoga and then taking a trip down to the creek. Oak Creek during the summer is the perfect balance of heat and cold. The water kept me refreshed, and the sun kept me jumping in the water all afternoon. I would regularly go up to Grasshopper point because it was a good place to cliff jump 20 feet into deep water. Plus, it was only a couple minutes up Oak Creek Canyon. A canyon full of beautiful swimming holes with incredible views, in my opinion, nothing in Arizona compares.

Now I did thankfully have the day off from work, meaning I could sit back and enjoy the day. I intended to take myself to dinner that evening. I started a ritual of taking myself to my favorite restaurant on my birthday. Not because no one would come but because I wanted the alone time. Too much partying in my youth would leave me recovering on my birthday. I rather enjoy me time, and what better day to do me, than on my birthday?

This birthday was going to be no different, and I was going to be taking myself to dinner at the local Vegan Eatery, Chocola Tree. I had heard positive reviews but never had the extra money available. I have never been vegan, but I would consider myself a conscientious eater. It matters how my food is grown. I continue to eat Non-GMO, organic, or more preferably local. I rarely eat processed food, and I try to cook as much of my food as possible.

It was a big treat to take myself out to dinner at a new exciting restaurant. I spent ten years working in restaurants so naturally, food is something I particularly enjoy. Trying new amazing cuisine is always an adventure for me. That dinner began an undertaking that I could never have foreseen.

It was a cute restaurant with tons of plants and greenery. The inside had walls covered in art and superfoods. The menu was full of tonics, teas, and an array of healthy elixirs. I had never seen such an extensive menu full of vegan food substitutes. There was cheese, burgers, and even vegan nachos. I decided to go with the mushroom Fantasy because I've always loved good fungi. With my delicious Pu-erh hot tea to accompany me, I was settling in for some fun people watching.

It was about ten minutes after taking a seat that I spotted a few women just wandering around the restaurant. One of them was walking around with a baby, and the other two were being incredibly social. The baby was not interested in the action because she wouldn't stop staring and smiling at me. The inner child in me exchanged smiles, waves, and some funny faces. It was at this time, a friend of the baby's mother approached from the back of the restaurant.

She was a beautiful, confident, and stunning woman. I noticed her from before, but she noticed me this time. There was almost an instant connection. She approached me without hesitation. Her self-possession was unrivaled, and her beauty breathtaking. It wasn't very long before she had a seat and joined me for what would be the rest of my meal. She introduced herself but I sadly, at the time didn't register her name, as I so often don't. I have never been the best at remembering names right when I meet people, I've gotten better, but it still happens. This new stranger was probably one of the most interesting people that I had yet to come across in Sedona.

I think what made her so appealing is that we could talk

about anything. I'm rarely able to open up and discuss serious topics with such openness. My views on society greatly differ from the mainstream view of worldly things. Well, this incredible woman was someone after my own heart. The friendship was immediate, but she remained so elusive to me. I couldn't read her the way that I could most people; there was something else about her that I couldn't place my finger. Either way, I was overjoyed to be having such an incredible random experience on my birthday.

I remember one of the first things she decided to do after hearing it was my birthday. She had me pull out my phone, not to get my number. Instead, she wanted to read my star chart. Little did I know that she was probably one of the most adept readers of star charts I have ever encountered, and I used to sell my art at psychic fairs. As she quickly looked over the chart, she was completely thrilled at what she discovered. While I wish I were a little more adept at what everything means, I do have a basic understanding of certain influences the planets have on us. However, I am most familiar with the planet retrogrades.

Anyone familiar with something called Mercury Retrograde has likely noticed the effects. Mercury retrograde is a three-week period where Mercury appears to start moving in the opposite direction in the sky. This phenomenon happens several times a year, causing many to experience something I have personally experienced many times. It is as if all the lessons from the past several months seems to resurface at the same time. It is recommended to proceed with caution during these times.

When I learn it is Mercury Retrograde, I heed the warnings. Many spiritual teachers offer advice about how to navigate life during retrogrades. My experience has taught me that many past issues are brought up spectacularly, only to test our current emotional reactions. In my opinion, the stars and planets affect our lives in ways that few people understand or even try to comprehend. I had previous star chart readings, most significantly a reading saying my ideal partner would be a water sign. My new friend and dining companion just happened to be a water sign.

Well, as she read my birth chart, she proceeded to tell me much of what I already knew about myself. I was a strong fire sign, and had many planets in the house of Leo, including the sun. I displayed the characteristics Leo's have, intelligence, warmth, and courage. Leo's also battle with arrogance, pride, and struggle to listen. It wasn't so much the Leo information that caught my attention, but it was the fact that she started saying that our other planets lined up with one another. My Venus was in an auspicious place on her chart, and my moon was in her mid-heaven. Honestly, even knowing that and writing it, I still barely understand what it means.

I have since discovered that studies on the subject have shown that most lasting married couples have favorable star charts. It is uncommon that two people with unfavorable star charts end up together, and if so, show higher divorce rates. (*The Astrology File" by Gunter Sachs*)

So now that we knew the stars were aligned, I guess getting to know each other was the next step. We started talking and talking and talking. I sat there across from her feeling the connection that we had. I am far from the person to make the first move and was just so blown away at how smart and insightful this person was. She was as smart if not smarter than me, which I loved. Her sense of humor was light and sweet. Although she also had this stoic presence that made her elusive to me. I honestly didn't know what to think, and I just kept talking with her. We talked until they kicked us out of the restaurant.

I offered to give her a ride home, which she explained was less than half a mile up the street. I walked her to the door and gave her a big hug goodnight. The energy between us was so powerful, but neither of us dared to make the next move. It was perfect just how it had happened. As I started my car, it began to rain, the drops hitting my windshield as I backed out of the driveway. She stood in pristine beauty at her doorway as I waved goodbye. It was now sprinkling as I drove away from this mysterious woman who had unknowingly stolen my heart. She was all I could think about that night and the next day. Although I didn't have her name, I saved her number in my phone as "Beautiful."

I was fascinated and couldn't believe how lucky I was to receive such a special Birthday Present. I felt terrible that I hadn't caught her name or remembered it, but it didn't stop me from thinking about her. She had truly captured my eye that night. We both knew there was something special, but I didn't make a move, and neither did she. It just wasn't meant to happen yet, but I wasn't going to let that stop me.

The next day came around like any other, up early and off to yoga. The one difference being I couldn't get this amazing woman off my mind. It made me feel again like a little boy at Christmas. My inner child was running wild, and I wanted to see her again. As I was driving to the store that day, I coincidentally drove past her friends from the previous night. I texted her right after I saw them because it just felt like a sign. After a couple of texts back and forth, I straight up called her. Thankfully she mentioned her name early in the conversation, and I never forgot it after that, it was Danielle Claire. So beautiful and so elegant, it fit her perfectly.

I knew this phone call was special because again, our conversation flowed so easily. Our second evening, we ended up talking on the phone for nearly eight straight hours. We truly talked about everything important in our lives. What made us unique, and what made us stand out from the rest of the world. Much entailed the problems faced by aggressive male egos. Something both of us had very strong opinions and experiences to share.

As a beautiful woman, she was repeatedly a target for the alpha male. All the smooth-talking, conniving, lies, and insidious means that these guys do and say to try and get in women's pants. This incredible woman told me stories of which I am unable to repeat; she was, after all, 007 dance teacher. Her purity and beauty were only masking her strength and awareness. She could smell out ill intentions like it was a sixth sense. This gift was as much a curse as it left her jaded to the abuses of men. I wanted to understand further, as I was never a victim of repeated abuse.

We talked about it for a while because she had been in one bad relationship after another. These guys would appear as good, honest, and caring individuals but instead were cunning deceivers. These guys are so good at putting on a front that most people don't see the person they are behind the scenes. Men have become super good at hiding their true selves from women and the public. So much so that I honestly believe that if women knew what their husbands or boyfriends thought or said, they would be hurt, devastated, or at least disappointed. Danielle and I both felt that there was something seriously wrong with the way men behaved, and the conversation deepened.

She told me that night over the phone many additional stories. She would have guys that would promise the world, would put

29

on the face, but when it came down to it, they were horrible people on the inside. They were cold and manipulative. They were secretive and would be people who many times had separate lives. We discussed men having other girlfriends or even wives. The bizarre stories that I have heard are cruel and a bit disheartening.

It was endless abuses that many of these men put Danielle through, and because they put up such a good front, it is impossible to convince other people otherwise. The topic of her many crazy past relationships was a hot issue. I've since learned, from her friends, her past boyfriends seemed so nice but were capable of such awful behavior. Throughout her life, men inflicted a large amount of psychological pain. She even explained how much it affected her when her father took his life when she was only ten years old.

We shared experiences that most people wouldn't share with a practical stranger. We talked about deep topics that have positively and negatively affected who we are as individuals. I was impressed at how much she understood the dark side of the men that are being created by our society. She was impressed that I was willing to stand up to those alpha males because it isn't easy.

I explained how much being a man whore is celebrated among groups of men. I even found it difficult to speak up against the behavior. So often men are conditioned to be accepted by the alpha male. If we disagree with the alpha male, we often become targets for ridicule. It has personally taken me years to develop the confidence to stand up against some disrespectful behavior, and rarely do I do it in a public setting. However, if I have communicated my feelings about a topic, I have no problem reasserting myself.

Over the 8-hour phone conversation, we also discussed to a great extent, the abuses women commit towards one another. Danielle had repeatedly dealt with attacks while running her dance studio. She was the victim of many different women in the local community, and I had sympathy. Her personal life dealt with men attacking her, but her business life was the exact opposite, the women reigned havoc.

I haven't personally experienced the cruelty that is committed from one woman to another since I am not a woman. I have, however, been the victim of a woman's jealous anger. I found it difficult when someone is spreading lies to make you look bad. Some women are even willing to say or do anything to cause your life pain. I even had one willing to turn my friends against me to prove themselves right and feel better about themselves. Some people want to put others down rather than put the time and energy to build themselves up.

Jealousy can be a very powerful emotion when women decide to use it against one another. Danielle expressed this is so many ways, and I think it was women who were the most defamatory. With men, it is usually right in your face with verbal or physical abuse; men are typically more direct. Women, I have found, are far more manipulative and conniving when it comes to getting what they want. It would blow my mind to hear how horrible women would behave.

Danielle said it was something that she has had to deal with more and more over the past decade. When she first moved to Sedona people were far nicer, and she didn't have to deal with half the headaches that she was dealing with when we met. I think the story that always sticks out in my head is about how a group of women would repeatedly show disrespect during dance practice. Problems that were so bad it made her question teaching dance in Sedona.

She told me there used to be a bench outside the dance studio. However, some mothers couldn't find the capacity to be quiet during practice. They found their social time to be more important than respecting their children. Danielle eventually removed the bench only to face ridicule from the mothers. The same mothers who couldn't remain quiet during recitals. Enraging Danielle, by their selfish behavior, only made their situation worse.

Danielle felt it was more important to provide a safe space for her students than to be popular. Danielle even implemented a requirement that all children must stay during the whole recital to prevent disrespectful parents from leaving early and disrupting the show. Yes, Danielle had to deal with parents who repeatedly would leave immediately after their child was finished dancing. No care for anyone else but themselves.

Danielle held the bar highest inside her studio. She wouldn't tolerate poor behavior from any of her students. She would kick girls out of her dance school if they showed any sign of being rude, or even exhibiting rude looks. She expected all girls to be respectful and supportive of one another. If a girl were hurtful to another, she would have the girls vote to see if the person should receive another chance. She included the girls too.

She wasn't the teacher who said, "I'm in charge, and you must do everything I say." She was the one who allowed girls to grow. She would inspire each student through the fundamentals of dance, to evolve into better expressions of individual talent. I would later witness this in action. Danielle let her older and experienced girls have far more freedom. Once the girls gave a conscious demonstration that they had learned structure and form, they were allowed freedom in their expression of dance.

Danielle could control the actions of those under her care, but it was her efforts outside the studio that truly fascinated me. I hadn't met many women who were outspoken and stood up for other women. These days I keep hearing more and more stories about how one woman went on a personal vendetta against another for ridiculous reasons. Most often it just appears to be one woman undermining another for personal gratification, were putting someone else down seems to make the other person feel better — digging for dirt, spreading false rumors, and a long list of other slights that I still find unbelievable.

I think what made me even more captivated by Danielle was when she told me about the horrible women in Sedona and how they treated her and her friends. Danielle, as I found out, was truly a best friend to everyone she knew. When one of her friends lost her mother, and as a result decided to close her business, Danielle was there for her. Danielle and I both wish that people weren't so selfish because the backlash that happened for Danielle's friend was possibly one of the most horrific community reactions that I have ever heard.

Danielle told me that since her friend decided to close the business that many of her clients were less than happy. It was purely selfish. They didn't care about the situation she faced; they were upset they would have to go somewhere else for services. The reactions were purely self-centered, which is sad that people would respond in such a way. They couldn't seem to understand why she would close her business, even though she had suddenly and traumatically lost her mother. Many women began to spread horrible rumors because they were unhappy about the outcome. Danielle would have to accompany this friend to the store to protect her from people who would say the most inappropriate comments. Honestly hearing about someone willing to stand up to others because it was the right thing to do was so heartwarming to me. I was falling in love.

Was this the girl I had been looking for all my life? Danielle Elise Claire was by far the most amazing, most intelligent, strongest, and on top of that beautiful woman, inside and out, that I had ever encountered. As we talked more about other topics, I think we both had realized that this was something special. Our conversations deepened, and we talked more about our past. We discussed my rather charmed childhood and her rather rocky childhood. I understood her, and she understood me. She could see that I had been on a journey of growth the past decade, and I could see she was ready to find true love.

I never expected that call to inspire me to change my life. I had my last puff of tobacco after I hung up the phone. Danielle made me want to quit, and that night, I did it cold turkey. I have tried to quit before, but it never seemed to last more than a couple days to a week. To say, cigarette addiction is tough to beat is a huge understatement. While I've never been the pack a day smoker, I still usually have two to four cigarettes a day. Still a decade long addiction that I wish I never started.

When I was twenty, I bowed into peer pressure and started dipping chewing tobacco. I struggled with that habit for years until I started growing my tobacco. After three years of chewing tobacco, I switched to smoking the plant instead. I haven't grown my tobacco in a few years, but I have been trying to quit smoking ever since. Danielle gave me a little more incentive to quit, mostly that she would feel ill if I remained a smoker, she was too sensitive, and it would cause her health problems. I enjoyed my last puff of a cigarette with my roommate that night.

Before we hung up, we had realized that this was going to be something more. We had made plans to make it official the next day; she wanted to set up a picnic for me at a park near her house. She wanted me to find her, and she would tell me when she was ready, where to find her. I waited in anticipation all morning to see her, we had planned on meeting in the early afternoon. At one-thirty, she texted me that she was heading out and that I should leave in thirty minutes. I can't explain how all the butterflies got in my stomach, but it felt like my stomach could fly away. I hadn't been that nervous since I was a teenager.

When I made it to the location, I found an eight-foot deep crack in the ground and through the middle was a nice little area to have a little picnic. I spotted Danielle off to the right further down the crack doing a little exploring. Even though I saw her first, I still had to find a way down to her. I quickly searched and found a little walkway that descended into the long deep crevice. I would never have known it was there even though I drove by it several times before. It was private and a perfect spot to meet for the first time. I spotted her just before we locked eyes. I don't know if it was just me, but I think we both went in for the kiss right away.

The kiss was truly powerful and memorable. Our lips remained locked for twenty seconds before we released. After thirteen hours of talking, we were ready for a little bit of action. The mosquitoes quickly joined our kissing party as very unwelcomed guests. While the mosquitoes weren't very kind, Danielle truly was. She had some incredible little snacks, all organic, non-GMO, and very delicious set out for us. We didn't hang out with our biting friends very long, but I can tell you that it was a beautiful first date. It was official; I was going to be spending quite a bit of time with Danielle. We were truly inseparable, from that point on.

4
A Quick Engagement

I am happy to say that we spent every available minute with each other from the moment we first kissed. Danielle became my best friend, and that relationship quickly blossomed. We could talk about anything. We could move through difficult topics with such grace and ease. Danielle and I shared a level of communication that I have yet to share with anyone else on the planet. Our conversations and our joy for life, while we were together was powerful, undeniable, and a display of the sincere love we shared for each other. We truly admired one another for the incredible individuals we were, and we also both had great self-love. The devotion between us was more than I can imagine. The first several weeks felt like a blur yet were some of the most enjoyable and intimate times in my life.

Danielle and I were also very passionate lovers who enjoyed adventure and deep intimacy. We spent many nights down at a local gazebo located in a beautiful garden surrounded by gorgeous flowers. The use of sacred geometry in the construction made it special to me as well. I appreciated it because Sacred Geometry has been something I have used as a tool for expanding my awareness for years. I felt it was having this effect on us as we made love in the moonlight.

People consider Sacred Geometry to originate from the sacred structures that create and influence the universe, giving real power to the idea behind, creative design. Using the sacred designs and structures from ancient cultures has brought about a revolution in our sciences. Cymatics is a new science that explores the potentials of using different frequencies to influence change. The patterns discovered in Cymatics are patterns we also find in sacred geometry. It was a sacred experience to share with my beloved.

One evening we were even graced with the presence of a family of javelina. For those unfamiliar with Javelina, they look

35

like wild pigs. While not actually pigs (they are classified in the Peccary family) they can be dangerous in a pack. They have large tusks that can do damage if provoked, especially if they have little ones nearby. I have encountered them numerous times in my life but nowhere near what this night would bring.

We were talking as we always did when we started hearing a lot of noise approaching. It completely startled us and brought us to high alert status. I grabbed the flashlight and shined it out of the gazebo. We could see about four or five javelinas running through the garden, although many more were present. I grabbed the mat we were resting on and used it to put up a barricade at the entrance.

At this point, my flashlight had spotted somewhere between twenty to thirty javelina wandering through the bushes. It was an overwhelming sight. We later looked up the meaning of Javelina as a spirit animal and found that they are a sign of strong connections with others. Danielle and I couldn't deny we were developing something strong.

The first couple dates I hadn't talked much about my passion for dance. It was probably halfway through the first week of dating that I decided it was a good time to show Danielle my style of dance. I have a unique approach that I would also say has very little structure. It is constantly evolving, and the form and movement very much depend on the music that is playing. So I chose to dance to a song called "Revolution" by Diplo. I had to look it up, but the song is classified as Electronic Dancehall. It is a song that starts slow and then has a very fast beat, slows down, and then goes faster and faster till the end.

Revolution is a fun and intense song for me to dance to, as I exercise every part of my body when I dance. My moves can be fast and interesting but unique and all their own. Danielle, an accomplished dance instructor, was blown away. She couldn't believe it in all honesty and told me that my form was akin to a professional dancer. I can't recall which accomplished Russian dancer she compared me to, but I was flattered.

We danced all night. It was a thrill to be able to dance with someone who could dance with me. It takes a talented individual to keep up with me, so I've rarely ever had dance partners when I go dancing, freestyle. I learned my dance basics by watching 2-step, salsa, and a little blues. However, my unique movements have evolved into something completely different than anything else. We still flowed together, displaying a unique approach that was electric. Danielle would choose a song, and then I would choose a song. The most beautiful night of dance that I have ever shared with someone. I wasn't anticipating what this night would also inspire. Danielle wanted me to start dancing in her classes.

It would be pertinent that I give a little more background on Danielle's class structure. Mostly I found it to be so incredible and a different way of teaching. She started many girls out as little dancers and had several classes of three to five-years-old. She was truly talented and gifted in her ability to handle the little ones. Several parents and friends commented on her natural ability as a teacher to instruct children of all ages. Mostly, because it was dance, she had a predominantly female class load.

Danielle had different levels set up for her students. As girls would advance through the levels, they would gain more freedom and chances for creativity. She made certain that the girls learned the basics, not just the basics of dance but the basics of manners, of attitude, and the character traits that make a smart and independent woman. As I said, she taught more than dance; she taught what it was to be creative, independent, and kind while seeing the beauty in everyone, which gave many girls a positive self-image. It was a big deal to be invited into the dance studio. The invite honored me because Danielle hadn't shared that part of her life with any other man. She had even switched up the classes she offered to teenagers because of the way teenage boys typically behave. She knew I was different from most men.

Danielle had to stop teaching teenage boys altogether because they would be crude or inappropriate. Our teenagers find it appropriate to act in sick and perverted ways, Danielle and I discussed this troubling topic extensively. It doesn't help that the massive availability of free internet porn, continues to twist the way many young boys view sex and sexuality. The comments that teenagers said to Danielle in her classes only proved this to us.

I was part of the start of this generation, a generation with access to unlimited sexual entertainment. So much porn and television vulgarity that it has torn apart the fabric of society. Sex lost its spiritual roots and now is seen purely for physical gratification. The University of Chicago is showing that sex, when performed with love in a monogamous relationship, is far healthier. In our male sex culture, there is no compassion; there is no consideration of the needs of others. Considerate lovers make better lovers than selfish ones. Consideration builds a deeper connection to create a higher level of satisfaction.

It didn't surprise me when Danielle told me that she hadn't had any other men in her dance classes. It is honestly sad that most are incapable of being respectful with their thoughts around young women, but it is the truth. Most men lack consideration. I aimed to be considerate in all my actions. The first class I was invited to be in was her P2 class, which included her most talented and advanced students. This class included girls that ranged from eleven to twenty-two years old. It was an achievement to be in the class.

Some spent years learning the art of dance, while others were truly incredible talents that earned it through hard work. It was incredible to see all the different techniques of dance that each person possessed. Danielle put on a display and had the girls show off their talent first as I was a bit nervous and didn't want to go first. It was exciting to see how Danielle controlled the class and allowed much of the design of the dance to flow from the girls; she was a great coach. I even made sure to bring snacks to my first class to win over the hearts of the girls.

Danielle knew I could dance, but she had made it a requirement that I audition for the class, and I was happy to oblige. I think she also wanted to show me off to her students, but I didn't mind that either. I was happy that I had found my dance instructor, the one who would make me a better dancer. She wanted me to dance to the same song that I first showed her, a "Revolution" it was going to be.

I had been warming up all day knowing that I was going to have to perform that evening. I was nervous, to say the least, despite having danced in front of hundreds of strangers and friends previously. I was even more nervous than when I first danced for my wife. I went in with 110% effort. I knew I had to impress them, and I did it with flying colors. I started the dance Revolution in the studio that night. The girls were blown away at my performance. However, I went too hard too fast. In total exhaustion, I had to stop dancing before the end of the four-minute song. I endured the next 20 minutes, waiting to catch my breath. I knew that it was worth it, as it meant I would likely be allowed to join the class.

I would have been a shoo-in if Danielle made the final decision. The girls had to agree that I was ready to be in class. Everyone voted. I believe it was a unanimous vote to allow me to join the class. It was more than an honor to me and something I wanted; I was finally going to receive some formal dance training. At this point, all the dancing I learned was from watching other people do it or just figuring it out on my own. I went to some classes for blues and salsa dancing but mostly learned by copying other dancers. Now I was beyond excited to be trained by one of the best dance teachers in the country. I was in love with our new life.

We did everything together, including errands, appointments, and sweeping her dance floor. When I met Danielle, she lived in her dance studio connected to her house. She had moved in there because it made it easier to afford to keep the studio open. Since the recession, she had struggled with keeping the business going. She even completely rented out the house and lived in an airstream on the property to pay the bills. Many students stopped dancing when times became rough for the country. Sedona was no different, and the economic downturn had a huge impact on extra-curricular activities.

The seven years before Danielle met me were filled with numerous financial challenges. She constantly told me about the struggle to keep the business going, mostly out of obligation to her students. She sold her car and started walking everywhere to save money. Many people, including myself, choose to bike or walk around the city. Danielle became known for walking the streets of Sedona in her big floppy sun hat. She was iconic in her appearance.

One of her biggest challenges was having roommates that respected the dance studio. Her students told me about Danielle having to throw people out for crossing boundaries or doing something completely inappropriate. A fierce protector of her space, a firecracker, she was an explosive force for good. It showed girls that it was okay to stand up and do the right thing. Danielle was a role model, unlike any other. I respected this about Danielle and always laughed about the way the girls would describe it. Kids say the darndest things. I remember laughing with them, trying to express her fierceness.

Danielle likes to call it her Kali side, her darker feminine energy that she channeled to triumph over evil. A side of her that I respected because I recognized similar energy when I was upset. Danielle showed far more control and direction with her anger, which was used to accomplish great good. I had much to learn.

Danielle was a protector. She repeatedly remarked that the little children that are constantly playing up and down the street don't have a voice. We both knew her actions led to protecting lives and made a difference to those who can't speak. It is a strange world we live in, but some work every day to make it a better place, Danielle was one of those people.

I learned a lot about the person Danielle was the more she opened up to me. The more I discovered, the more I loved her. I never stopped being amazed by the incredible stories or the passion for life she embodied. Everything we did was an incredible experience. I didn't see this relationship ending, so when my parents told me they were visiting several weeks after my birthday, I knew they had to meet Danielle.

My Mom, Dad, and Sister had not been to Sedona since we were children. They were in for an unexpected adventure, as I planned to introduce them to my better half. Although, I dropped the news on them as they were pulling into town. I wanted to avoid silly questions or potentially give them time to do something embarrassing. Having my family visit meant embarrassing moments were unavoidable. They arrived around dinner and were famished after the 4-hour drive, so we met at the restaurant.

Dinner was fantastic. We had a great time discussing how we met and the apparent connection we had. Danielle also really connected with my dad due to her top-secret past. My dad was a fighter pilot in the Air Force. Danielle had no problem "shooting the shit" with him. It was entertaining to watch. I was glad my parents liked her seeing as Danielle didn't have a father most of her life. The family connection brought us even closer together.

Danielle loved being able to hear about all my embarrassing moments growing up. It was equally entertaining as it was humiliating. It made Danielle feel like part of the family. Danielle loved it, and my family had made her feel welcome. It was a great feeling to get such positive feedback from my family. She impressed them beyond words.

The weekend consisted of my sister taking an obnoxious

number of pictures. I didn't enjoy all the pictures at the moment but will forever be grateful for the memories she preserved. She took pictures of every adventure we went on. We enjoyed some light hiking and a lot of good food. We didn't take my family to the Vegan Restaurant for a meal but did go in for some chocolates. Everyone loves chocolate, and not everyone loves a vegan hamburger.

My family doesn't share the same concerns about food like me. To my family's dismay, I have changed my views about many ideas I had growing. My awakening to certain issues has caused tension and strife within my family. No longer do I force my new views on my family, and no longer do they expect me to behave as they expected. We have come to a better mutual understanding. However, this understanding was only a recent development with Danielle entering my life.

Danielle helped revitalized the connection between all of us. I know my family supported my decision to date this amazing woman, but they were also shocked. I don't think they had ever seen me so head over heels in love. They knew something special was there, and I knew they were happy for us. Even my sister throwing me under the bus made Danielle feel more like part of the family. The truth was we were both completely head over heels in love with each other, now it was a bit more official.

I think the biggest thing I realized with my family was how truly enamored I was with Danielle. My parents made sure to point that out, embarrassingly. I felt they approved of my relationship. I even for the first time, received open support for my orgonite and medical marijuana careers. They gave me an amazing mold for my orgonite in the shape of a marijuana leaf. I couldn't believe it after years of ridicule. Showing me, everyone has the power to change, even if it isn't as fast as we may hope. I couldn't escape the change that entered my life.

Inescapable. Was this it?! Were we both waiting for each other? After three weeks, our lives were becoming entirely intertwined. Life just flowed effortlessly, and we were perfect together. Everyone around town thought we were adorable, and we brought smiles to many we encountered. We genuinely had fun together. I loved everything about her. What happened next only made sense.

I decided to ask her if she thought we should get married. It wasn't an immediate proposal but more of an idea. Danielle was so excited that I wanted a secure future together. She practically said yes right away, and with that, we were going to get married.

We both just knew we loved one another, and it just felt right. We were on a rocket ship relationship and were past the point of no return. I can't explain how we fit so much life experience into such a compact amount of time. One of the biggest hurdles being a huge shift in my line of work. Which without her help, I would never have come to such deep realizations. A big life change was still a small part of the events that propelled us those first couple weeks.

The deep discussions about our lives continued, showing us new and interesting challenges. Most problems or issues from a new relationship happened. We discussed living situations, children, life goals, aspirations, and even looking at the things that we didn't like about ourselves and each other. We worked through all of it with such beauty. We understood how to communicate with each other. It was beautiful. We both agreed that we had lived a lifetime in our first month together. Most relationships take months if not years, to progress as far as we already did. So now we had to discuss the details of making it official.

Our planned wedding day was fast approaching, and we spent practically every minute possible together. She would even come to hang out at my work, that brought me to Sedona in the first place. At the time, I was working at the local Medical Marijuana Dispensary. It was my second time back in the industry, which I enjoyed. I loved getting paid to sell weed legally. Moving to Sedona was a massive improvement to my previous job in downtown Tucson. The views from inside the new office were magnificent. The people were even more pleasant. I felt at home when I first arrived.

I have researched the most successful dispensaries in the Nation, the ones that are providing free Wellness Center options to their patients. These include yoga classes, acupuncture, healthy eating seminars, and so much more. I saw potential in Sedona to provide those benefits. The location had a perfect space that was being completely unused. It felt like an opportunity, but I would find the opposite to be true.

Due to a problem I had with a coworker, I had to inform the manager at the time that I felt a coworker was mistreating clients based on if they tipped or not. Seemed like the proper thing to do since I take a lot of pride in customer service. The result was not punishing the employee but removing the tip jar completely. I hadn't realized the jar was gone the next time we worked together. I had volunteered to work the front desk, so I never noticed it was missing the entire day. I was only trying to avoid talking to her.

Danielle showed up an hour before closing to hang out with me. It wasn't until I walked out the door that I realized that there wasn't a tip jar. I wanted to blow up, I was beyond upset, mostly because it was a $250-400 per month pay reduction. I was at the time making $11 per hour which was $2 short of the originally promised $13 per hour. I hadn't worried before since the tip jar would usually make up the difference. The pay cut made me furious.

Danielle was with me as this happened, and it was the first time she saw me angry. Now at that time in my life, I would say I still lacked control of my anger. Often my temper could get the better of me, and I would not be my usual pleasant self. She was able to see me at my worst, emotionally out of control. Everything that I was hoping to get from working there was crumbling to nothing. I wasn't going to be making near enough money now to accomplish half of what I wanted to accomplish with my life. It was devastating. Danielle helped me come to several realizations.

I realized that upper management only cared about trying to supply inexpensive marijuana. The idea of an integrated wellness center was never going to manifest at this job. Danielle helped me to work through all of it, and she helped me come to some big decisions.

Now I wasn't making enough money to thrive in Sedona at $11 per hour. I was barely getting by before. Danielle reminded me of this and other issues that bothered me. I felt the managers that worked over me had zero say in the direction of the company. They received all direction from our Phoenix office that also rarely showed up to our location. We did only do $1 Million a year in business compared to the over $12 Million that the Phoenix location did. The company didn't show much care or attention to our location.

It bothered me that my manager would communicate the lack of concern the home office had for our issues. I could see the focus was not on the patients. The concerns were focused on profits for the company, not in providing proper medicine. Never was it about giving back to the community or the employees for that matter. With my wife talking me through everything, I finally concluded, I needed to quit.

The next day I was super surprised to see my General Manager working. He was filling in for the assistant manager for the day. It was perfect synchronicity because I needed to talk to him about what happened. He gave me the worst reason to why he thought it was pertinent to remove the tip jar. He decided that since the other locations didn't have tip jars, he would remove it to stop the problem. I proceeded to ask about getting the $13 an hour originally promised. He then told me that the Assistant manager only gets $13 an hour. The option of promotion to a manager just meant that I would officially get paid what I did with the tip jar.

That was all I needed to hear. I was looking forward to less money than I was making with tips while having more work and responsibility. I was not interested. Honestly, I couldn't believe that managers at a business that grosses over $1 Million a year in sales, on a plant that our company grows, only pay their top managers $28,000-$34,000 per year. It was embarrassing, and I couldn't take pride in the job anymore. I put in my month notice because someone needed to be retrained to work there. I still took pride in my performance as an employee.

At the time, I was very knowledgeable about how to help most people with managing pain, sleep, anxiety, and many of the other problems that MMJ can remedy. One of the biggest being the constant influx of Cancer patients looking for relief from many of the side effects of chemo. I told Danielle it was eye-opening to see every week the new Cancer Patient that the Cancer industry failed. It is hard because many of these people were struggling so much, but it felt good when I could help a patient find the proper medicine for their problem. It isn't rocket science, but there is a science to it. Since I started in the industry in 2012, Arizona has seen huge leaps in the quality of medicine available, but it still needs more development to see the plant fully utilized.

With my revelation that it wasn't time for me to continue to work in the MMJ industry, I knew I needed a change. Considering my soon to be wife was also a local dance teacher, and we had discussed silly rumors that small towns like to spread, it just seemed right that I move on. She was very outspoken to her students about staying away from drugs, considering she didn't do them. She walked the talk, and she took great pride in that. She taught it was okay to be pure even when everyone else is doing the opposite. It's okay to stand out and do what is right, especially if it is for yourself. Standing up for yourself is not always easy when one doesn't have a foundation to stand on.

I was shifting Danielle's perspective of Marijuana used medicinally. We both still feel recreational abuse, as with all intoxicants, is harmful to many people's lives. Danielle helped girls build that foundation being a role model we could all aspire to achieve. She changed many lives in her mission to keep kids safe. As much as I was teaching her about the things I understood, she was sharing with me far more about the wisdom she possessed.

When I said Danielle read my astrological birth chart on my birthday, I had no idea the level of her understanding of astrology. She understood unreservedly how the planets could affect people. When my parents were visiting, she practically nailed my mom and dad's personality just by reading their birth charts. I also found when she read my sister's that she saw a lot of the struggle that she and I had throughout our lives. Danielle would also read charts for birthdays, for special events, and even in the event of a death. She let the stars guide her, which was no surprise when it came to choose a wedding day.

My wife wanted to choose a day that was right according to the stars, an auspicious day, one that she felt she could get married. We had a couple of limitations because of her teaching schedule and my work week. We decided that a Friday would be the day of the week to get married. After referring to the next month's star charts, we decided to choose the date, Friday, September 18th, 2015. The stars told Danielle this day was the most auspicious, and it was only two weeks away.

The first thing I had to do was switch shifts so that I could have the weekend following our wedding off. Switching shifts meant my work weeks would run back to back instead of having a break in the middle. That meant I had to work seven days straight to return to my four days on three days off schedule, but I knew it was worth it. My request for days off came halfway through my final month of work. Regardless of the issues, I was having with work, the idea of getting married made it worth any price I would have to pay. Danielle and I were having such a great time that nothing else mattered. Every day our friendship deepened, and the knowledge of each other continued to grow

. We evolved, in part, because she saw a big reflection of herself in my anger. Danielle had far more experience and lessons to teach me about anger. She understood me, and I understood her, we both were reflections of the deep anger that existed inside both of us. Not that we ever let the anger rule our lives; in fact, our love kept most of those feelings far away from both our minds and hearts. We lived in a bubble of love, and only when opportunities for growth occurred would anything that could be conceived as not loving, enter our world. So interesting things did happen often, but it wasn't anything the two of us together couldn't conquer. It is overcoming those challenges that made both of us stronger and closer.

The next thing we needed to figure out was what was going to happen to her school. To Danielle, her house and the dance school were her main concern, and rightfully so. Obviously, after three weeks, I wasn't expecting her to split everything she had accomplished and worked so hard for her entire life. It caused her much concern to think the potential risks she ran if things didn't work out. So we decided to sign a prenuptial. I would get nothing in the slight chance that we were too hasty. We agreed to keep things separate, which made her feel secure, so it made me feel good too. Possessions don't overly concern me, I appreciate nice things, but I prefer living a simple life.

We had a couple of serious decisions to make. First off, we had decided that our marriage wasn't something we wanted to announce or make public. We wanted it to be about us, and we didn't want our families saying anything about it. Danielle and I decided to tell no one except some friends. Mostly just friends that we encountered since we couldn't keep our mouths shut. However, there were certain people she didn't want to know yet, solely to avoid a large wedding. Deciding who should and shouldn't come was, by default, almost entirely up to Danielle.

We told the dance class first, so all the girls knew right away that we were getting married. Since they all had hoped Danielle would get married one day, Danielle decided that they should be able to come. Miss Danielle was getting married, and it was a big deal for a lot of the girls. They decided they were going to perform a special dance for us at the wedding. It was all finally decided. Our wedding would be small and beautiful, with a non-denominational

46

minister performing the service.

    The only thing that was missing was my actual proposal. It just so happened that I came across the most beautiful heart-shaped crystal I've ever seen a couple of days after our big decision. Seeing as we weren't doing things the traditional way, I decided to change it up a little. I choose to give my wife the most beautiful heart-shaped stone I had ever seen. Obviously, when I presented it to her in the dance studio on one knee, I already knew the answer, but I also knew that it was beyond official. Danielle Claire and Brandon Strabala were engaged, and we were going to get married on September 18th, 2015.

5
Wedding Day

The wedding quickly approached after a brief three-week engagement. While our love continued to deepen, we didn't question the choice we were about to make. It was as if we just knew our destinies were intertwined. Life was in a state of perfect synchronicity. A permanent honeymoon phase that never diminished because our lives would not allow it. Danielle and I had that special magic all-the-time. We were both very present in our lives before we met and that intensified when we were together. We gave each other strength- strength we would both soon need.

Danielle woke up, twenty-four hours before our wedding, with pain in her stomach area. She explained that she felt something the past week. I was clueless until the pain sharply intensified. Danielle never showed discomfort or pain. She explained that if it didn't start to dissipate, then she might have to get it checked out. I was a little concerned, but she hid the pain, very well. The real agony she was feeling, was not fully communicated. Danielle is the strongest woman I have ever known, so I wasn't nearly as concerned as I probably should have been.

I had the whole day off and some errands to run to prepare for the ceremony the next day. When Danielle's classes started, I was off to finish gathering up what we needed. I picked up some glass containers for the sand ceremony that we were having the minister performing. I also had to pick up some flowers, a belt, and a few other things. Including a run to the MMJ dispensary, as a favor for Danielle's friend, whose husband was also a patient at the dispensary.

The gentleman recently had surgery and was immobile. People must go into the dispensary to pick up their meds in Arizona, which can be difficult for people, at times. Although now there are delivery services. They had expressed concern that he couldn't make it into the dispensary, so he wouldn't be able to get more meds.

I picked up some that were great for pain relief and sleep. I made sure to pick up edible and topical medicine because it was far more effective at relieving physical pain than most of the medicine that patient's smoke. As it happened, I couldn't deliver that day. Too much to do, and I still had to prepare for class.

The thing I was most excited about that day was dance class. It was delightful to have my fiancé teaching me how to dance. I wouldn't say it was her that I was learning from, most of the time in class I was learning the dance moves from her students. Danielle had an eye for dance and would assuredly bring the best out of everyone. Shouting in approval or disapproval, when students do or don't hit their precise mark. It made her an amazing coach, albeit a little intimidating.

I will admit that class always made me a little nervous because often my fiancé would put me in the spotlight for a solo performance. While all the students normally did this, it was all very new to me. Most of the girls had four to fifteen years of dance experience with Danielle. I felt very honored that they thought me talented enough to train with them.

Danielle called me thirty minutes before class saying that she was canceling class, something I knew she never did. I knew something was wrong. She asked if I was on my way; thankfully, I was. Danielle bragged about sitting through class after most of her previous serious health concerns. Nothing could keep her down when it came to her obligations. She was selfless in giving herself to her students. Something was different.

When I arrived at her house, everyone had left except for one parent and her daughter. She had noticed that Danielle was showing some pain and discomfort during her previous class. She had no idea Danielle was hiding such an immense amount of agony. I imagine she did this for the girls because she always liked the girls believing she was invincible. (Honestly, I thought she was at this point too, but that story I'll save for later). I knew that, if she was canceling class, then she should go to the ER because this might be something serious. We were both hoping it was just a UTI or something else minor. What we were in store for was far from what we were expecting less than a day before our wedding.

The Sedona ER was not busy that Thursday night. I practically had to carry her inside because she was unable to walk on her own. The waiting room was empty, so we walked straight to the front desk. They checked us in right away, and we were put in a double room by ourselves. Immediately they checked her stats and blood pressure. I could tell, at this point, that my wife was very knowledgeable about her health and knew her normal blood pressure better than the doctors or nurses. She knew her blood pressure was high, but considering the pain she endured, it wasn't a surprise. Danielle and the doctor agreed.

The nurse assisted with drawing blood and taking samples for the tests. The doctor ran us through the long list of health questions that needed answering. Danielle ended up asking the doctor about as many questions as he asked her. Most of Danielle's questions were speculative, so the doctor couldn't answer directly. Sadly we were going to have to wait on answers.

Resigned, albeit nervously, we waited for the blood tests to come back. The doctor also wanted to run a full scan of her abdomen. We agreed it was a good idea, but I also couldn't go with her. They were taking her away for about forty minutes to perform the scan, and I had to sit and wait patiently. After they brought her back, we had to wait another hour for the scan to be analyzed.

The entire time we were talking about how we were still going to get married the next day. We kept expressing our undying love for each other, which made us stronger. I am extremely glad that I was able to be there for her. I kept reassuring her that it wasn't going to be serious and that it was all going to be okay. I didn't even consider the possibility that this could be serious. I was going to maintain a positive space that things were going to work out, and we were still going to get married in her studio. I wanted to be strong for her because she feared the worst.

The moment the scan came in, we knew it didn't look good. We could tell the doctor was not looking forward to sharing the results from the scan. Danielle saw the nurse had a tear in her eye. I missed that cue, just feeling Danielle squeezing my hand. I embraced her as we both braced for the news. He proceeded to tell us that the scan had turned up several masses on her ovaries. While the doctor couldn't tell us if it was just minor cysts or full-blown cancer, he did say that we would have to do further investigation to figure that out. He had more news too.

The blood tests had also come back and shown an elevated

blood marker that they use to diagnose ovarian cancer. Explaining this also is inconclusive, and a biopsy would have to be performed to figure out exactly what it was. I prayed, hoped, wanted, and wished that my wife did not have cancer. I wouldn't entertain the idea until we had total confirmation. I reassured her at every step that I was going to be there for her, and we were still going to get married.

At that point, I called the minister to cancel the ceremony for the next day. The hospital was still trying to figure out which hospital was going to be the best one to send us. We needed an oncological surgeon, which is a unique specialty for surgeons, from what they told us. We had some time before they could arrange a transfer.

Since I had the time, I decided to pick up the marriage license. It looked like we were going out of town for the weekend and there was so much I needed to grab. I was in such a rush that I just threw a bunch of stuff in a couple of bags at my house and did the same thing when I stopped at Danielle's house. I attempted to predict everything we would need for the next couple of days. I forgot so much in my anxious haste. Most importantly, I wanted the marriage certificate ready for something special.

I returned to the hospital as the ambulance was putting Danielle on the stretcher to take her to Phoenix. While I was gone, they had found a great hospital with a surgeon that was first class, to help my fiancé. They told us that he was one of the best specialists in the country, which was a small relief. I was planning on following the ambulance down in my car, so I didn't get stuck in Phoenix.

In my haste, I had only thrown ten dollars in the gas tank. I was out of time and prayed a quarter tank of gas would get me to my destination. The entire hour and a half trip between Sedona and Phoenix was smooth; I followed the ambulance the whole way. However, when I arrived in Phoenix, I was met with the most shocking billboards I have ever read.

"If you have any information about the I-10 shooter, please call 555-555-5555." At that time, there was a psychopath that was shooting people on the I-10 freeway that runs through the heart of Phoenix. It didn't occur to me, I was on the wrong freeway, so the entire time I was bobbing and weaving my head. I wasn't about to give him a clean shot. I continued praying that my wife and I would make it safely to the Scottsdale Honor Health Hospital. We did make it safely, and I made it with a little gas to spare, which was a double relief.

It was about 2 am when we arrived at the hospital and checked in. They moved us into a suite. The room was bigger than most hotel rooms and had a nice fold-out couch for me to sleep. Danielle's had a fully loaded bed with all the bells and whistles, such as cooling, heating, and adjustable everything. We were in one of the newest and most state-of-the-art hospitals. The nurses were very nice and helped us settle in for the night.

We knew we faced a lot the next day, but we had no idea just how crazy the next day would be. I don't think we could have imagined what would happen on that Friday, September 18th, 2015. We were about to have one hell of a miracle, pun intended.

We both had a little shut eye from total exhaustion, but neither of us slept through the night. We were woken up by the morning nurse crew. The two nurses introduced themselves, but it was Kathy that would stand out that morning. After running some tests and talking with us, we told her that we were supposed to get married that day in Sedona. She was heartbroken to hear that. We told her we weren't too worried about where we got married and that we just wanted to get married. Kathy told us she was going to check on some things, but we didn't think much of it at the time.

The doctor showed up not too long after that. He wanted to discuss with us the possibilities and what we would want depending on the outcome of what he found. We all agreed that if it was cancerous that we would want everything removed and any other signs of cancer removed as well; this meant a full hysterectomy. The other possibility of a cyst meant a similar surgery. We essentially decided that, unless it was beneficial to leave her ovaries in place, then it was probably best to take them out no matter the outcome.

At this time, my fiancé also asked for the surgeon's birthday and where he was born so that she could read his star chart. She wanted to make sure this doctor was supposed to be her surgeon. After reviewing his star birth-chart, she was certain that this was the doctor for her. She even told the doctor a little about himself that slightly surprised him.

I also did some internet research and found that the doctor we had was world-renowned for the procedure that Danielle was due to receive. The staff had a nickname for the actual procedure, and the nickname was also a play on the doctor's last name, the Janisecktomy. I was happy that we had what appeared to be the best surgeon in the world for Danielle's situation. It felt almost perfect in this imperfect world we were spiraling into.

We had no idea that, within the next twenty minutes, the hospital staff would be preparing for the first wedding ever performed at the hospital. Kathy came back to tell us some great news: she had checked with the resident chaplain and found out that he is also a fully ordained minister. When we met Carl, the minister, my wife and I both knew this was the guy who would marry us. He was a tiny older man who was incredibly soft-spoken. Carl told us this was due to some throat cancer he had beaten a couple of years ago.

Carl felt bad that he could only perform the traditional Catholic wedding ceremony because it's all he knew. I'm sure the nurses told him we were hippies from Sedona and likely weren't practicing Catholics. We didn't care, and we were happy that we were still going to get married. We were given an hour and a half window before the ceremony would take place. I made several calls, but the quickest anyone could get to Phoenix was about two hours from Tucson or Sedona. We were forced to recruit two hospital staff members to be our official witnesses.

We hadn't even picked out rings because we were going to take a trip down to Tucson to do that after the wedding. Carl, being the outstanding gentleman that he was, offered to let us use his wedding ring. Forty years of marriage and he was willing to let us borrow the ring. We were hoping it meant a good omen for our future. We had a ring to use for the ceremony that we could exchange. We had a minister. We had witnesses for the ceremony. It was all working out so strangely perfect. The next thing that happened blew us away completely.

We were not at all, expecting the staff to jump on board in such an incredible fashion. Some of the nurses ended up putting together a bouquet, a flower headdress, a boutonnière, and a garter belt with a blue ribbon made from hospital equipment. Everything was hand made by the nursing staff and other hospital staff. It was an "all hands-on deck" kind of moment. When I made a quick run to the car, I saw them rolling a podium through the lobby and setting up chairs on the patio. It was rather exciting, and the energy was electric.

The staff even covered the podium with flowers. We couldn't

believe what they had pulled off in an hour and a half. They even bought Danielle a white blouse to wear at the hospital shop. I will be honest that, in my packing haste, I was more practical and wasn't thinking about what clothes to wear to a wedding. The best thing I had to wear was jeans, a black shirt, and flip flops; not what I expected to be married wearing.

Thankfully, the staff bought Danielle the white blouse so that she was more comfortable with the fact that she would also have to be in a wheelchair. They had set up the most incredible setting in the hospital courtyard- it had such greenery, and the staff enveloped it with flowers. The location was called "The Healing Gardens," which is exactly the type of marriage we were embarking on: a marriage of healing.

When the ceremony was ready, and the staff finished setting everything up, they separated us. According to tradition, it is supposed to be bad luck to see the bride before the wedding, so one group of nurses took me down to the gardens one way, and another took Danielle down another way. We were aware our wedding was going to be far from average.

The administrative staff asked if we would mind if the staff watched the wedding. We encouraged it. Danielle just asked that they do not take pictures, and any pictures taken would be sent to my email and would never be made public. Danielle was always concerned about her image.

They walked me up to the center podium in front of the crowd that had gathered. There were about fifty people we didn't know sitting and standing around the garden area. We had several rows of seating and an aisle up to the center. One of the administrative staff members rolled Danielle down to the back of the aisle. She looked beautiful when she arrived. I could see all the joy radiating from her, which hid the incredible pain she endured. She was the strongest.

They rolled Danielle down the aisle with a smile across her face. I received her in front of the crowd of spectators. We locked eyes and just kept looking into each other's gaze. It was really happening. I just held her hand through it all.

We said our vows, through sickness and in health. Sealed with a huge kiss, we officially married at 10:10 am on September 18th, 2015 at Honor Health Hospital, in the Healing Gardens Courtyard. It was still a beautiful Friday.

Our hearts were overflowing with love that touched the hearts of many witnesses who gathered to join in our celebration. We saw many with tears in their eyes, completely touched by the commitment we were showing each other. It was important to me because I wanted to show her that I was committed to her no matter what. No matter the outcome, I was going to be there for her. It gave both of us the resolve to stay strong for what laid ahead of us.

After the ceremony, we went back to the room briefly before they took her to surgery. At this point, Danielle felt it was important to notify her family about what was happening. The pending surgery topped with a surprise wedding would be a lot to handle. We hadn't expected to tell our families so soon about the marriage, but the circumstances had called for an audible.

I gave both families the update and told them what was happening. It was a huge shock to everyone, and emotions ran high. Danielle wanted to talk to her family because she was going in for very major surgery. She kept the conversations short as I shared most of the details with everyone. After that, it was just the two of us again.

We had about two hours after the wedding to spend with each other while they prepped her for the surgery. It was a time of deep love, immense pain, undesired sadness, and topped with joy from our wedding. It was so confusing yet strangely comforting. I knew that the commitment I demonstrated was one of the biggest factors to calming any fears that I might abandon her. I guess you could say she suffered from some serious abandonment issues throughout her life. It was a gift to show her the assurance that she deserved.

When they took her to surgery, I was beyond an emotional wreck. I didn't know what to think as my whole world was getting turned upside down. I didn't want to leave the hospital, but I also realized that I should probably get some additional meds for my wife. Thankfully and coincidentally, I had purchased the medicine for her friend's husband, which is legal, since it would have been patient-to-patient. We weren't making it back to Sedona, and my wife needed the exact medicine I had purchased. Since my wife didn't have her MMJ card yet, I would have to bend the rules to help her.

There were a couple of other products that I felt would help her as well, so I decided to take an adventure to the closest MMJ

Dispensary. I didn't want to leave the hospital for very long, but I also knew the surgery would be at least three to six hours. I needed something to calm my nerves, and my wife was going to need some natural pain meds. I knew she wasn't going to be thrilled about all the prescription pain meds that the hospital was going to provide. Even upon our arrival, when they offered the meds, she was very cautious and showed incredible apprehension. Danielle asked about using Medical Marijuana. The nurses and doctor gave us approval but not officially.

I also used a little bit of the MMJ the first night in the Hospital on Danielle. It helped her relax and get some rest. It also showed me we needed stronger products. Phoenix had several unique products that I couldn't get in Sedona, so I made sure my adventure was very productive.

Upon my return, I wandered around the lobby for a little bit, simply waiting. It felt like forever. I don't think the possibility of losing Danielle that day ever truly crossed my mind. I just wanted to know she was okay. It was very hard not being able to do anything. It was the first time, I admit, that I felt helpless. Like nothing I was doing could help, but the universe would remind me otherwise.

I had mentioned that there was someone called the I-10 shooter, killing Phoenix drivers. Well, it just so happened the same day were married, was also the day he was miraculously captured. It was all over the local news channels. The synchronicity almost made me feel like we had played a small role in making the arrest happen that day. I couldn't stop thinking that all the people that were at the hospital would be spreading all the love they had experienced with us across Phoenix. Love is a powerful feeling, which is contagious.

It reminded me of the power that Sedona had, the special energy that people would experience and take with them. We brought that energy with us and shared it with the entire city that day. We spread so much love and showed people something they had never seen. It was something special, something magical, and I felt that magic was responsible for helping conquer the city's greatest fear. Some say that love conquers all, and that day, I felt our love did just that.

While waiting in the lobby, I read every magazine I could to keep my mind off things. I was waiting and wishing. I kept checking in to make sure they hadn't received any updates. Finally, after five and a half hours, they sent word that they had completed the surgery. I was ready to see my wife; I missed her so much. I didn't realize I was going to have to wait another twenty minutes before I would even speak to the doctor. It was the longest twenty minutes of the entire day. I was so nervous and so hopeful that they didn't find cancer. I knew the odds were high that it was cancer, but I was still ever so hopeful.

When the doctor called me back to the consultation room, I was a wreck. I had ridden more emotional rollercoasters that day than most of my life combined. I knew I was in for some big news and that I needed to be resolute. It still feels like a blur now, just like when it happened. I sat down on the couch, and the doctor proceeded to tell me that he removed the cancer. I couldn't believe it. I was shocked and so scared for my wife. I couldn't believe I would have to tell her that it was cancer.

He also told me the procedure went smoothly. The doctor did have to perform a full hysterectomy and said he removed any visible signs of cancer as well. He mentioned something about installing a port for future treatment. Beyond that, I don't remember the rest of the conversation. I was crushed and knew we had quite the journey ahead of us.

I had to wait for another twenty of the longest minutes of my life for them to finish getting her ready after surgery. I was fully expecting to have to share all the information that the doctor told me with my wife, and it made me so nervous. The doctor told me I could break the news to her. When they finally called me back to the surgery discharge area, I was full of so many mixed emotions. Most of all, I was excited to see my wife. It was our wedding day, after all.

When I got there, she was awake and alert. The first thing she said to me was that it was cancer. She said the doctor told her right after she came out of surgery. I couldn't believe it. The doctor said I would have to tell her. She told me that the doctor told her too, but that just confused me. I gave her the biggest kiss, and we held each other's hands until they sent us back to our room. There wasn't much to be said after that.

Once back in the room, they hooked her up to the machines that monitor her and helped her adjust the bed. Danielle, while very good at not showing her pain, was in incredible agony after the surgery. We talked a little with the nurses who mostly discussed the treatment with my wife. They supported the use of chemotherapy. Danielle was truly scared for her life, and the nurses weren't giving her the answers she wanted. The next day, we would get our answers straight from the doctor. The answers my wife so desperately needed.

After the nurses left us alone, I knew it was time to pull out her alternative options. I knew we needed to start pain management. I knew my wife was very opposed to using the pain killers that the hospital provided. She didn't want to use the button they supplied for the medication drip. Mostly because she suffered from many adverse side effects from medications throughout her life, and this experience was no different. The pain meds were already making her nauseated. She didn't want to take the nausea meds because they would cause her seizers. I knew a better way to beat nausea.

At that moment, I unpacked the medical marijuana I acquired that afternoon. I knew that my bride couldn't eat, so I would have to start topically. We did this secretly because the hospital couldn't officially approve the use of MMJ.

My experience in the MMJ industry taught me about Rick Simpson Oil. Rick Simpson used it in cancer treatment in Canada for over a decade. It is named after the founder and is one of the most medicinal products that people have developed for the MMJ industry. It retains much of the activated cannabinoids which have shown to provide different medical benefits. It can be eaten or applied topically.

Most people are familiar with THC, which is the cannabinoid that gives people a high feeling. The second-most popular, although quickly becoming the most popular medical cannabinoid, is CBD. CBD is being used to treat childhood epilepsy and many cancers as well. I had purchased a high CBD topical cream that day, applying it with an accompanying foot rub. Including a little Rick Simpson Oil that we had already begun to use.

With topical absorption, I found it best to put it on her feet, specifically in-between her toes, where there were the most blood vessels for maximum absorption by the patient. Immediately we saw the benefit, and Danielle also preferred it to how the pain meds made her feel, which thankfully was an option for her. She also appreciated the foot massage.

All the pain meds she had the first night allowed her to be able to also reach a unique state of bliss with me. It was, after everything, still our wedding night. I couldn't imagine being with a more incredible person at that point in my life. I knew we had a journey ahead of us, but, for a moment, we still had our magnificent love to carry us through. We had a beautiful evening in each other's embrace. I wouldn't have traded it for anything except maybe the miracle to make the recent problems disappear. I will admit that Danielle and I made the best of our honeymoon suite.

In all the pain of the day, we honestly did find a deeper connection through extreme hardship. Our bond deepened to a level that neither of us could have anticipated. It was a miracle. It was as if all the problems did, for a moment, disappear. The love we shared between us gave us both the strength to share a promise that still brings happiness to my heart.

6
Not So Honeymoon

Danielle and I both had the entire weekend off. We were fully expecting to spend a nice quiet weekend with each other, certainly nothing too crazy. It was supposed to be a micro honeymoon, but it had turned out far different than either of us could have expected. It was a far wilder experience than I could have ever imagined. The day after the surgery was anything but a honeymoon.

I was grateful that I was able to stay with Danielle in the hospital for the weekend. I was able to be by her side almost twenty-four hours a day except for when I grabbed some food. I know it made it easier on her to have me there with her. We were in a huge brand-new hospital with the staff being especially attentive and kind. Everything felt new, and peace surrounded us.

As I mentioned, there was a beautiful garden in the center of the hospital where we were married. The building was several stories tall and located on the North Side of Scottsdale, which is the upper-class area of Phoenix. I've never been a huge fan of hospitals, but this one wasn't bad in my book. It felt like at least we had our little honeymoon suite. We had privacy and some space in the room, even though we weren't expecting to be there this weekend, it wasn't the worst place to spend time recovering.

I was also happy because there was a Sprouts Grocery Store down the street where I knew I could buy Danielle fresh organic juice once she could start eating again. I went to the store and purchased all the organic fruit packets I could find. I bought her fresh-squeezed juices and made sure to have some organic oatmeal too. Danielle was very strict about her diet before her diagnosis, so after this occurred, the dietary regulations became even stricter. She had some knowledge of proper diets because she worked as a health assistant for some time with a local MD/ND. The hospital food was far from anything that Danielle would even consider consuming. I did end up making several trips that weekend to purchase everything that she needed.

The first day went as expected, beginning with the nurses waking us up early for the shift change. So far, we had had very nice and helpful nurses. Most were talking to us about chemotherapy because my wife was constantly asking questions. I too had a long list of questions of my own. Most of the advice that we received said to get started as soon as possible. I was a bit concerned about starting treatment so early. Danielle expressed a lot of reservations about any treatment.

From my research, I found that chemotherapy basically stops the division of cells, the hope being that the cancer cells die off first because they have a quicker metabolic rate than our normal cells. I also realized that it stops all cell division, which means it should also halt the healing process. My wife was recovering from the most intense surgery that a woman can receive, she was in great pain, and preparing for several weeks to a month of convalescence. We each had our concerns about what to do next, and we were waiting for answers from the Doctor.

The doctor arrived around 8 am to talk to us about the surgery. We had been anxiously waiting and were nervous beyond all belief. He was a very pleasant and professional surgeon, very truthful and forthcoming with his answers. He immediately told us that it was Cancer when he opened her up. The Doctor was surprised to hear that Danielle remembered anything after the surgery. He told us that no one ever remembered what he told them after they came out of anesthesia. Which is why he told me I would have to tell her. He sat for a moment in amazement at the revelation. The Doctor even asked if she was a trained government agent, she just laughed and said nothing, as he proceeded to explain the surgery.

He explained that he had to make two incisions that went across and up her abdomen. He opened her up and performed the full hysterectomy. Additional exploration showed several inflamed lymph nodes, but there weren't any significant signs that it had spread. I trusted his words as this was what he did as his specialty; we all felt confident that he had removed any visible signs of cancer. He didn't consider surgery alone to be enough for her survival. He was dropping the big news bomb on both of our days. He told us that without chemotherapy, she would survive less than a year. This was a big blow to Danielle and a reality check. We were devastated. Immediately we had questions for him. We were foremost concerned with the side effects of the chemotherapy. Danielle had a bit of a complicated medical history. For my wife, this was also not the first time that she had faced a terminal disease or a life-threatening prognosis. She had at one point in her life suffered from Lupus and Addison's disease, but both had gone into remission and no longer affected her. She suffered from some problems because of the disease and had to take cortisol, a synthetic hormone, that assisted her when she had Addison's disease, and her adrenal glands failed. If the lupus were to return, it would cause additional complication.

Another problem being that if she started throwing up and didn't control it quickly, she would continue to vomit until death. Throwing up might require immediate medical attention. Vomiting and Nausea are the two main side effects of chemotherapy. When we asked the doctor what we should do about this, he said not to worry there were medications to help with that despite Danielle's reservations about not responding well. The Doctors final recommendation was to try the chemotherapy and see what happens.

My wife and I had discussed before he came in what options we would consider. We both had very strong feelings against full blown chemo. However, the doctor had previously mentioned that there were less harsh versions now available depending on the outcome. I didn't understand what he meant; this was new news to me. We were hoping the doctor was going to discuss the other options, but the only option he gave was full blown heavy dosage chemo.

During the surgery, he even installed a port into my wife so that they could pour the chemo into her insides. A more aggressive but potentially more effective method of treating the source of cancer. It seemed like a very intense treatment option. On top of that, Danielle was upset that he installed the port in the first place. It made her feel disgusting having something coming out of her. The port never bothered me, I never felt it took away from her beauty. My concerns were on the source of her cancer.

The Doctor only told us he was looking for genetic markers in the Cancer as he didn't have any other answers as to what caused it. It would take several weeks to discover the results too. He never showed any sign or concern at the cause of the Cancer. His sole and main purpose was to sell his treatment. Encouraging Danielle just to give it a shot, as he explained it was the only option that would offer her a chance for survival. Trust me when I say that the number of times, he reassured us that my wife would die without doing chemo was disgustingly scary.

I had done my research, and on top of that, I had personally experienced the failed chemo patients at work every week. I heard the horror stories. I saw the struggles many of them faced. The hopelessness in their spouse's eyes, I still didn't get it at this time, not fully but I started to understand it. I began to see how hopeless the answers were making Danielle — constantly being reminded by the nurses and doctors that she didn't stand a chance of survival without chemo.

The backlash from the staff, had us stop voicing our disapproval of the treatment options they recommended. Resistance was Futile. It was a group effort we realized we couldn't compete against and win. They all had the same programming, and nothing we said was going to get them to think otherwise. Hopefully, this book will.

However, I expressed serious concern that they wanted to start treatment the first week after surgery. It upset me how fast the hospital wanted to start treatment while the recovery was still an issue. The doctor conceded that within the first month was fine, but for some reason, the doctor and staff wanted to push for more aggressive treatment. The doctor told us to expect about a two to three-week recovery time from the surgery and that we should immediately start treatment then. I was also wondering how long she would be in the hospital, and he said it would be another four to five days.

The apprehension continued to mount throughout the first two days. Danielle was uncertain about the answers from the doctor, as she didn't feel that they took her conditions into account. First, she worried that her past illnesses would resurface if she were to do chemo, and in her condition, those problems could cause life-threatening complications. The only solution that they could provide was a long list of medications they use to combat side effects. It was literally if this is wrong, they give this drug, if this happens, they use that drug.

My wife became repeatedly upset because she would have such bad reactions to medications. She had many in her life already that showed adverse side effects; all pain killers would cause severe constipation, while Advil and Tylenol would cause nausea. Then anti-nausea meds would cause seizers. The doctors were facing a complicated patient, but the treatment never changed, the treatment they used was universal, and they never discussed a single other option. This enraged Danielle. She was furious that they hadn't offered a single treatment option that took her health conditions into account.

I was still caught up on the lack of discovery process involved in the cause of her cancer. It upset me to have no answers to the potential cause of cancer. It felt like more should have been done to address potential causes of cancer, but that didn't happen either. I anticipated that there might be toxins or chemicals that may have caused it, but there were no tests, no survey, no investigation whatsoever. I left me so angry that I had a difficult time discussing the issue calmly.

Thankfully I received a little reprieve when my mom and sister arrived. Danielle had several friends visit that Sunday too. It was nice that one of her very close friends lived near the hospital. She was able to come by and show some additional support, often giving me a couple of minutes to take a smoke break. I didn't want to overwhelm my wife with too many visitors or conversations. I could tell after several minutes that my wife was not responding well to my family's questions. I didn't find it appropriate to go over traumatic experiences in front of Danielle, putting too much stress on her. Danielle's friend was visiting, so I was able to excuse the three of us.

I thought that grabbing a burger and watching the football game would be nice to get my mind off things. We coincidentally joined the family friend my mom and sister had driven up with at a local restaurant. His wife was strangely enough in the area, visiting a friend who was losing the battle to Cancer. I couldn't help but feel life had called us together at that moment for support. Synchronicity was playing its cards again, and I couldn't help but notice that we were all called to the same restaurant. It was a tough time for everyone, but we found comfort in each other.

I said a big goodbye to my sister because she was leaving to teach in Thailand for the year. My mom was returning home to Tucson 2 hours south of Scottsdale. When I got back to the room, I knew my wife was a little upset about my sister and mother's comments about her having a full hysterectomy. I never thought they would make such horrible comments.

My mom and sister were concerned about the type of surgery and the type of cancer. After discovering it was ovarian and she had a full hysterectomy they were showing immediate concerns. I knew their concerns were that we weren't going to be having children. I had to tell them that we were planning on adopting anyway to get them to shut up about the kids. Instead, their response was, "Good to hear; we were so worried about that." Danielle was beyond upset and couldn't believe they would comment about my wife not being able to have kids.

I didn't understand the damage and trauma it caused to Danielle since I'm sure she felt bad enough about being robbed of the ability to have kids. This was a very sensitive subject for Danielle, and a source of much immediate sadness. This experience taught me how important it is to be mindful of what we say, and how we say it. Sadly this was just the first of many insane comments that people would say to Danielle that were completely inappropriate or disrespectful.

After my family left, we were back to dealing with the pain. The surgery left my wife unable to move on her own. The first couple of days involved convincing her to use the medications that the hospital had provided because the MMJ wasn't strong enough to manage all the pain. The MMJ would help, but it wouldn't make it go away like some of the prescription pain killers could. She needed to rest, and mixing the medications were helping. Still, her fear of constipation was overruling her need to control the pain; she had a high tolerance for pain. It made more sense to her to handle something that she could manage if it meant that a bigger fear could be averted. Danielle did things her way, and there wasn't a lot I could do to convince her otherwise.

I went to bed Sunday night dreading Monday morning; I was in for the worst case of the Monday's ever. The reason I wasn't looking forward to Monday was that I had to work a ten-hour shift in Sedona on Monday morning. Typically I worked normal forty-hour work weeks with four days on three days off. This week I was in for a little more because I switched shifts to have our honeymoon. I would have to work for the next seven days straight.

Monday morning, we were up around five a.m. The nurses started coming in to check on us around 6. I had already applied the topical pain meds that I had bought. We saw better results every day. I was thrilled that it was making her recovery a bit more pleasant. She was still using an occasional dose of the pain meds they had on a drip. She wasn't thrilled with how it was making her feel as every dose kicked up her nausea. I had to make a quick run to Natural Grocer's to pick her up some supplies for the day before heading to work. Danielle needed some organic shampoo and conditioner, as well as some more juice snacks. It had to be quick if I was going to make it to work on time.

I promised that I would be back that evening because I wasn't going to leave her alone a single night. I made a vow that day to always spend my nights with her. I gathered my things together that I needed for the day, and I was off.

I left early enough to miss rush hour traffic at 7:00 am. It was a little more than an hour and forty-five minutes back to Sedona, and I had to work at 10:00 am. I knew that would give me 45 minutes to an hour to get ready and get to work, which was plenty of time. That day at work was particularly hard, I didn't say much and wasn't feeling very talkative. Thankfully it wasn't a busy day, so I was able to send a bunch of "I love you texts to my wife." After nine hours, my boss let me out a little early. I did tell him about what had transpired, he sympathized. I grabbed everything I had forgotten to grab in our first crazy trip to Scottsdale. I ran by both of our houses, finishing little chores. We did have several days before Danielle would be home.

After I gathered everything, I was back in the car. I made sure to bring plenty of music with me so that I would stay alert. I've done some wild long-distance road trips by myself several times, so this just felt like it was going to be a bit of an extended one. I knew I could do it. Life had prepared me for this challenge with many solo road trips.

I'll mention a notable few. Once, I drove seventeen hundred miles in less than twenty-four hours, making the trip from the Illinois border to Arizona. I also made a twenty-four-hour round trip to San Diego from Tucson to make it to a family reunion, Sunday was the only day I could get covered at work, so I left after a fifteen-hour shift at 3:00 am, then drove five hours to surprise the family at breakfast. I believe only my sister knew I was coming. Sadly I also had to work the following day. So I spent eight hours with the family took an hour and a half power nap and drove another six-hours home. It may not have always been fun, but it was always worth the trip.

My favorite adventure was a day trip from Tucson, AZ to Los Angeles, a short eight-hour drive each way. All to watch a US vs. Mexico soccer game with my roommates. Knowing full well I had to drive back immediately after the game to make it to my 8 am soccer game the following day. A game that we just so happened to win down three players. I guess you could say that long-distance road adventures have tested my commitments to the extreme, and I knew this was going to be one of my greatest tests of commitment. I committed to being with my wife every night, and I wouldn't let her down.

The first trip back wasn't a challenge at all. I was so excited to see my wife that my adrenalin just kept me super alert and super anxious. I sent a text or two to let her know my progress, but after an hour and 40 minutes, I was at the hospital entrance. Still had to take the elevator to level 3 and then go to the other end of the building, but I was just so happy to see my wife.

When we saw each other, we kissed and hugged and cried because we were so happy to be together again. It was about 10:00 pm at this point, but I wanted to stay up with her and talk. She told me how her friend from Phoenix had stopped by to show her support. She also talked about what she was going to do about telling the girls in her dance classes. She didn't want any rumors getting out. I told her that wasn't something we needed to worry about right now.

One of her friends and the parent of a student showed up over the weekend and drafted up an announcement while I was having lunch with my family. It didn't reveal anything other than Danielle was temporarily closing the studio because of health concerns. She knew that it was going to make a lot of people worry because so many saw her as indestructible. It was a miracle she survived most of the events of her life, and many of her friends knew this. Danielle was miraculous in every sense. It always appeared like nothing could keep Danielle down, the cat with nine lives. Danielle never wanted to show weakness to the community, a community that she said loves to spread rumors.

Coincidentally, the friend who was now living in Phoenix had to move away from Sedona to avoid small-town gossip. When people make choices with their lives because they lose a loved one, it isn't right to expect that person to go back to the way things used to be. Loss changes people, and many choose different paths when confronted with death. Danielle and I were reevaluating our situation faced with our new challenges.

To some, it could be a wakeup call; each of us must choose how we deal with the grief. Support is what people need, and asking inappropriate questions, or making any selfish comments are just unacceptable. Danielle wouldn't stand for it. Sadly, people are so selfish that they would impose their needs or desires above another person's. Too often, Danielle would push her desires aside to help others; she was the definition of supportive.

Support comes in many forms, it can be a kind word, showing up for someone, a home cooked meal, it can be a simple compliment, or offering to sit down and listen to someone, and when I say listen, I mean listen. Most importantly, any information which is shared is confidential, and should never flow into gossip. Today people spread crazy rumors to feel better about themselves. It is talking about the worst in people versus encouraging the best.

We don't compliment random people unless they really stand out, but it's the people who are not standing out that most need the encouragement. It is the homeless person that needs the reassuring word. We give all our energy to the glitz and glamor of life and compliment the pretty people but forget to compliment the person who is trying and struggling. Danielle would see these people and would offer support.

My wife made everyone feel special. I know that was one of the things I loved so much about her. I would like to believe I made her feel as special as she made me feel. It felt like I owed it to her to make her feel extraordinary. To provide the support and understanding she needed most. I felt beyond protective of her and didn't want her to experience any additional stress from outside sources. We had enough to deal with at the hospital. She was constantly being scared by the nursing staff, convincing her that she needed to do Chemo.

After my first day back at work, my wife's attitude towards

chemo was already shifting. I was a little concerned, although I figured it wouldn't hurt to get some more information. That night I went to bed on the fold-out couch as I had over the weekend. It was just nice to be with her and show her the support she deserved. We still had our intimate moments, despite the hellish nightmare we faced. It proved our love was deeper than anything purely physical. We had an emotional connection that neither of us had ever shared with another person in our lives. Neither of us had ever known such genuine love, and she knew at that point that I wasn't going anywhere.

The next morning, I was up at 6:00 am again. Danielle and I spent an hour with each other. We talked more, and we said a lot of "I love you's." However, I had to head back for day two at work, and it was another hour and forty minutes home. I threw on some music for another smooth trip home. I Cleaned up, changed into my work clothes and I was back out the door. At work that day, I did a little research on Chemotherapy.

I started with cancer.gov, which is pro chemotherapy. I looked up all the information I could. The main thing I was looking for was more clarification on potential side effects and what we could expect while going through chemo. We hadn't received many answers that satisfied my wife or me for that matter. I knew that no matter what we decided, we were going to make an incredibly informed decision. I read all the material that they provided on the website and printed out the information that I thought Danielle would want to read as well.

I thankfully got out of work early the next night as well, and I was heading home quick before going back to Phoenix. I was still feeling good and was ready for another trip back down the mountain. I packed up some snacks and hit the road. At this point, my wife was always anxious and wondering when I would be there. I arrived around 9:00 pm and was able to spend a nice evening rubbing the medicine into her feet. It had become somewhat of a ritual that I would give her a foot massage every time I applied her meds, well since I didn't use gloves, I guess it was both of our meds.

I know at the time that I did use Medical Marijuana for anxiety, sometimes sleep, and for pain as well. I have used it more often recreationally, but I understood the medicinal benefits as well. The application of the Rick Simpson Oil, it was having a calming effect on me too, which was a good state for me to be of service. Danielle needed me to be calm, cool, and collected, because I was her rock, for the times when she couldn't be calm and collected.

Four Days after her surgery, she stopped using the prescription meds, she was constipated, which was a common side effect she had from those meds and the anesthesia. She also had developed a bad case of ascites, which is when there is fluid buildup in the abdomen. The doctor recommended that they install a drainage port to take care of the issue. So my wife would have to be put under again for them to install this. I would have to say that the anesthetic they used gave her the worst side effects. The nurses constantly reminded her that it would take several weeks for that to clear the body. It was going to make her feel completely awful all over again having to go through this procedure, and they were going to do it the next day.

That night we discussed a little more about the treatment options. She was becoming increasingly supportive of trying chemotherapy. It was quite the shift for her considering that initially she had said there was absolutely no way that she would be doing chemo, but She didn't want to tell them that. We felt forced to play along with doing the traditional treatment. Now she wasn't playing. Danielle was serious about Chemo.

I pulled out the information sheets I found from the American Cancer Society; it was a lot of information. The first and most important thing I thought we should go over is the Side Effect Worksheet that is used to monitor and tell how you are responding to the treatment. It was literally four full pages of nasty side effects such as vomiting, diarrhea, constipation (yeah you can get both apparently), swelling, allergic reactions, and about twelve other side effects that all list levels of severity. We were supposed to use it to track her negative reactions.

Danielle's immediate response was, "Fuck That." She proceeded to say that most of the side effects and the main side effects were practically fatal with her pre-existing conditions. If she started throwing up ever, we would have to go to the ER, and they would have to administer a drug that helps her stop vomiting but makes her feel horrible. A coworker and neighbor confirmed to me that he had to take her non-stop puking to the ER one night. He definitely made it sound about two hundred percent funnier than it was, but that was just the type of guy he was, always making jokes.

Danielle and I decided it was probably best not to tell the Nurses that she wasn't interested in doing chemo. If she did, it was clear that they were going to continue to pressure her into doing it. They practically scared my wife into starting chemo; thankfully, she didn't succumb to the fear, and her rational mind won over. I should also say that according to the most recent statistics at the time, stated that she only had an eight percent chance of survival with chemo or radiation. I have noticed the statistics have drastically changed to closer to forty percent. Eight percent didn't inspire hope.

The hospital could not provide most of what my wife needed and didn't carry chemical-free, organic, or non-GMO food. The hospital couldn't give her any information on available alternative treatments. They wouldn't discuss alternative options even though over one hundred different alternatives have been shown to fight cancer in one way or another. I knew it was in Danielle's best interest to get out of the hospital.

However, we had a problem. Danielle was still constipated. It had been about five days at this point, so it was starting to become a concern. The next day she had to go under for a small procedure, which meant more anesthesia. Creating more worry about the continued constipation as a result. The nurses reminded us that she hadn't eaten enough to have a bowel movement.

We tried to get some sleep that night, but we both found it rather difficult. Most of our nights had been restless, and by day three of work, I could feel a bit of the emotional exhaustion. I was wiped out, but at least I had the drive and some music always to allow me to re-center myself to be the best I could be for my wife.

The following several days were very similar; I was driving every morning back to Sedona for an eight to nine-hour shift then hopping in the car to drive back to Phoenix to spend the night with my wife. Friday was the big exception, I didn't work early in the morning, but I also hadn't gone out looking for a new job either. I was slightly more concerned about making more money at this point. Especially considering we were facing the cost of alternative treatments which is never covered by insurance. I knew I needed to make more money.

I left a little later that morning around ten a.m. to head back and get cleaned up so I could apply to several restaurants. I was completely exhausted at this point and didn't have the energy for job hunting. I didn't have an option, and I needed to find a better job. I wished at this point in my life that I had a more stable foundation because much of this additional stress was because of financial need. It was an added stress because we were going to be out her income for several weeks, according to the doctor. I was seeing that it could be even longer than that for her to be able to teach again. So I decided to do what I could.

The first place I applied to was the restaurant at the end of Danielle's street. I figured the menu and the style of dining was a perfect fit for me. I walked in and asked to fill out an application. I sat down at the bar and started filling it out, soon afterward the owner walked in. I said hi and introduced myself and told her that I had just married Miss Danielle.

Right away, she was impressed and told me that she absolutely loved Danielle. I didn't feel it was the time to tell her what had happened yet. At once, she gave me the job, but I knew I still had to fill out the application for her records. I was so happy that at least I had accomplished what I came home early to do. I immediately went home for a needed nap before work that day.

After a five-hour shift, I went home. I was truly feeling the exhaustion setting in, and I was starting to worry about the drive. I wasn't feeling my usual strong, vibrant self. Facing exhaustion, I couldn't give up now. I hate to admit, but my secret weapon for extended road trips is nicotine or cigarettes typically. I gave up chewing tobacco seven years ago, but it wasn't until I met Danielle that I was able to kick the smoking tobacco addiction. She made it easy, and after six weeks, I could really use one.

The stress was getting to me, and the need for a cigarette was at an all-time high. I knew I could safely drive anywhere if I had a little nicotine. I broke down and bought a pack of cigarettes. I wanted to keep it a secret and fully intended to give them up as soon as I was done driving like crazy. Loaded with my secret road trip weapon, I made it safely to Phoenix that night.

I brushed my teeth when I arrived and went up to see my beautiful wife. I am sorry I haven't mentioned it more, but when I say she was beautiful, she was still beautiful. People couldn't believe how lovely she looked, especially after her surgeries. Danielle always maintained that natural inner attractiveness she had inside.

Even though Danielle was tough on herself, she would always get the best compliments from everyone who met her. Most said they wished they looked half as good when they weren't sick. It was cute but still made Danielle feel like she was still missing some of that allure because of the circumstances.

We had another great evening together, but I also tried to get some rest. I had brought up all the orgonite that I had made and put it in the room. I immediately noticed that I slept better when it was in the room versus when it wasn't. I made sure to always leave it in the room with Danielle because I'm sure it was helping her too. For those unfamiliar with orgonite, it is a substance that can be made using metal shavings, a resin, and crystals that helps protect from harmful EMF radiation. The radiation from all the devices was unavoidable in the hospital.

Most people tell me that they sleep better when they put a piece orgonite next to their bed. I never had a sleeping problem until now. I needed the rest, and so did my wife. I knew that I needed to do what I could to assist. The first night we both slept was the first night I brought a bag full of orgonite in the room. I later decorated the room with tons of pyramids. The addition had created a noticeable difference in my ability to sleep.

When we woke up on Saturday morning, it was another beautiful sunny day. We always seemed to wake up around sunrise. It also gave us an hour or two to talk before I had to go to work. I left that day, knowing that it looked like Danielle would be released on Monday. It brought me a lot of relief because I had Monday and Tuesday off so I would be able to take her home.

The next two days went without a hitch, and finally, Sunday night arrived. I was just relieved to have completed my endurance challenge for the week. It was nice just to know that we were likely to be discharged the next day. We could finally return home together.

We woke up with high hopes that we would be able to get out of the hospital quick. It ended up taking about five hours longer than expected but at least when we were able to leave Danielle was doing much better. The previous ten days had been enough, and she was pulling together all her strength for the car trip home. She was still suffering from extreme pain from the surgery, it had done a number on her, and the ascites was still causing severe discomfort too. My only goal was to make it home safe. I took it slow, making it home in about two hours.

We made it back to my house that evening around eight p.m. It was fantastic to get her settled into bed finally. I made sure to double dose her with medical marijuana. She was able to start eating the MMJ by this point, which was better for sleep and anxiety. I had to be careful not to give her too much because she didn't enjoy being "super stoned," as some might put it. In the evenings, it was a very useful tool to help her sleep and rest her thoughts. My home would be our new home. We had a journey of recovery and healing ahead of us.

7

A Healing Home

Danielle and I decided to stay at my house for several reasons. First, she didn't want people just showing up and checking on her. It is a small town, and if people saw she was home, they would have been knocking on her door. The second reason we decided to stay at my house was that we had a little more space to move around in, and that was also sort of the third reason. My roommate was a massage therapist and yoga instructor, so she had tons of pillows to keep Danielle comfortable. Plus, it was the right energy for us to be around while healing. I was subleasing a room from her, but she had made the house feel very peaceful and serene.

I had enjoyed living at the house since practically the moment I moved to Sedona. It was just off the Thunder Mountain trailhead, in fact, I would walk out my back yard and across the street to reach the entrance. Thunder Mountain is the mountain Walt Disney modeled his ride Big Thunder Mountain Railroad after. I loved that I could freely explore Sedona out my back yard. I hadn't spent much time at my house after I met Danielle, we spent most of the time in her dance studio. She still had two Roommates living at her house. Danielle didn't feel they were ready for the burden. My roommate was the exact opposite, so staying at my house put Danielle the most at ease.

Keeping Danielle comfortable to the best of my ability was my top priority. My roommate thankfully had a nice collection of hard pillows and body props from her time as a bodyworker and yoga teacher. Danielle felt most comfortable being propped up in bed, similar to the way the hospital bed would have her sit. It was the best position to provide the least discomfort. Managing her comfort levels was the most challenging task at this point. I was giving her MMJ foot rubs at least 4 or 5 times a day. Not only did the medicine usually help relax her, but the feet have connections to all parts of the body, and I would notice an improvement every time I would give her a foot rub. I still felt rather helpless, so I did everything I could to help Danielle feel better.

After a week in the hospital, we were both very eager for additional answers. The hospital hadn't provided us with the answers we both needed. Danielle had a Doctor friend who we were going to be meeting with as soon as we returned to Sedona. It would take a couple of days before we would see him, but the questions needed answers. Most of the questions that we had were about alternative treatments and other radical options. Doc was a man who had spent years providing solutions that the medical industry declined to offer. Doc was a little radical, and I would also say one of the most knowledgeable individuals about Cancer. He knew his stuff and at the same time was a very complicated individual. Doc was also someone who was tormented by loss. Our situation wasn't making things easy for him.

Looking back now, I truly sympathize more than anything; he too had lost his spouse and best friend several years prior. He lost his license to practice as a doctor because he was willing to do anything for his wife. Danielle and I both believe that what he did helped keep her alive longer so that they could share the special time they had together. The Doc was an eccentric genius type, and it took all the smarts I had to keep up with him.

Much of what he discussed was very familiar to me. Most of my online reading usually involved educating myself on topics about healing, diet, and disease. If I was researching a topic, I was truly confident in the validity of what I had researched. I often look at all perspectives, and then I use discernment to conclude. I will admit that I have been proven wrong from time to time, but for me, it just is ever-expanding my truths.

Doc's knowledge was overwhelming and humbling. After a week of disappointing answers and general lack of general health treatment or knowledge, I was relieved. The Doc, in my opinion, was our first set of real answers from an experienced doctor. I had spent the past nearly two weeks, begging my wife to start using some of the treatments I would recommend. Monoatomic Elements or Ormus had been shown repeatedly to cure cancer; they use the platinum elements in chemotherapy; they use platinum and palladium mixed with toxic chemicals. I had read papers that said the metals themselves if used properly in the right doses could help cure cancer. Danielle wouldn't take any until the Doc said it was okay. If she wasn't already familiar with it, she didn't want to hear about it.

I failed my first Test. I think it is important that I tell people that I messed up at this point in the recovery process. I did what we found to be the biggest mistake that so many people make. I was pushing the treatment that I thought would help cure her cancer. Feeling helpless made me believe that I could gain control if we did my cure to cancer. It didn't matter to Danielle what my choices would be.

I didn't make that mistake for long. I started to understand that Danielle was going to do things her way. It didn't matter to her that my way was to use Electro-Magnetic Therapy Devices, something she couldn't do because frequency treatments could trigger her Addison's disease, and we couldn't have her going through Adrenal failure while trying to recover from cancer.

I had to learn to keep my mouth SHUT. I had to respect what my wife wanted to do for her treatment. It wasn't up to me to decide what was best for her. She was the only one who could make that decision. The only thing I could do was talk her through the decisions that she was making. I could help make sure that she felt they were the completely right thing to do, even if it wasn't the way I would do it. I feel every person has a treatment that will be most effective for them.

Belief in the treatment or vice versa, the lack of belief in the treatment, can decide the outcome. The Placebo and Nocebo effect have repeatedly shown that sugar pills can cure people and a belief that a sugar pill is poison can injure or even kill. A belief in sugar has the power to heal or kill, depending on what the person believes is fact. It doesn't work all the time, but it works more times than Science could pass it off to chance. I think this was my biggest lesson and something I would continue to learn and refine through the course of our ordeal.

After our first meeting with Doc, I was convinced that we were going to beat this. He had confirmed that we needed to do lots of antioxidants, which was something I strongly supported. Including making sure she had proper clean water, we were banned from drinking tap, although I had stopped drinking tap water years ago.

I would go thirsty versus drinking tap water while I was staying at Danielle's, not really by choice but instinct. I know the difference between water that makes you feel good and the dead water that is passed off as water these days. I was drinking structured water, from my roommates work so that it would provide a healthier charge. Danielle immediately switched to this water.

The next thing we were going to be doing was alpha lipoic acid mixed with palladium. Another dietary supplement that has been shown to beat cancer as well. I was excited it had one of the platinum elements in it because it helped me bring up using the Ormus and colloidal minerals. Doc said no harm would come of using those supplements. I was finally allowed to start using some of my techniques to help beat this cancer. I wish I had checked my ego to start. This behavior created much tension between Danielle and me.

I knew that what I wanted to give her had no negative reactions, but it didn't matter to her. It was purely a beneficial supplement that has so many benefits that it was crazy to me that she wouldn't take it. She wanted to know for sure that it would help her and nothing I said could convince her otherwise. I was more than persistent, and the constant pressure I applied to get her to take it was met with more and more resistance. It created such resistance that it almost created a fear of the supplement.

A fear that I knew she also had towards using Electromagnetic Therapy Devices. My roommate had a very subtle EMF device at the house, and my wife, before getting sick wouldn't even get near. I knew she had some apprehension, and because of her medical history, it was set in stone. I knew better than to try and change her mind on this subject. If only I realized that applied to all subjects, then I might have avoided some problems.

Despite Danielle's beliefs, I also asked the Doc his opinion about Rife Electromagnetic Therapy devices. He told me that he personally only trusted the original device that Dr. Rife created. Some of the other new devices have such a mix of frequencies that they may or may not be helpful. In my research and experience, I was noticing the same thing. This was another interesting confirmation from a knowledgeable doctor.

I had a simple rife device, but it wouldn't allow for precise tuning to certain frequencies and that shortcoming I felt made it far less effective. I still wish that it was something that we could have tried, but the lack of support from the Doc and Danielle's left that treatment on the shelves. According to Danielle, there wasn't going to be a chance in Hell that she was going to try EMF treatment.

All my research and understanding of the disease had not prepared me for cancers greatest challenges. Nothing could have equipped me for the experience of going through Cancer with a loved one. It felt like a crash course with a lot more crashing than staying on course. I would make many mistakes along the journey, mistakes I always hoped to grow through.

First thing I learned to respect my wife's decisions, no matter what. I didn't have to agree, but I always needed to show her the highest respect. In no way would I disrespect her decisions by telling her to do something opposite to what she decided. I couldn't push a single Opinion about any treatment without ample supporting proof. The truth is that most of what I had studied and read was still something that I would classify as, "In my Opinion."

In my opinion, what I discovered is that people have a hard time respecting other people's decision, especially if those decisions are contradictory to our own. Just because something is true in my life and not true in yours, it doesn't make either of us right or wrong. For example, in my opinion, Clowns are funny and joyful. A doctor would be wise to prescribe me, clowns, if I'm feeling depressed. However, if he prescribed that to someone scared of clowns, he could end up sending that person to a mental institution. A silly metaphor, but sadly, our medical system doesn't consider belief structures despite belief playing a fundamental role in the Placebo effect.

Our talk with the Doc resulted in many insights and revelations about what the plan of attack should be. Cancer is a disease that consumes and eats the food of the body. By stage 3C, there was a chance cancer had started to spread. We had no proof that it progressed to any other part of her body, but the risk with stage 4 is that the tumors start to develop everywhere.

My theory is that tumors develop where the body is weakest. My wife's most traumatized area was her woman parts. The repeated abuse of men and the constant jealousy of women made the area a prime spot for Cancer.

The Doc told us that, "Cancer was an opportunistic disease." His statement resonated the most with me. Everything I had seen in my studies showed that it would attack weakened parts of the body, broken hearts would lead to breast cancer, control issues or a life that is out of control would lead to pancreatic cancer or people that had communication issues would be at risk for Thyroid cancer. These weren't sole causes, but if a disease was opportunistic, I could see the life patterns that would weaken certain parts of the body. I was learning, and I knew that the path the Doc sent us on was the right one.

I would say that a sense of relief set over both of us as we finally knew what we were doing to combat Danielle's Cancer. It was a mix of nine different dietary supplements that were all known to be super antioxidants. We also were going to start using the Hyperbaric oxygen chamber to help increase her healing, and we were going to start doing an IV treatment as well. There were also other treatments we were going to implement as her healing from the surgery progressed.

The priority was getting her diet dialed in, while also making sure she got lots of rest. Rest I could tell was the most important factor in how strong she felt daily. Alternatively, if she spent too much of the day stressed or worried it would wear her out. When Danielle was worn out, the pain would increase, and she would suffer the most at night.

Immediately after returning to my home, we began a late-night shower ritual to help her deal with the pain. I set up a stool for her to sit on in the shower, and I would sit next to the shower for support. I was usually the temperature control for her, so she didn't have to get up or move. It was impossible for her to stand for any length of time so she would have to sit for the entire shower. Rarely did we not use all the hot water in the house for a therapeutic session, but we would spend ten to twenty minutes in the shower.

The improvement that the water would provide was worth the time involved. The gentle stream would melt the pain away. My wife found the warm water very soothing and helpful in her healing process. During the first couple of weeks, sleep was always a big challenge. She took some naps, and the MMJ was helping to put her to sleep from time to time.

I can't forget that while all this was happening, I was working two jobs for a time. It might have seemed overwhelming if it weren't for the fact that I decided I was going to rise to the occasion or at least give it everything I had, failure wasn't an option for me.

I loved Danielle with all my heart, and she deserved one hundred and ten percent of the love I had to give. It was clear to me she also needed the support.

My priority was being there for my wife, nothing else in my life mattered to that degree. So in between shifts, I would run home to let the dog out and usually indulge Danielle with a foot rub to re-apply meds. Often, I would also have to help her to the bathroom as she could not walk on her own without a walker for the first several weeks.

The ordeal physically and emotionally drained Danielle. It was difficult to face the people in her life with the new reality she was facing. Danielle didn't want to share her problems with the community. If people were having trouble in their lives, Danielle was the person many people would turn to when times were tough. She knew how to listen.

Danielle gave people a beautiful space to share their deepest pains. Most people who interacted with her would be left a better person because that is what she did. She never gave up on anyone that she cared about and for her, the community was her family. I learned all families by blood or otherwise have their problems. She shared her problems about the community but started hiding her conversations with her Real family.

I had shown some concern that she was getting upset with her family. Primarily how upset her mother could make her. It bothered me that most interactions I observed would end with Danielle being upset. Much of the stress stemmed from the fact that her mom expected Danielle to do or at least try chemotherapy. Her mom did not understand the risks or practically anything about chemotherapy at that point.

Like many people who still have faith in the Medical Establishment, they don't ever acknowledge the risks or dangers associated with our prescription pill medical industry. My wife would repeatedly explain the risks she was facing because of her previous medical issues. Danielle's sensitivities made chemotherapy potentially life-threatening. Even her mother showed zero respect for her decision, causing unnecessary stress. Danielle knew what was best for herself, and no one was going to change her mind.

Never once did our families show a sign that they believed Danielle was doing was the right thing. Danielle, most of all, wanted her mother's support but struggled to gain it. Danielle was constantly looking for ways to win her mother's approval. Her mother wanted her to go to the oncologist, and Danielle hoped that would earn her cooperation. We were willing to try anything to change her mind.

Danielle's mom, like many other people, feels that Chemotherapy is the only solution to cancer, and she wouldn't entertain that there were other options. Everyone her mother knew did chemo, some survived, and for that reason, she thought it worked. I can't blame her for her experiences, but not everyone responds well to chemo. I can attest to that personally working in the Medical Marijuana Industry.

Additionally, many cancer patients suffer due to complications caused by chemo. The facts show chemo kills people every year because it can cause such serious reactions in a sick or weakened body. Danielle and I even had several people tell us about relatives that had to stop chemo because it made them too sick. Others told us that the chemo did so much damage that it ruined their quality of life, leaving most in medicated comas before passing.

I couldn't handle how upset her mother was making her and that they were calling every day, expecting a full update from Danielle. I told her she needed to cut back on talking with them because it was stressing her out. She started to make sure that she would talk to them while I was at work. For a week, this had been going on, and the daily updates with her sister and mother were becoming problems. Even though she wasn't telling me, I could tell something was stressing her out. It wasn't very difficult for me to deduce what was causing her additional stress, but I said nothing. It was her decision, despite my reservations.

Danielle's sister did not help the situation. Repeatedly Danielle would complain to her sister about their mother's behavior. Emotions always ran high during their conversations. Too often, Danielle had to curb her sister's emotional outbreaks. Danielle was using her emotional strength to handle each interaction. Danielle rarely felt like her sister was on her side. I tried to keep my opinions to myself, but it was difficult.

Danielle's family upset me the most because I always had to deal with the repercussions. Especially when I was home for an argument, and I could see the immediate impact. It was so much more obvious the impact anger and stress were having on Danielle's recovery. Stress would keep Danielle up all night in unbearable pain. I would wake up every hour or two to apply more medications or shower her. I always did everything she needed.

Danielle finally told me she was hiding that she was talking to her family. Telling her, I already figured that out. She was surprised I didn't say anything, explaining I was trying to respect her space. We always talked about everything, and until the previous week, we would even talk about how much her family would upset her. So when I could tell she was upset, without any reason, I started to have some ideas. So if she wasn't telling me about what was stressing her than the stress must be her family. I told her how obvious it was that they were straining her recovery.

It was so difficult for me to maintain a positive attitude towards their behavior after this. I was barreling into one of my first major mistakes. It finally happened, and I snapped on Danielle's sister. There wasn't anything special about their disagreement, but I finally had enough. I quickly repossessed the phone. Danielle knew I had a couple of things to say, but she asked me to be calm. I was not in the mood to be nice. My first major error in judgment.

I had a few rather choice words for her sister, and when I'm angry because I feel wronged, I can get rather righteous. Practically yelling into the phone, I told her sister exactly how I felt. I couldn't believe how much she allowed her mother to treat Danielle poorly. Also repeatedly causing Danielle to be upset was so heinous, in my eyes. It all happened in a blind rage, a rage that I wish I never let loose. I felt she was a huge problem, and I let her know, as aggressively as possible. A fatal error on my part.

Danielle's sister didn't think she had a problem, and nothing I said changed that. My aggression immediately had her sister on the defensive. The conversation was a complete failure on my part. I only showed an unhealthy expression of my anger to her sister. I regret ever behaving in a way that would cause such massive repercussions down the road. My first regret is that it was not helpful to act that way in front of my wife. I should have at least walked outside. I wish most of all that I had communicated my issues calmly versus an all-out verbal assault.

I rarely showed my anger to anyone, but Danielle and I had plenty to be angry about. Danielle's anger was more than enough for the two of us. When it came to anger, we had a lot in common. I did my best to hide my anger, hoping not to let her suffer. I knew that I shouldn't be around people if I'm angry. However, this experience was testing my capacity to control my anger to the highest degree. It was important to me that I not make my wife suffer my emotional outbursts. Finding a way to control my emotions was imperative for Danielle's healing.

There was enough stress in our lives that we couldn't control. Danielle faced mountains of obstacles in her recovery. Even the thought of having to go to the hospital would cause severe anxiety. People or Doctors questioning her treatment stressed her out. Convincing others to support her decisions would anger her. It was impossible to avoid all the problems. The best we could do was handle them to the best of our abilities.

Danielle didn't think I would support her in setting up an appointment with the oncologist. I feel bad that she felt that way. She had secretly gone with a friend to schedule the first appointment. Her friend had to convince her that it was the right thing to do. Danielle said her friend literally held her hand the whole way. She still needed me to take her to the appointment, so she informed me of her decision. I didn't mind at all because I wanted to see if I could find some more answers too. I obviously wouldn't have wished that she needed to go through that experience, but I was going to make the best of it.

Danielle and I agreed that we needed more answers. Answers that could provide the reasons why Danielle was choosing to forego traditional cancer treatments. It was a long shot to find the answers we were looking for in a place that promotes chemotherapy. Without a visit, I didn't see any other way to get her family off our back. The pressure to go was too much stress for my wife, and she gave in, causing more problems than I anticipated.

The other big stressor that was hanging over Danielle was making a formal announcement to the dance community. For the first two weeks, we had just given a general, "Danielle is temporarily in the hospital, and We will let you know as things develop." Danielle knew this wasn't a satisfactory answer for her students, and Danielle had to get a real message out to the community.

Thankfully one of the mothers stepped up and helped with contacting all the students. It was too overwhelming and exhausting for Danielle or me to handle. Knowing the silly, rude, or stupid comments that people make, it would have been far too much stress for either of us. It was nice that someone offered their energy and time to handle all the responses or headaches that came up. Which surprisingly more rude comments came back in response than we anticipated.

There was a general show of support, but surprisingly, there were some that Danielle's friend wouldn't even share with her. The one that got me was one wealthy parent that had just recently bragged to Danielle about spending $40K on a home renovation, even asked about a couple of hundred-dollar refund. Considering at the time Danielle was out of work, and we didn't have enough to cover the six months of treatment, it felt thoughtless. It is hard when people are more concerned about themselves than others.

Thankfully not all people behaved poorly, and many people just showed their unconditional support. We received a dozen gift cards to the local healthy grocery stores, which were such a relief for us. I still can't express the gratitude we felt. Danielle also loved the people who sent her a text every week, saying they were thinking about her. Most were wishing they could see her, even though she wanted her privacy. Although we found through experience, there is a fine line to being respectful of people's boundaries and pushing individual needs over those boundaries. Making someone feel guilty for wanting their privacy is a behavior that we found appalling. Danielle dealt with this issue from both friends and family.

We choose to live at my house for an extra level of protection from the public. No one knew where I lived except the friends she told. My roommate was also a saint and helped us out immeasurably respecting Danielle's privacy. She didn't tell anyone at her work what was happening because she didn't want loose lips to tell people anything that wasn't the complete truth. It was important to her that the message she gave everyone would be perfect. There was no room for error when it came to communicating with the community. Danielle said misheard rumors were common in Sedona. Maybe rich people have nothing better to do.

I think Sedona suffers from Elitism of all types, elite super rich to ultra-spiritual hippies. The super-rich live above everyone in their mega mansions, acting in life exactly how they live. Sedona throws a different level of elitism into the mix. The self-proclaimed gurus who proclaim their beliefs above all others. These people believe that they are always right and will not listen to someone who challenges them. They will often find it important to force their opinion on you if you think differently from them.

My wife told me she has told off several people who were preaching from a place that put themselves above all others. I too see the behavior throughout our society. The irony in our spiritual community is that many of the spiritual guru's are behaving the exact opposite of how Jesus or Buddha taught people to behave. Acceptance and Love with humility while forgiving those who know not what they do.

The rich tend to force their desires because those with money tend to use their money to get what they want, and if you have enough money, there is almost no limit to what you can buy these days. So the rich don't understand the concept of No, they only believe more money and power are needed to attain a yes. So my wife has had to put a few rich people in their place because they were using their money to control or manipulate people to get what they want, even if it put her at financial risk. Danielle would do the right thing no matter what, at times, she had to show restraint to protect her business, but she still would do the right thing.

The other problem with Sedona is that it is also a small town. People that have lived here for a long time know everyone else through maybe one or two degrees of separation. It's quiet and slow-paced, but it also has its share of problems. Local business owners face many problems when operating in a small town. Public opinion plays a huge part in if a business will make it or fail. I watched this happen to my roommate's business that she was managing. The owner would take pride in being an asshole to customers he deemed unworthy. The behavior I would never want to be listed on Yelp.

In a world where business can succeed or fail based on online consumer reviews, it is a terrible idea to give people a reason to write a bad review. In restaurants, it was a common understanding that people who have a bad experience would tell eight to ten people, but people who have a great experience will only tell one or two people. So bad experiences will ruin a business reputation, and in a small town, this is doubly true. A bad rumor could ruin someone's reputation or business. Danielle cared about her business deeply, which is why it was so important to communicate properly with the community about her condition.

It took about three and a half weeks for Danielle to finalize a statement. We had to tell everyone that Danielle was going to be in treatment for Cancer and that we were going to have to cancel classes for the semester. We didn't include the fact that her healing was taking far longer than we had anticipated, and the stress of teaching would not be beneficial for healing either. Danielle felt it was important to let everyone know that she had also gotten married, and I had been caring for her with a small group of other ladies. We asked that people respect her privacy through everything. The next couple of days after the announcement would be highly emotional.

Many people were shocked to hear the news that she had cancer. We were overwhelmed by the show of support. We received many letters and gift cards that were crucial to relieving any stresses we were facing emotionally and financially. After weeks of isolation, it was good to have a change of pace. Danielle was relieved to get the burden off her chest start moving forward.

It took a month before she had the strength to start talking and telling people what happened. It was hard for her to talk about it, and she always feared people would say something upsetting. People don't always respond well to bad news, and for that reason, they don't always behave appropriately. It was a chronic issue we faced.

The other fun challenge we had was the "Baby," as Danielle referred to her. Her real name was Andora but being a miniature blonde Pomeranian, she was cuter than a baby. She wouldn't even allow people to refer to the Baby as a dog. Her mom had trained her to be the perfect child, she would sit in a chair, she would wear sunglasses, and her mom would have her do other fun tricks. Andora was truly a Diva, and like her mother loved to be the center of attention.

Andora was the most intelligent and complex dog that I had ever met. She ran me through the ringers when I first met Danielle. Andora was jealous of all the attention we were giving each other, but Andora made her needs known. It didn't take long before I won Andora over. She messed with me until I started giving her a lot of attention too. Andora and I already had a strong bond before we decided to move her into my house.

We picked up Andora the day after we got back to Sedona. For the first two and a half weeks, she was quite the perfect angel. My roommate was concerned with Andora causing us to lose the security deposit. Since she was trained to sit in the chair, we would only have her in the chair or on the bed when she was inside. I took her for a walk four to five times a day so that we didn't feel bad about keeping her confined. It was working fine, but then my roommate broke down and allowed the dog to run around.

I made a mistake and didn't take her out before I fell asleep and Andora had an accident in my roommate's bedroom. After that, my roommate was rather upset with her. On top of all the help she provided, my roommate was dealing with a crazy boss who was causing so much unnecessary stress. Andora being a rather sensitive individual started acting out the more my roommate would ignore her for misbehaving. It was a circumstance that eventually drove us out of that environment.

Andora wanted attention and would do anything to get it. My roommate was played into her manipulation. I don't find Andora misbehaves if she receives the proper attention, as she taught me. As I mentioned before, Andora messed with me when I first met Danielle. She pooped and peed on my side of the bed in a bid for attention, so this wasn't completely unfamiliar. Andora started a vicious cycle of misbehaving for attention, causing me to forfeit my security deposit.

Thankfully while that problem was occurring, we received a message that Danielle's tenant was moving out. She had another tenant that didn't appear to be using the house. We could move back into Danielle's house with the privacy she wanted. It would thankfully be an easy move.

Several of Danielle's friends offered to clean the house before we moved in. It was perfect timing for us to move back into her house. It was obvious the increased stress of our life was causing some serious additional stress in my roommate's life too. It wasn't fair to continue to ask her to put up with the extra stress that we had brought into her world, especially if we had a safe place to continue her recovery.

Our return to Danielle's home was actually the first time I was able to wander the house freely. She had made it a rule with her tenants that she wouldn't have other people in the house, especially other men. When we met, we didn't need to use the rest of the house. Now the studio was completely inadequate to support Danielle in her healing. We would need access to the whole house, and somehow it had manifested one month before we expected it to happen.

It felt like divine intervention transpired to make it happen. One bad situation pushes us one way, and life provided a solution. A very common theme throughout our journey. I refer to it as synchronicity, but I think most people refer to it as a miracle. Every day felt like it was a miracle, but we were still praying for the big miracle.

Now we had to take advantage of the miraculously clean house that had manifested. We were heading back to our home, a first for us as a married couple. It felt like a dream to finally be home after our previous month's journey.

8
Homecoming

The trip from my house to hers was only several miles, but it was still one of Danielle's first trips in the car since the trip from Phoenix. We hadn't needed to leave for treatments because the Doc would bring everything we needed to the house. Danielle particularly liked this because she didn't have to be seen in public, even though I thought she still retained such radiant beauty. She maintained a beauty that few people could even explain other than it seemed almost otherworldly. Now that she was home, she glowed even more. Her home was a place that brought her much happiness and pride.

It was great to finally get her back in her house, which meant so much to her. It was where she taught dance for the past seventeen years, but to her, it was far more than that. It stood for all the struggles and hardships that she faced to keep the dance studio open. It also stood for the independent woman that she was. She bought it herself and had worked her heart out to keep it open through the recession.

Danielle decorated her home masterfully. Beautiful artwork graced the walls, cool artifacts, and unique antiques she would dig up in her second-hand shopping adventures made her space divinely unique. She didn't need new things because she would see the beauty in many discarded items. It says something about her general character because she would also see the gold in the people that society discards. Her house stood for more than just dance; it was a complete expression of herself.

Danielle's was happy to be home, but we faced some immediate challenges. First, we had to figure out our sleeping situation, and our options were limited. We had a single bed that met Danielle's quality standards, but it meant that I would be a little crowded sleeping next to her. The other bed in the house was old and included some broken springs. Danielle even mentioned it might have had mold. The only other thing would have been a memory foam mattress to lay on the floor. We decided that the floor was a really bad idea, and the mold was out of the question. Leaving only the single bed as the best choice.

I could manage the discomfort because it felt more comfortable always to sleep next to my wife. I couldn't leave her alone, no matter where she would sleep. I could endure if it meant we were doing what was best for my wife. The tight squeeze just created more intimacy, so it wasn't all bad. It was just a matter of time before I would bring up my queen size bed in storage up from Tucson.

The second challenge was adjusting to the new surroundings. We didn't have access to the main bathroom because technically, the second roommate was still there but hadn't been home in a month. Considering the roommate left her bathroom filthy, we weren't about to start using it yet. So we had to make do with the little spare shower located in the laundry room. It was a far smaller shower than at my house. I found a tiny stool that she could sit on in the shower while I would hold her hand for support.

At some point, during the shower, she would request that I remove her stool and she would sit on the ground for the remainder of the shower. I worked it down to a science. I could almost predict when she would ask me to turn up the temperature. I would then bundle her up in two or three towels and get her to a warm bed. During the autumn keeping Danielle warm and comfortable was never an issue. Sedona has such beautiful warm weather for eighty percent of the year, which is what led to one of the biggest problems we faced living at Danielle's.

As December approached the temperatures in the evening began to drop significantly. Danielle had lost a lot of weight and was far more sensitive to the cold. She would even spend afternoons in the Sun to keep up her body temperature. Danielle realized that being cold was not good for her recovery. It was better to keep her bundled up, which was not a problem unless she had to use the restroom. Danielle's home, like many in Arizona, didn't have central heating.

Built in the '20s the house's electrical system hadn't seen an upgrade in several decades. Danielle had almost lost the house to an electrical fire if it weren't for the dog bringing a small problem to her attention. After repairs, the technician informed Danielle that she couldn't use high wattage electrical heating elements. Leaving us with only two small heaters that met those standards. Danielle also made sure that we only had one heater plugged in per circuit breaker. I made it work by running some extension cords through the house so I could easily move the heaters to where we needed them. I would use them to warm up the bathroom before we had to use it at night, and also would bring both in the room if Danielle was too cold.

My final challenge was moving out of my old rental and into our beautiful home. Between shifts and running errands for my wife, I was able to grab most of my stuff over the following two weeks. Due to the circumstances, my roommate let me out of the lease a month early so I could handle treatment expenses. It was such a blessing, and I am still grateful for that.

The first week settling in was a bit overwhelming for me but eased by the convenience of my new job. The restaurant I was working at was less than a quarter mile down the street and directly across the main road that runs through the Heart of West Sedona. It took me less than a minute without traffic and three minutes with heavy traffic to drive to work. Normally if I worked that close, I would walk or bike to work. I always drove, concerned my wife would need me, and I wanted to be able to get home quickly.

It was at this point that Danielle also started connecting with more people. It had been about five weeks since the surgery, and she was now able to walk and move on her own. She was more confident now that her health was improving. There was a lot of personal pride that Danielle had that she wanted to maintain. On top of that, the opinions and comments of the Spiritual Community had Danielle angry and in fear.

Danielle witnessed ignorant comments people would make about Cancer, and that the person invited it into their lives. Danielle was upset by this way of thinking, as her cancer wasn't something, she intentionally invited in. She knew she wasn't the cause of her cancer, and positive thinking was not going to make everything go away. I am reminded that positive thinking guru Dr. Wayne Dyer also passed from a six-year battle with cancer. Cancer is nothing people consciously bring into their lives. It is an attack on the weakness of a person. The weakness could be from trauma, toxins, or a multitude of other sources. It is in this that each person's journey is different.

Humility is something I gained in this process. I needed to respect my wife's journey even though I would have done many things differently if I were in her shoes. I even had to learn the hard way why it is important to keep our opinions to ourselves. It was hard for me to realize that pushing my beliefs on my wife was violating her free will. So I had to start respecting her decisions if she was also going to start respecting my opinions about those decisions. No matter how much I wanted to help my wife if she didn't see my actions as helping then I really wasn't helping her. Despite me believing that I was being helpful all the time.

One of our first interactions with someone who was rather oblivious to others, was when the last roommate came to the house to clean her room and the bathroom. We were expecting her arrival because she had been texting Danielle about paying the last bit of rent. The roommate was made aware that Danielle was facing serious health issues. So we didn't need any explanation there. However, it was her first response that sent Danielle through the roof.

The roommate commented that Danielle had lost a lot of weight. Danielle was absolutely beyond offended by the remark. I actually didn't understand her offense initially but realized quickly why it was so inconsiderate. Danielle at the time was trying her best to gain the weight she lost during her recovery. As much as the comment was made in good intentions it was received as a sign of her failure to return to normal. The last thing she wanted to hear was she was looking thin when she was trying to get back to her ideal weight.

I realized quickly how incredibly rude it was to comment on the appearance of someone sick or recovering. We shouldn't point out problems that may be causing serious stress to that person. It is almost like squeezing a lemon in an open wound. I maintained an extreme cool during this time, and the roommate said nothing and went to her room to start cleaning.

After finishing, she tried to apologize by saying she didn't realize that would upset Danielle, because she would be happy if anyone told her that she lost weight. It was a big wakeup call for her to realize that sick people might not want to be called skinny. I helped calm the tension between Danielle and her roommate with the highest level of calm. I then told the roommate it was time for her to leave and thanked her for cleaning. My wife was impressed at how I handled the situation.

It was a huge improvement compared to how I had handled Danielle's sister. I only wish I had half the grace and elegance I used at this moment. Immediately I stopped the conversation saying it is clear that both parties are upset. I noted that we were thankful that she was sorry and that she needs to be more mindful of her words, next time. I told her that it was best for Danielle if she just accepted the lesson and left us alone. I thanked her again and sent her on her way. Sadly, not all encounters ended this smoothly.

By far, the most upsetting visit for Danielle was a parent who just made a surprise stop by the house. For the sake of her involvement in the rest of this story, I will refer to her as Narcy, because of her extreme narcissism. I was sadly at work when she unexpectedly showed up. Otherwise, it would have been a much different interaction. I had previously threatened to excuse people from the property for not behaving properly. My wife's health was more important than another person's needs, even my own.

I would never wish a Narcy into anyone's life, but she still plays a very important role in the story. Narcy brings awareness to behavior that is truly harmful to others. Sharing this encounter will help more people recognize the behavior and protect themselves from it. I couldn't protect Danielle from Narcy, but Danielle did share how hurt she was by her.

First, Narcy used her daughter to force a visit while I was out. Not only was Danielle having a tough day, but she wasn't in a place to take visitors. It was a serious sign that some people have zero respect for other people's boundaries. Danielle was not allowed to decline the visit either, as the child was used to gain entry.

This parent also broke every single rule that you could during her visit. Narcy questioned all of Danielle's treatment decisions, she even said, "if the treatments don't work, you are going to try chemo, aren't you?" Truthfully, I think, it is this exact behavior that made her constantly question whether she did the right thing. It upsets me the most because it was a pattern that she repeatedly dealt with from her family as well.

Danielle constantly faced people who didn't support her decisions. I even learned Narcy questioned all of Danielle's ideas about returning to teaching dance. Considering the performances were something that stressed Danielle out more than any other part of her job. Danielle thought it would be best for her health to stop recitals for a while. Narcy did not like this because the recitals were for the parents. She was stating in her opinion that Danielle must put on the performances. It seemed that Narcy could not do anything but push her wishes and desires.

Narcy also made some inappropriate comments about me. Danielle had a picture of us taken during our wedding on the table, and Narcy thought it was okay to make a slightly sexual comment about me. Not in words but in the way, she said it and insinuated. I'm not sure exactly what was said, but it was done in a tasteless fashion. Narcy's lack of concern threw Danielle over the edge. Danielle stuffed her reaction due to the child being highly sensitive. Danielle seemed to garner jealousy in many forms.

Another neighbor, while doing a walk up the street, said she was jealous of Danielle's situation. After explaining her condition and the wedding that also happened along with the hell she was going through. The woman still said she was jealous. I understood where this woman was coming from as she gave a brief explanation. Stating, "How lucky Danielle was to have found someone who would do everything she needed." Again, like her roommate, Danielle did not want that in her life. She wanted to be healthy and to contribute equally to the relationship.

Danielle was so mind blown that someone would say something so thoughtless. Danielle couldn't imagine why someone would say they are jealous of someone who has cancer. These people assume that because they wish their life could be one way that all people want their lives to be that way. Also, in no way shape or form did Danielle want to be dependent on someone. It humbled her being forced to count on me. Although it upset her that she couldn't help me more and made her feel inadequate knowing she couldn't work and contribute. My wife wanted to be a productive member of our relationship. In no way did she want someone to take care of her. It offended her for someone to think that of her.

Danielle and I were plagued by people who never thought before they spoke. I can say that it was made worse by the situation we faced. The tragedy we faced made people uneasy and nervous. I too find it hard to control my emotions when faced with uncertainty.

It was a perfect storm for people who are ill-prepared for expressing their emotions. I learned a lot from navigating that storm in myself and through watching others. It would be in the positive examples that I would find my strength.

One family that came over truly leaving a positive imprint because of their presence. One of Danielle's students was Church of Latter-Day Saints, and she was a very gifted and longtime student of Danielle's as well. Her family had planned a visit with Danielle, and I didn't know what to expect. The one thing I did notice when they entered was that they were all emotionally positive. None of them showed the pain or sorrow that I knew they all felt. The same pain and sorrow that so many people showed to Danielle.

This family did not behave as so many others, and they held the highest space for my wife. They prayed with my wife, even though my wife was not someone who believed their faith, she loved their prayers. The whole experience left my wife filled with joy, with happiness, and with something no one else had ever brought to her before. It was something special, and I will never forget their kindness. It was such an honor to witness a good example for support. It is rare to meet people who know how to behave when someone is sick or dying.

The main culprit I identified was that most people are completely unprepared with how to behave in highly stressful or emotional situations. The lack of experience means that many people behave as if like a child getting angry for the first time. They don't know how to control their temper, and as a result, their behavior can be quite offensive. Most people have little to no experience helping people through the death and dying process, this means that the emotions that come up are very new to most people.

Expressing emotions poorly often happens when people are overwhelmed. Witnessing a loved one suffering is one of the most overwhelming experiences to endure. When people are not prepared, their suffering is greatly amplified. Rather than focus on the suffering of the sick person, most people start to deal with their own suffering. People end up dumping the emotional overflow on everyone around them. I'm guilty too.

When we are suffering, it is hard to ignore it. It is a survival response versus a compassionate response. However, sharing our suffering with others creates the same biological response in all parties involved. The leading science is showing this happens when we watch TV and listen to music — proving that sharing suffering is one of the most selfish and destructive things you can do to some who is trying to heal. It takes compassion to set aside our suffering while we attend to the suffering of others.

Sadly, most people couldn't leave their emotional baggage at the door and left it all with Danielle every time. Danielle couldn't hide it either, and I always knew when she had a draining encounter. It was obvious every night she didn't sleep. Danielle pushed many people away because she recognized the problem too. Which led us to not having the support we needed.

Danielle felt many friends abandoned her in the process, we had a big show of initial support, but few people continued communication. Danielle felt the people she showed up for didn't do the same for her. It was devastating for Danielle. She had hoped to have someone else in her life that was capable of being there for her. Someone to support her in all the decisions she was making and keeping opposing opinions to themselves. The opinions of people who visited upset Danielle the most.

People loved to share their opinions without ever knowing the truth or special circumstances Danielle was facing. The problem with opinions is they rarely are valid for all people. If people were more concerned about the needs of others versus pushing their opinions, we wouldn't have seen so many problems. This behavior is why Danielle decided to withdraw from society. People can be unconsciously cruel these days in an attempt to feel better about themselves.

I see it more and more throughout our society, people who feel bad about themselves and put others down to feel better about their circumstances. For Danielle, it was as simple as dwelling on all the problems she was facing. Many people wanted to know everything that happened to her, without realizing it was all at Danielle's expense. I don't feel people are doing it intentionally but intentional or not; I feel the behavior needs attention. In my opinion, there is no excuse for this type of behavior, and I hope this story conveys that message.

It didn't change the fact that many people that Danielle had hoped would reach out didn't. I'm not sure if it was because I was in the picture, but the lack of support was bizarre. The people that were reaching out were people that she didn't want to be around, or they were asking to bring their children over. Danielle wasn't having any students over because she found children were ill-equipped. The few students that had come over had proven this to her.

Another reason she avoided having students visit was to keep up her image. Danielle didn't want to subject her children to the suffering she was going through. Many parents and students didn't understand this, causing added stress when Danielle had to explain. It may have been a little superficial, but it was also her choice, and it wasn't anyone else's decision to make. It wasn't easy to accept for many people. I didn't always agree with her either, but I knew I had to support her decisions.

The only people in Danielle's life that were supporting her decisions completely were the Doc and me. Since the Doc was in charge of her treatment, it was clear he was on board for everything we were doing. After educating myself on the treatments, he recommended, I felt confident in his recommendations too. It couldn't have been easy for Danielle only to have two people on her side when it came to beating cancer, especially since Doc and I were having a tough time too.

The Doc and I were both emotionally taxed by the situation. The Doc had lost his wife to a chronic illness not long before. Danielle and I both knew it was still very hard on him. It isn't easy to lose a loved one, and it feels even worse when you feel like you may have failed that person. Danielle told me that Doc did everything he could to keep her alive. She said it wasn't his fault, he likely kept her alive far longer than she would have if she hadn't met him. It was clear he still felt the loss.

Danielle was a hot button because we no doubt triggered his own experiences. Danielle and I could see he was having a tough time. We could tell it was becoming increasingly difficult for him to be there for us, as we started seeing him less and less. He started having more frequent times that he would need to disappear to regroup. Danielle could feel the stress of it all too.

I too was feeling a bit stressed and overwhelmed by everything that was happening. It didn't matter to me because I knew that I had to stay strong. I made sure to do everything that Danielle needed of me. I did all the cooking, shopping, cleaning, and driving her to most of her doctor's appointments. I always had to assist with all showers, including taking the dog for several walks every day. With a full-time job, I was pushing the limits of my endurance. I didn't feel overwhelmed because Danielle always seemed to have it much worse. She gave me the strength to endure the stresses.

Before Danielle, one of my biggest stresses was around money. I have found the more money I'm making, the less stress I have in my life, but the stress increases exponentially the less money I have. For the first decade of my adult life, I was financially stable because I always worked at successful restaurants. The abundance I had experienced for so long didn't prepare me for the stress that being broke would bring.

Before meeting Danielle, I had spent the past several years attempting to get myself back on my feet financially. Due to many choices I made, that I don't regret, but also wouldn't repeat. I don't regret those choices because I learned so much from them. Danielle and I were finally in a place to rebuild before our lives drastically changed. Since the day of our wedding, we had become increasingly concerned about covering all of the expenses. I had to make more money.

I would never have supported us if I had stayed working at the Marijuana Dispensary. However, my new restaurant job wasn't quite as lucrative as I had hoped. We were not as busy as I was hoping. If the restaurant was busy, it would have easily covered our basic expenses. I still decided to stay at the new job, even though I wasn't making as much money as I wanted. Other perks made it an ideal option for me.

Primarily, I did have a lot of flexibility in my schedule. Also, because it was often slow, I could take nights off or even close early. I felt more inspired to be with my wife versus work all the time. The restaurant was also facing hard times and needed some experienced help to keep things running. I still don't know how they would have done it had I not showed up. I was scheduled six days a week, but my schedule was unique.

Besides waiting on tables most nights, I also did cater deliveries for the restaurant most mornings. Since Danielle and I were usually up at sunrise, going to work at seven a.m. wasn't a problem. I often would deliver both breakfast and lunch to different locations. It was one or two hours of work for each delivery. I made fifty dollars per delivery, creating a far more consistent income. The final reason I stayed was that I could easily run home. It was never a problem in-between shifts to take care of Danielle and Andora. It worked for the schedule that Danielle needed me.

I would usually get an hour or two in between shifts to spend with my wife. After I finished the chores, we would usually cuddle. We spent many afternoons just holding each other and talking. If she wasn't feeling good, I would give her a medicinal foot rub. Things had started showing some improvement. She even started to give me back scratches as it was something I truly enjoyed, and it made her feel like she was giving back in the relationship. Plus I would never let her do it long or to the point that it was making her tired. I only allowed it when she was doing well because I do also feel that it is important to be active to aid in recovery.

We continued to discuss the concept of how Gabby Gifford's husband forbid people to show any negative emotions after someone shot her in the head. I completely understood the importance of this factor in our current situation, and the problems were that many people in her life weren't respecting those boundaries. Most visitors often acted the exact opposite of proper behavior. People expected the same relationship with my wife regardless of her condition. This expectation was very stressful and exhausting to my wife. Since we both had to pay for it at night, we tried to manage stresses the best way possible. The one area where I had practically zero control was with her family. I stated my opinions, but that still never stopped the interactions.

For over a month, I had dealt with Danielle getting upset with her mother regularly, which typically led to arguments with her sister about the issue at hand. Often, it was about their mother bringing up chemo, but other times, it would be a cold or rude comment. I understood the importance of family because we needed all the support we could get, so when they offered to come out, I figured it was a huge opportunity. Danielle and I were both concerned about the visit. Her mother planned on coming out for a day while her sister was going to come out for the weekend with their son, who was being deployed in the Navy.

Danielle, before they even came out made it abundantly clear, that if their intention to visit was to talk her into chemo, that they shouldn't come out. She asked that they don't bring it up anymore and that while they are visiting it not become an issue. It took a little planning on their part because her sister couldn't take any time away from work and her mom was going to take the train. Danielle's nephew was going to pick up her mother from the train station and visit too. Finally, a real show of support for Danielle from her family. I was relieved but also a bit concerned about how the interaction might turn out.

Her mom and nephew arrived first for less than twenty-four hours. Her mom could only stay for a very short period, not any good excuse other than she had to get back home. She did brag about the other people she visited along the way and was her usual self for the day. I ended up grabbing some lunch with both her mom and nephew at a local restaurant. It wasn't an organic menu, so I knew we couldn't take anything home to Danielle. I was impressed that her nephew picked up the tab, which was very generous of him.

Her mom ended up leaving that afternoon to go back to Philadelphia, but I'll still never forget the last thing she told Danielle as she was leaving. I should give you a little background before I tell you what she said. Danielle told me that her mom, for many years, had been caring for an individual as his caretaker. Danielle told me the relationship was also more complicated. I don't know all the details, but the fact is that she had spent many years taking care of this man. So it blew my mind when she was in the front yard, and she told Danielle that she was tired of being a caregiver. To say that to a daughter who is recovering from Cancer not only seemed heartless, but it was just plain cruel. Her mom made it crystal clear that she didn't want to help.

I believe her sister arrived later that day with her husband. We spent the evening talking and after everyone left her nephew returned to talk with us. He was very respectful and inquisitive. I thought the conversation went well, and we talked about the options that we were choosing as treatment. We were aware of the concern that the family had, but they weren't considering the circumstances that led us to our decision.

The reason we decided against chemo was because of Danielle's specific situation. Many nurses told us off the record that there was no way they would ever do chemo, especially if they had my wife's diagnosis. We knew what we were doing was right for Danielle, it may not have been the right choice for the average person, but for Danielle it was. I supported her, her other Doc supported her, and Danielle supported her own decision. We talked for over an hour before he went back to Flagstaff because he was being deployed the following week.

The next day I worked the entire day, it was a Saturday and one of my longest days of the week. I had three shifts, a breakfast and lunch catering delivery, and I had to work that night at the restaurant. I worked the morning shift and came home to check on Danielle. She was getting ready to meet up with her sister, but I only had an hour. I came back later that afternoon for another break. Danielle was out and about with her sister.

At this point, I took the garbage out that had piled up over the weekend. I also cleaned up the kitchen. I had been cleaning all week to prepare for Danielle's family, or at least in the extra time, I created to make it happen. No one had lifted a finger all weekend, and I couldn't believe it. Then Danielle informed me later that they did nothing but complain it wasn't good enough. Thankfully I finished everything and took a rare moment for myself.

I returned to work that night, and after I got off, I called Danielle because she wasn't home. Danielle informed me she was staying at her sister's hotel. Danielle had taken them on a sightseeing trip around Sedona, and she was resting. Her sister, after all, hadn't been to Sedona in the 18 years that Danielle lived there. It blew my mind that they would think my wife was capable of such a big adventure. I was a bit concerned about how the evening would go.

Danielle was already having a healing crisis when I arrived at the hotel, so I didn't stay very long because Danielle's pain was through the roof, we had to take three showers, and she was completely miserable the entire night. I still remember how hard that night was for her because it made me so angry. It upset me that her health problems were the result of interacting with her family. I, as usual, had to work at seven a.m. and eleven a.m. the following day, but still made it home just in time to say goodbye to her sister.

Danielle and her sister had gone into our room to talk privately. Within several minutes Danielle came storming out of the room screaming at her sister. She had decided to bring up trying chemo. At that point, I lost it. I got in her sister's face and started yelling at her. I told her to quit acting like "A Fucking Child." She was completely out of line, and her emotions were all over the place, she was a complete emotional mess.

I could tell that her sister lacked any emotional strength and her behavior because of that was usually horrendous. At this point I had only dealt with it over the phone but now to see it full-blown, I wasn't about to stand for it. However, my reaction to the situation ultimately didn't help the problem. I made it much worse by getting involved.

I excused myself from the encounter quickly, avoiding everyone until they left. I stewed in a moment of pure rage outside. I never thought at that moment how destructive my anger could be. As much as I wanted to believe I was protecting Danielle, I had no idea how I had the opposite effect on the situation. It was becoming harder and harder to control my emotions, and my emotions out of control can be a force of harm. I resorted to my medicines and smoked myself out of an anxiety attack, just in time to be there for my wife.

After their visit, my wife was livid. She couldn't believe their behavior explaining how selfish they were. She was mind blown that her family would treat her so poorly, although, it didn't surprise me after observing present actions. Danielle's stories from the past just confirmed this to me. I started to see the vile person that her mother was. I didn't need any more convincing, and it was clear her sister was toxic too. I couldn't stop Danielle's desire to have a better relationship with her family, so I tried to support healthy interactions as much as possible.

It was a tough couple of weeks getting back to normal. Little did I know that expressing my anger through yelling would have such serious consequences. I would have to make many more mistakes before I would realize the full gravity of my situation. My mistakes were adding up, and Danielle was keeping track. However, my continued support outweighed the mistakes — the support she so desperately needed.

Danielle and I were left very much on our own at this point. The Doc was coming over less and less. Our families were unwilling to offer the support we needed. However, we weren't asking for help either. Danielle and I both were victims of our pride. Only when we both started humbling ourselves did we find the answers we were looking for all along.

9
What's up Doc?

Danielle was constantly reconnecting with friends as her health began to improve. One friend had recommended that we meet with one of their mutual friends who was a Naturopathic Doctor (ND) in town. Danielle and I agreed that since we couldn't get in touch with Doc as regularly that it might be best to have a back-up doctor. We decided to set up a consultation with her friend. Danielle was very familiar with the new doctor since she had worked as a front desk secretary for her and Doc some years prior.

I was very impressed at the first consultation with our new ND. She was incredibly professional and on top of that highly knowledgeable. I would say that she was not an expert on treating cancer, but she had hands-on experience treating it with alternative methods. We talked while she took Danielle's vitals. We discussed the treatments that we had already started.

We told her that we were using the hyperbaric oxygen treatment to help with healing from the surgery. We also had used an alpha-lipoic acid supplement. There wasn't much that we were doing that she had any problems with except the oxygen chamber. She wasn't sure if the increased oxygen would also increase the growth of cancer. She supported it to help with healing from the surgery but didn't recommend it for further treatment.

She had a couple of other options she wanted to present to us. The first was a light therapy device. We had investigated another device in town because of the data that has shown these light therapy devices can shrink cancer tumors and even rid the body of cancer completely. However, the device also uses additional Electromagnetic Fields during the treatment, which means Danielle wouldn't use it. It isn't that she couldn't use it, but her phobia of EMF treatment made it not worth trying. The ND explained her light therapy was just light and no other frequencies. Danielle was on board for adding this treatment as soon as possible.

She also told us about a new IV treatment derived from a turmeric extract. It was called curcumin, and there was a doctor in Phoenix who was using it extensively to treat Cancer. She had a patient that had used it, and it put his stage 4 cancer into remission. She even told us that he was a McDonald's diet type of guy, so she was very optimistic about Danielle's situation. I learned turmeric was showing incredible anti-cancer properties, but now they were creating a more concentrated extract administered through an IV.

The big issue with this treatment was that insurance wouldn't cover it. Each IV was also going to run between three hundred to six hundred dollars per treatment. Depending on the concentrations, it was going to be more or less expensive. Danielle would also have to run the IV once or twice a week. The price tag was daunting. I would have to start making far more money to pay for it myself.

The next item that she provided us with was a list of things that we should avoid. The list was extensive; it told us to avoid soy, gluten, and other refined sugars. The biggest thing that caught my attention was that memory foam mattresses, according to her, could be cancerous. I was a little bothered because the mattress I was planning on bringing up from storage was a memory foam mattress. So now we were left with a single mattress as our only solution.

Igniting the start of a crazy struggle to find a mattress solution. It wasn't something that fit into the budget in the immediate future, so I just put it on the back burner. I was still sleeping fine on the single mattress with Danielle. A solution we didn't need to focus on now.

The solution we decided on was starting the curcumin treatment as soon as possible. The additional research I had done showed that it was not harmful to the body, but it was highly anti-cancerous. It was a more natural form of chemo without all the crazy side effects. Danielle was confident it was the treatment for her. I just wished her family showed the same support. The price was our primary concern. I certainly couldn't pay all the bills and pay for treatment. Danielle's insurance didn't cover any treatment that wasn't chemotherapy or radiation. Additionally, we weren't receiving any financial support from either of our family's, but that wouldn't stop us.

The first step we decided to proceed with was to have a chemo port installed. I know it sounds a bit strange, but it was necessary for Danielle. We had initially declined this after her surgery because our goals were different. Now a port was the best option. Danielle had trouble with people being able to find her veins, so if we had a port, running IV's could be far easier to administer.

The insurance would only cover the port installation for chemotherapy. So it was decided that when we visited the surgeon, we would set up an appointment to have a port installed. Danielle decided to tell the Doctor that she was going to do Chemotherapy. It was all working out, but we still weren't sure how we were going to cover six hundred to twelve hundred dollars a week in IV's.

The ND also told us many other things to avoid, including stress to give Danielle the best chance for recovery. The plan included a modification to her diet and some chemicals to avoid. After going over everything, the ND also decided that the water could have been a huge culprit and that tap water could potentially be very harmful. The ND also informed us that the unmonitored estrogen doses that her other doctor was giving her might have been a huge contributor to the development of her Ovarian Cancer.

Now, this is where one of the first big arguments happened that put some serious stress on our relationship. Mostly due to my ignorance and expecting an answer about what caused Danielle's cancer. We still had to meet back with the Surgeon for a check-up on the surgery. I was fully expecting to hear back from the surgeon that they had figured out what might have caused cancer to develop. I wanted answers from someone who promised me answers.

Danielle discussed her entire medical history with her doctor friend. She went on to explain her extensive use of IV's for vitamins and estrogen. The ND explained Danielle should have been monitoring her estrogen levels during that time. Danielle confirmed the doctor never tested her levels. Leading Danielle to conclude, that a doubling of her estrogen doses six months prior was a contributing factor to her cancer. A possible cause was not quite the answer I wanted.

Nothing could convince Danielle differently. The doctor who gave her years of IV's was at fault. It broke her to learn that her friend didn't run the proper tests, tests which were required. The years of trust vanished in an instant. Danielle did nothing but vent about how angry she was at the situation she was in, and that it apparently could have been avoided. I couldn't have understood the level of betrayal that Danielle felt. She became upset that I didn't take her side completely on the matter.

Our arguments were explosive and never ended well. There was no doubt in Danielle's mind, and I couldn't accept that. I still wasn't sure and didn't want to be blaming someone if there was another cause. I didn't want to jump to conclusions. I wanted answers, I wanted proof, and the surgeon was the man to give me those answers.

Danielle was not looking forward to the meeting like I was. Leading up to the doctor's appointment, Danielle showed increased health problems, especially through the night. I could easily tell when she was stressed about something because her pain would intensify, she would have more digestive issues, and on top of that would end up sleeping far less. I always tried to provide positive reassurance. I constantly wanted to show her the love she deserved, especially during times when it was so important I do so.

This trip required a lot of support for Danielle on my part, she not only wasn't looking forward to the 4 hours we would spend in the car, but she didn't enjoy going to the Doctor's. Every time we go to a Doctor's, they must tell us that Danielle is going to Die if she doesn't do Chemo or Radiation. Even our Naturopathic Doctor had to tell us "by law" that Danielle was going to die without doing treatments that are approved by the American Medical Association. I can't imagine the fear that comes with confronting people who repeatedly reminded her she was going to die.

This trip to Phoenix was a little tense, but we both managed to make the journey without any serious issues. Danielle's comfort level was way down, her pain was constantly increasing, and we were less than halfway through our journey. We met at the doctor's offices instead of the Hospital. I hadn't realized that we were going to a different location about 20 minutes further down the road. Meaning we had to take an extra bathroom stop, setting us a little behind schedule.

We arrived at the offices to find accommodations far nicer than we were expecting. The office had a much nicer atmosphere than the huge cold hospital. It put Danielle a bit at ease to not have to walk through the long hallways. I was thankful that they had tea and snacks in the waiting room. We welcomed anything that put us both more at ease. I was rife with anticipation, but Danielle was anxious and terrified.

The surgery to get the port scared Danielle the most. However, the surgeon sold us on having him perform the surgery. When I say he sold us, I mean he sold us on using him to install the port. Danielle and I decided there wasn't another surgeon in the country that we would have used. We already witnessed his work once, and Danielle was satisfied with his current remarks. After his inspection of the area, he operated on, and he expressed healing was progressing well and that she should expect a full recovery within a month. A huge relief to us since we hadn't "officially" consummated the marriage yet. Thankfully we didn't wait till the wedding.

The Surgeon knew his stuff about Surgery. However, I would be disappointed with his answers about my wife's cancer and potential treatment options. Danielle and I both inquired about the less harmful options that he had mentioned, but again, we were told that those options weren't available for us — telling us that the abdominal port that he already installed was a new type of chemotherapy. The same new treatment that we had already had aggressively pushed on us. At the time, I didn't think it was best to start treatment until her body had fully healed. Now it was different.

Danielle was mostly healed, and in a place to honestly look at the options. So we asked more questions about the abdominal port chemo bath, which was set up to put chemo right into the location of where he removed the Cancer. It seems like an effective possibility except that he finally informed us that some people end up only doing one to three treatments because it is so intense. I could tell right away my wife was scared, pissed, and mad that they would attempt to put something so toxic in her without disclosing this huge truth.

Danielle told him that she would pass on that treatment option but would proceed with a more traditional approach. We would have the port installed in Phoenix by this incredible surgeon, and she said she would receive treatment in Sedona at the local oncologist. We made appointments to get the port installed, and we also set up a consultation with the local oncologist.

When the Surgeon finally decided to go over the tests they had run on the Cancer, I was thrilled, well initially thrilled. I was hoping to find the answers we were looking for, but instead, I was completely disappointed. Not only did they have no answer to the cause of her cancer but that they weren't even going to investigate further. The DNA test had turned back a negative so there was no answer that the Medical Establishment would or could provide. I was pissed off. I had held out blame in hopes of any additional information.

I felt horrible at my stance towards the cause of my wife's cancer. I was truly sorry for any strife I caused between us. I was expecting answers, and the only answer we had was basic malpractice. It did bring some peace between us, but it did create mutual anger towards the doctor who administered the estrogen IV's. Truthfully this is the first time I officially felt let down by the Medical Establishment. I wanted to know what caused my wife's cancer or cancer in general, but the truth is that the entire Medical Industry didn't care. I was so angry.

Despite our issues, we scheduled our appointment back to Phoenix. The rides were rough for Danielle. The hour and forty minutes between Sedona and the Hospital was very strenuous on her fragile body. The 03' Mustang wasn't the easiest car to get into or out of after surgery. However, the ride was smooth enough not to cause much more discomfort.

I stayed strong through these trips because I knew my wife needed me to be. With all the energy I could muster, I made sure that she had someone present for this new operation. Undergoing surgery struck fear into Danielle. I knew she didn't look forward to the side effects of the Anesthesia or the meds that the hospital would provide. It is difficult when the side effects can be worse than the original diagnosis. Prescription Medications were one of the most harmful substances that my wife consumed while sick. The problems forced Danielle to use them as little as possible.

Installing the port was the smoothest adventure so far. Danielle was stressed about the surgery while also relieved that she would be able to start treatment. It also meant that drawing blood would be easier. Since Danielle suffered from very thin veins, she always had nurses that needed help finding her veins. So often I felt like they used her like a pin cushion before consenting to additional help. On several instances, we had to have an ultrasound machine to find her veins.

I had to leave the room whenever they would draw blood or

insert an IV. I would get so light-headed around needles that I would nearly pass out. It was the same my whole life with piercings or even worse injuries. I don't think I could ever be a doctor because of those issues. One time I did pass out during my blood draw. The nurse was surprised but continued the procedure since I passed out sitting up. I thanked her and spent the next hour recovering. My wife was nothing like me when it came to IV's or needles.

After another routine week of recovery time, we were scheduled to talk to the Oncologist. I was a little more excited about this meeting because I figured an Oncologist would have all the answers. We needed to have all the answers so that anyone who questioned us could see we did the fact-finding ourselves. I didn't see any way to stop her family without all the answers. Danielle was willing to do anything to gain her family's support. It was crucial to me that we find a way to stop the stresses caused by the lack of support.

Danielle even canceled the initial appointment because she didn't want to be pressured to do the chemotherapy. I supported her decision, but I guess that wasn't enough. The pressure from her family caused her to set up the appointment secretly. I didn't mind either way as I wanted to answer more of my questions.

Several days before the appointment at the oncologists, I could tell she was getting nervous again. Talking about it would cause her to stress; she would constantly question if she should even go. I would constantly tell her that we were going to get more answers, and answers we desperately needed to bring some peace between her and her family. I didn't tell my family any details about the treatment we choose, mostly because I didn't want to deal with their opinions. I knew my family knew nothing about cancer treatment. If I'm going to find some answers, I will get the answers from the professional or expert.

The trip to the Oncologist was not the same experience for me as it was for Danielle. I wasn't scared to hear what she had to say. I fully intended her to answer all the questions I had about chemo. I was genuinely a bit excited to see into the lion's den. I thought it was going to be a very informative visit, no matter the outcome. After an hour wait to see the Doctor, I was in for a huge disappointment.

The doctor came in as most do and ran through the usual patient checkup and went through her records. We again discussed all of Danielle's previous illnesses. We even discussed that Danielle had lost over a pint of blood and had chosen to decline a blood transfusion, meaning she rebuilt all her blood naturally. It was not something most people walk away from, but after surviving several life-threatening illnesses, it wasn't unusual for Danielle to survive the impossible. We all joked about her past medical history, and that led to our concern with using such strong chemotherapy.

We were hoping for a new solution. The Surgeon had told us that there were new, less harmful chemotherapies now becoming available, and we asked her if that was an option. She said that the only one that she recommended in our case was the strongest and potentially most dangerous treatment option. The problem is they didn't let us choose, and they only offered one treatment. It felt like there was no consideration for my wife's personal medical history.

The medical establishment could only provide one option. There was not going to be another alternative. Danielle was upset to learn there were no other choices because we were expecting to hear about a safer version of Chemo. As Danielle put it, we were facing the Cadillac of Chemotherapies. The frustration came with the lack of other options and a complete lack of support for alternative options. I anticipated that would be the answer we would receive. What I didn't anticipate is how the doctor would respond to my other questions.

I think my first trigger was when the Doctor asked if Danielle was eating enough. I proceeded to tell the Doctor exactly what she was eating daily. When I finished, I asked if that was enough? She responded, "I don't know. I'm not a dietician." I couldn't believe that diet was not a primary concern for cancer patients. My research showed how helpful diet was in maintaining proper health. So why wouldn't a cancer doctor be educated on the topic?

It was game time for me, and the gloves were coming off. I started asking serious questions about what we could expect from the chemotherapy the doctors recommended. Such as what potential health problems could we be facing? The doctor was not interested in disclosing the side effects and avoided the question completely. She decided it was best to print out the medical disclosure. I was somewhat satisfied knowing I would have the information I wanted. It still upset me that she wouldn't discuss that with us.

To skirt the issue, our oncologist said something I still can't believe. The doctor proceeded to tell us that chemotherapy was derived from the bark of the Pacific Yew tree. The doctor explained the medical industry created a synthetic version that works exactly the same, to protect the tree. As if to inspire a positive response from us. I said, "If there is a more natural version, then why can't we try that instead?" She didn't have an answer.

I don't even remember the questions I asked next, but I can clearly remember my reaction to her response. I was expecting an experienced professional to provide me with answers. Instead, she looked up my remaining questions on WebMD. I was beyond upset at the apparent incompetence that showed. I couldn't believe that the doctor had to look up answers online. Considering I could answer further questions this way, I decided to stop my questioning. I was in utter disbelief. I lost all remaining faith in our for-profit cancer treatment centers during this visit.

After learning that the doctor didn't think diet was important to cancer treatment, I was appalled to find buckets of candy throughout the cancer ward. They were feeding high fructose corn syrup in copious amounts to patients who have cancer. Considering cancer thrives on sugar, and even more on refined sugar, I couldn't believe my eyes. Doc and our ND had confirmed this fact. It was a huge reality check for me.

The whole show was about money, not health. I realized that the cancer industry doesn't care about the health of people, near as much as they like being able to provide expensive treatments to patients. Our doctor would have made over one hundred and fifty thousand dollars for the treatment she wanted to give us. A treatment that she was required by law to recommend. A law that utterly violates any sense of medical freedom. It made me think, but it also made me mad. My anger toward the Cancer Industry continued to grow, and it looks like it was not going to stop growing either.

Danielle was not satisfied with the answers that the doctor provided, and she declined to move forward with any further treatment. This choice was a surprise to the doctor, and she proceeded to tell us just like all the other doctors, that we faced a high probability of death if we didn't proceed with her recommendations. Sadly considering our circumstances, I felt the same way if we did try the chemo. Danielle didn't want to face a potentially more destructive foe if the solutions were going to cause worse side effects. Again the solutions were nothing more than putting band aids on problems as they arose. It didn't fill us with a bit of confidence.

Danielle asked one more question before we ended our appointment. She was concerned about monitoring her cancer markers and was hoping to reschedule another appointment. The doctor's response threw both of us a curve ball. We were informed that the doctor was very busy with training students, had many patients, and also, we were not pursuing treatment. Due to these reasons, we would only be scheduled for another appointment six months from that date. Danielle felt this was unacceptable. The doctor did not concede, leaving us both confused and angry.

After another terrible experience in a hospital for both Danielle and I, we knew there was no way that we would ever do chemo to fight her cancer. Not only did the sheets she provided show that there was a possibility of death, but it also showed serious side effects that Danielle, still, was not going to sign up for. We weren't going to do something that felt so wrong. It didn't matter that some parents, her mom, and sister were pressuring her to try Chemo. I had no problem standing my ground on the topic, and neither did Danielle. After this appointment, she made it excessively clear that she was done talking about chemotherapy. I could see that the decision was not a solution for us.

Danielle and I didn't need to find any more answers from the mainstream medical industry. We knew what we were going to do. While I probably would not choose the same options my wife chose, I undoubtedly supported her decision. We poured through mountains of information to reinforce our belief in making the best choice. The experience helped my knowledge grow exponentially. Talking to professionals and receiving insights taught me more than any of the hundreds of medical articles that I previously read. I learned how we were going to treat my wife's cancer. I had to support her decisions.

I knew that my wife was going to do it her way. It wasn't about me or my way, and it had to be all about her situation. I had to put my ego aside and support my wife in her decisions, even if I didn't completely agree. I could offer my input but had to allow her to use it or not. It wasn't easy for me, but it was something that I learned to do in even the most stressful of circumstances. We all need to learn the skill of supporting people in their journey without putting our projections and desires on them too.

It was becoming more difficult to face the fact that the medical industry was never going to support our decision. Made even more frustrating that by law, doctors and nurses had to tell Danielle she was going to Die. I hoped that was it for Mainstream doctors, who constantly reminded Danielle of her demise, and the uncertain future she faced. Danielle faced all the additional trauma because we needed to convince her family that her decision was the right one. Danielle so desperately wanted the full support of her family in her decision.

I find it imperative to unify in support of a treatment option, and we cannot be divided. The division leads to doubt, and doubt can be the real killer. I find it criminal not to support treatments, especially in a world that scientifically recognizes the placebo or nocebo effect. Which states that treatments work or fail based on belief. All medications must beat the placebo effect to become available to the public. Sugar pills have been proven to cure more times than any pharmaceutical company would ever care to admit. So why does a law exist that creates a nocebo effect?

Despite the stress of the adventure, we walked away more resolute in our undertaking. There was no doubt in my mind that Danielle was making the right decision. However, despite both of us going through the same experience, Danielle did not walk away, completely satisfied. If I had known, I might have made changes then and there. It was at this point that Danielle needed to believe in her treatment. There weren't enough people in her life that were showing her the support she wanted. Something needed to push us in the right direction, but I didn't know what.

Then probably the second biggest miracle possible happened. The friend she had reached out to and that put us in touch with the ND showed up and offered to pay for the treatment. She also wrote my wife a check to pay for other medical expenses too. It was a huge relief to me since I only started getting paid at my new job. It took all the pressure of making sure we could afford treatment, off my shoulders. It would have killed me if we weren't able to do treatment because we didn't have enough money. Now we had more than enough to proceed with all treatment regimens.

Danielle's friend truly showed her support in making sure Danielle would have the best chance to return to full health. Danielle even turned away an extra check she was going to write to me, but we both agreed that was excessive. I've always worked hard and earned what I needed or wanted, so bailouts have always made me feel uncomfortable. We welcomed the assistance and were incredibly grateful.

10
Treating Improvement

After several weeks of being at home, we started to see gradual improvement. The process was slow and rigorous for Danielle. She was not healing near as fast as she was expecting. The doctor said it should take two weeks to heal after the surgery, but at a month and a half, we were beginning to see the improvement we both so desperately wanted. Improvement was a constant judge of the progress we were making against the disease. All the new treatments had us convinced Danielle was going to beat the Cancer. I did not doubt in my mind that we would lose the battle.

Danielle's doses of curcumin intravenously through her port produced immediate results. While it wasn't quite the results we expected, it did show us that it was doing some serious work in her body. The IV's were far more intense than we initially expected. The side effects varied depending on where it entered the body. Itching and slight burning were common side effects but typically when administered into the arms. Since we were using the port to administer the IV, we expected the irritation and itching would be less severe.

The biggest issue we faced was the reactions to the IV itself. The first week went by without a hitch. After a week, we started seeing more results, and these were very unexpected results. Danielle would explain it to me that it felt like her insides were burning, especially where the disease was. She also noticed that she would get pain in her gall bladder because of all the die-off from the treatment. From what I read in the supporting material, it was great at cleaning out the body, and sometimes the gall bladder would become overwhelmed. The ND explained it was something similar to gall stones but not quite as painful. Danielle felt the pain and having endured both agreed with the doctor.

I felt so bad for Danielle for having to go through such an

intense treatment. The thought of even trying something more toxic or problematic seemed ludicrous. I knew that we might have been facing more dire problems during a chemotherapy regimen. Despite the potential comparison, we still were facing a powerful treatment. The intensity would wear Danielle out, and the nights after a treatment would be particularly rough.

Danielle found sleep rather difficult because of near constant discomfort. She would occasionally nap during the day, but mostly, she would try to stay up and sleep at night with me. Obviously, because of her pain, she often stayed awake while I slept. However, I would instantly wake up if she needed me. Most of the time, we would wake up several times a night to use the bathroom. The surgery had made her less regular with bathroom breaks.

It never bothered me being with her in the bathroom. It was more important to make sure she was safe versus worry about silly cultural taboos. She usually needed a little assistance to the bathroom, especially at night when she was often much weaker. Truthfully it was a great time to talk since the distraction helped with the discomfort. Some might have thought it was a shitty situation, but I enjoyed every minute with my wife. Thankfully, for her sake, she was becoming increasingly more independent with every passing day.

Danielle started taking short walks up and down the street. She was constantly trying to move to help with the rehabilitation. She felt so helpless because of her condition and what it prevented her from doing. The limitations pushed Danielle to accelerate her rehabilitation. The doctors had told us that walking regularly and keeping the body moving would assist in the healing process. So Danielle, even immediately after the surgery, was up and trying to walk around. After a month and a half, she was becoming far more self-reliant. I no longer needed to provide constant support, and she could easily walk a couple of hundred yards before exhaustion. I was so impressed.

The progress wasn't without setbacks. Two separate instances had shown how important it was, for Danielle, not to push herself without assistance. Both accidents occurred while she was trying to take a solo walk. It was almost disastrous as she fell both times injuring herself. The added stress of making the injured journey home was likely more damaging. Danielle became increasingly cautious after the second incident, but that never stopped her from moving forward.

It would fill Danielle with great joy every time she showed improvement. Walking further day after day filled her with a great sense of accomplishment. Danielle appreciated and recognized the small improvements. Then she constantly tested her boundaries as she felt more and more capable. Typically we would do two to three hikes down the street every day, assuming the weather was cooperating. The cold weather was not Danielle's friend. Her body couldn't handle the shock of being cold, nor could it deal with the stress caused by prolonged exposure. Even properly dressing for the cold weather became a hardship. Despite the challenges Danielle gave her recovery every bit of strength she could muster.

As her physical strength began to return, so did her desire to help around the house. Even though I would discourage her from doing household chores, she still would find time while I was working. She knew I would never let her strain herself while I was home. Even though I knew it wasn't the best thing for her to be doing, I could also tell that it made her happy to be a contributing member to our marriage. It always made her sad that she was unable to be of service. Danielle was truly an independent woman and a driven go-getter when I met her. I couldn't imagine the struggle she faced with having that independence stripped away in such a traumatic series of events.

Danielle's internal struggles were a constant stressor. I could see and hear the pain when she would talk about the things she wished she could be doing. She clearly missed all her students the most. She missed the dance, and because of that would completely avoid listening to music, something she did very regularly before the Cancer. Even texts from students would remind her of how much she wanted to teach. So many parts of her life reminded her of the things she had lost.

I even reminded her of everything she wished she could do as a wife. We were technically still newlyweds, and her health had prevented a proper consummation. There was so much she wished she could do for me, even though I didn't need anything from her. The truth is that I had zero problems stepping up to the plate to be the person my wife needed. The satisfaction received from doing the right thing and the gratitude I received was all I needed to keep me going. I didn't think much about the things we didn't have because I fully expected we would have a lifetime to indulge in the physical pleasures.

I did everything I could to make sure that she didn't feel inadequate. Danielle had never allowed herself to be so dependent on someone. So it was not an easy transition for her to let me fill those roles. There were many roles that she never thought I would have to fill. I don't think either of us expected our relationship to evolve into a caregiver/patient union. However, when it came to the kitchen, I learned it was best to keep Danielle out, healthy or not.

I learned very early in our relationship that Danielle couldn't cook, especially after eating my first boiled steak. So, it wasn't a problem for me to prepare all the meals that Danielle needed. Her diet had greatly simplified, with overall guidelines being organic, non-GMO, and Gluten-Free. She also avoided sugars like the plague. I had no idea how much food has sugar added until I had to start reading every label. Where I could go, shopping was limited to Natural Grocers or the Local Health Market. Danielle ate loads of superfoods, smoothies, and super grains. Another staple in Danielle's diet was gluten-free muffins and Free Range Organic Local Eggs. It was simple but rather expensive.

Thankfully due to the additional financial support, we were able to afford the best of the best when it came to food. I know how important diet is, and Danielle was even more vigilant in making sure everything she ate was up to her standards. I would often have to clear any new food with her, and even temporary food replacements needed approval. The ND was a vital part of making sure we had the best food for Danielle also. There were many products she recommended for us that I believe helped. Due to the surgery, Danielle had become hypersensitive to many different foods.

Dietary restrictions were one of the biggest challenges we faced with making sure that the food I purchased wouldn't make her sick. A big challenge was to make sure her sensitive digestive system didn't take in anything that would cause a negative reaction. Too much oil would cause digestive problems causing additional pain in her gall bladder. We practically removed all oils except for a little raw coconut oil. Most things were baked or steamed to preserve the nutrients. I did my best to meet or exceed all of Danielle's requirements.

Gluten was obviously a big no-no in her diet. The smallest amount would cause extended abdominal pain. I also made sure that anything I prepared was free of onions, garlic, and spicy peppers. These were all of Danielle's previous diet restrictions before the surgery. The only exception was a very nutritious Bone Broth made with garlic and onions. If we veered off the path, Danielle would experience more pain, more discomfort, and further bowel issues. Digestion was one of Danielle's biggest concerns.

To keep the digestive concerns under control, we kept a strict diet. Most mornings would start with a completely plain gluten-free waffle from the restaurant we first met. I would also procure several internationally famous raw chocolates from their chocolate bar. I would usually call in the order so I could drive down the street and return within ten minutes. I never wanted to be away from Danielle a minute longer than needed. Upon my return, she would usually eat the first half of her waffle then put the rest in the fridge. Simple and small meals were common.

Other mornings included buckwheat oatmeal with three soft boiled eggs. I perfected the amount of time it would take to make a perfect soft-boiled egg because they were Danielle's favorite. If she didn't have oatmeal, she would often accompany the eggs with half a gluten-free English muffin. There were very few companies that made an English Muffin that was tolerable to my wife. An issue that was constantly an issue when shopping, thankfully, we isolated the problem ingredients and avoided them no matter what.

As she healed, she tried to consume more and more food. It was very difficult for her to eat because of the nausea that she constantly felt. The curcumin treatment made it even worse, and Medical Marijuana only reduced the symptoms. We faced a constant struggle with making sure that the nausea was never more than she could handle. Danielle knew her body so well and knew its limits and would only eat as much as she felt strong enough to eat. Many times she would have to put the rest of her meal in the fridge for later. She would always make sure to finish it when she felt capable, so food rarely went to waste.

Most of her dinners and hot meals entailed brown or black rice from regions that produce highly nutritious superfoods. I would also boil the rice with ionic mineral and monatomic elements — both shown to help overall health. I did everything in my power to provide the best food possible. We started buying in bulk the items that we knew were satisfactory. It was a process, but we had each other through everything.

We were constantly studying and reading material about the foods and supplements that we were consuming. Sadly there was not a double-blind study showing a proper diet does or does not cure cancer. However, the anecdotal proof from the people who are trying alternative treatments is abundant. The stories vary, and there is a lot of proof that some treatments work for some people while for other people they don't work. I did a lot of reading about the subject before I met my wife, so this was an even more in-depth research assignment than I had endeavored before. Not only was I reading the material, but I was also putting that knowledge into action constantly.

I knew that through my research and talking with the doctors that controlling inflammation and providing the essential nutrients to the body was crucial in a full recovery. We didn't spare any expenses and made sure that Danielle was receiving a super dose of antioxidants every day. I would make her a super green drink that would include a little fresh fruit, greens, mineral whey for protein, chia seeds, hemp hearts, and a superfood powder, with just a dash of honey. I figured her diet alone would have cured her cancer, according to other reports.

After a couple of weeks of treatment, there was an improvement but not without consequences. Every time that Danielle would have a treatment, she would have about six to twelve hours of extreme discomfort to intense pain. She explained it to me that it felt like the cancer was "being burned" out of her. Cancer at this point would have been moving into stage four, so if that were the case, it would be very active in her body. The burn-offs, as we called it, were intense but showed immediate improvement. The most dramatic progress was during any healing crisis. The pain reduction alone was worth the initial discomfort, according to Danielle, which helped significantly with her moral and mental well-being.

After a couple of months of being incapacitated and incapable of caring for herself, she was finally starting to show real signs that she was healing. Every day that she had more energy was a miracle. Many afternoons she would relax in the front yard. October through November had beautiful days allowing Danielle to sit outside without causing any stress. Environmental stress being something we constantly made sure to keep at a bare minimum. Super cold weather meant very little travel outside. Road trips in the cold required preheating the car before we left. A quick trip from the door to the car was about all the cold that Danielle's body could handle. Shivering was something that would wear her out incredibly fast, so I made sure that happened as little as possible.

The biggest challenge was late night showers. Often the hot water would help reduce the pain. I didn't care if she wanted a shower in the middle of the night. All she had to do was wake me up and let me know. I would almost like a rabbit jump up and throw a heater in the bathroom and turn the water on to get the room super warm for her. Evenings were still always cool, and the trip to the bathroom was challenging for Danielle. Once in the shower, she would sit on the shower chair until she would request the chair removed.

It brought her comfort to sit in the shower on the floor, although she was still super self-conscious. So she wouldn't want me to even look at her, even though I found her absolutely beautiful, she felt like she was now less than she once was. The surgery left her scarred, and the way her body had changed was still dramatic to her. The tone and fitness that she cherished her whole life was gone, the natural beauty was still there but not to the level that she wished.

She had high standards for herself, and it disturbed her, seeing that she now fell short. Danielle was ashamed despite my constant reassurance that she was still the most beautiful woman in the world to me. That wasn't a lie either. Danielle truly possessed a beauty that I still find incomparable. I told her constantly.

As time went on and her health continued improving, so did her desire to do more. Even though her physical limitations were a huge barrier, she still wanted to be a wife who was of service to her husband. I never felt once that she neglected me. I think she made a huge effort to be the best wife she could be, which helped me to be the best husband I could be for her. For this reason, she made sure that when she was strong and feeling good that she would do one of my favorite things, give me a short back scratch.

I love having my back lightly scratched, and it is so relaxing to me. I never asked for one, but Danielle would always be the one to offer, and wouldn't take no for an answer. In the afternoons, when she was strongest, she would tell me to lie down next to her. For several minutes I would slip into a state of pure bliss. It always made me feel so refreshed, and I could see she was satisfied at being of service to me. She would constantly say that she knew how to take care of her man, but I always said, "I don't need anyone to take care of me. I got this, and I got you." Usually followed by a kiss.

We never stopped kissing from the moment we started. The Truth is we shared a deep love that I still can't explain. The connection we shared, and the friendship we cultivated was marvelous. Many days just involved laying with each other when I wasn't working. I loved cuddling in our little single bed with my wife. In everything we were missing, we still found so much to appreciate. There was so much to appreciate while spending time with Danielle.

On top of that, I swear my wife had the softest smoothest skin I have ever felt. Her skin was perfect and never lost that perfection even through her illness. The sensation of just having her there with me was so powerful, and the companionship made us both stronger. I still look back at all the roles I filled and can only attest that true love carried me through it all. Love gave me the strength to persevere, maintaining the happiest and most loving attitude around my wife. The ability to maintain that space is one reason that our relationship grew even stronger.

We would constantly talk, during the time we were together, never running out of topics to discuss. The conversations were usually deep, not just simple small talk. We always talked about interesting and unique topics. Often, we discussed behavior patterns of others and discussed the reasons why people behave the way they do. Between the two of us, we felt we knew how to read people.

We both had our unique talents at reading people, and she was far better at spotting the dark side of someone, while I tend to bring the best out of people. I believe all people have a good and a bad side, and we observe the one that we encourage. I also don't feel like I was blind to shortcomings, but I rarely spent time focused on them. I feel I would experience more shortcomings if I spent more energy focusing on them. Danielle could smell those with dark sides like a hunting dog looking for the kill. She excelled at her protective motherly instincts. Still, she would tell me that my ability to read between the lines was uncanny.

Danielle was very impressed by my simple conclusions. I

try not to make judgments just observations. At the time, Danielle was concerned about a meeting request. The inquiry came through Danielle's friend, who was helping us out with treatment. The invitation was a bit strange and vague. Danielle was concerned because it seemed like the woman wanted to offer advice for using social media. I did a little research online and found that the woman contacting us had a GoFundMe set up. I also think crowdfunding is great when done for the right reasons. I found some questionable motives that raised some red flags.

The GoFundMe on the surface seemed normal. A single parent is facing a potential cancer scare while looking to cover expenses. I was in support until I reached the end of the post. An update added said that the test came back Negative. Thankfully my wife's friend was not facing cancer like we were. However, she was still asking for over twenty-five thousand dollars, which in itself wasn't the problem I had. The problem I found was that she was solely requesting to purchase a twenty-five-thousand-dollar electro light therapy device.

After my months of research, I knew that the treatment option she wanted to have others pay for was considered the most expensive option online. There are many other less expensive treatment options, and the websites that advertise the device she wanted even states that finding a device in your area is far more economical. We even have one here in Sedona, which is why I was so concerned why it was imperative that this woman purchases a machine for herself.

Anyone here in town could get ten years of unlimited treatments for fifteen thousand dollars. It would need to be used for over fifteen years to recover the investment. So why was the option to use the local device never mentioned? If Danielle were able to use that treatment, I would have pursued an unlimited pass for her. I came to only one conclusion to why this person was marketing the GoFundMe as such. This person wanted other people to pay for her business, and she was using a tough situation to gain sympathy.

It was her goal to have people buy her a twenty-five thousand dollars machine. I could see through the pity story, and it was obvious to me what the goals were. I didn't have a problem with the goal either, but I didn't approve of the method to attain that goal. I would expect someone to be more honest about their intentions. Sadly the funding stopped after she learned that she did not have

Cancer. Apparently, having cancer was far more profitable than not having it.

A motive had appeared, which I shared with Danielle. Danielle already expressed her doubts, but now I had some proof to back up her doubts. The message she received about social media made far more sense after reading the GoFundMe campaign. It was clear that this woman wanted to make a proposition to Danielle. I truly felt like this woman wanted to use Danielle to get what she wanted.

It appeared the dreams of a light therapy machine were gone when the diagnosis changed. People stopped donating large quantities. Now she figured she could use my wife to get the rest of the funds. My wife, however, was not interested in being public about anything. When she told this to her wealthy friend, they both confirmed this suspicion of mine. I could tell this would have been a pushy woman from reading about her and hearing Danielle talk about her. We decided to pass on any further communications considering it would not have been a positive interaction for Danielle.

We were always trying to limit exposure to people that would cause additional stresses. For this reason, I ran most of my errands to the store without her. She didn't want people to see her and spread rumors about her appearance. Many women in town had histories of spreading rumors about my wife, some true and some not, but almost always done maliciously. So we limited exposure to anyone who might instigate that trauma. I still find the behavior women show to each other sometimes so much viler than even the most sleazy, deceitful guys.

Women mistreating women was another huge topic we talked about extensively. It was a common theme among many of our conversations. We would discuss the way Danielle's students would treat each other, mostly how the recent generations were far more problematic than in the past. Rudeness and elitism were chronic problems in her studio. Danielle would never stand for it, but our observations came to several conclusions. The behavior seems to stem from poor parenting or simply a lack of parenting.

Danielle was far more upset about parents disrespecting the rules of the dance studio. The anger she had towards the behavior of the parents was something I constantly endured. Sometimes it was a stupid text, or sometimes it was the complete lack of texts. While she distanced herself from her students, she had many who couldn't respect her privacy. This caused Danielle to push even more people away. The opposite of what we needed. If only more people were concerned with what Danielle's wishes were instead of worrying about their own needs.

The Naturopathic Doctor was one of the few women that supported Danielle through everything, including the friend who paid for the treatment. That friend was a great reassurance to her constantly. Few people were regular about letting her know that she was in their thoughts. However, the few people that did make that effort were huge mood boosters for Danielle.

Some of the girls were very good about sending loving texts, but still, some would push to see her. As much as she wanted to see her children, she didn't want them to see her sick. It could be traumatic to many children, and Danielle certainly couldn't handle that trauma. I didn't understand it at the time, but it makes a lot of sense now.

Danielle constantly struggled with her slow healing and her inability to get back to teaching. A mental struggle that I tried to assist. Talking it through, we could often help her come to peace with some of the behavior. My unusually positive outlook on life was a big help in making sure that we would come up with a positive understanding of the problem. I didn't just want to play the blame game like most people. It takes a different level of thinking to own our part in any situation. We could only control our reactions to each situation, despite Danielle's efforts to control all aspects of her recovery.

Some situations were just unavoidable, such as the time we were driving to the Bed Store and Danielle hoped out of the car and ran over to say hi to a friend. I parked the car and went to introduce myself. The friend was super surprised to see Danielle, and from what she had heard, this meeting was completely unexpected. She proceeded to tell us that Narcy, the one who showed up and caused a bunch of problems, was spreading rumors around town about Danielle's health. One of Danielle's greatest fears had come true.

Narcy was telling people that Danielle looked terrible, and her treatments weren't helping. I can only imagine it was because she didn't believe in Danielle's choice of treatments. Including judging Danielle based on how she appeared during a random surprise visit. Danielle's friend, who stood in the street was surprised to see Danielle in such good health. The fact that Danielle was able to run over to her friend had shown that her health was improving. It was just devastating to hear a woman was spreading false rumors around town. As upset as I felt, I knew Danielle was a million times more upset than I was.

Avoiding conversations or communications with certain people was a big part of eliminating suffering. Some people know how to push other people's buttons while others live stressful lives spreading that stress everywhere, they go. Both kinds of people were highly toxic to Danielle literally causing health problems just from a simple visit.

Danielle was the go-to person for people who live stressful or overwhelming lives. Sadly these people could not leave their problems at home. Combined with the sadness surrounding Danielle's Cancer, these people were walking time bombs around my wife. My wife's sister, even though most of the relationship existed over the phone, was a "star stunning" example of someone who couldn't control her emotions. That was the main reason I didn't reach out to my mother for assistance. I knew she could be an emotional mess, as she has demonstrated at most events throughout my life. She always told my sister and me that she simply couldn't control it. Now I see how important it is to have some level of control of our emotions.

The second type of stressful person that my wife encountered was the one who somehow got joy out of another person's misery. I had a family member who I witnessed deriving joy from the misery of others, so I know it exists. I have observed this behavior all across our society. In Danielle's and I story, Narcy was a prime example of this behavior. My wife and I constantly referenced her behavior when we would encounter other people who behaved similarly. Finding peace in turmoil was always the challenge. We could discuss the problems all day, but without solutions, we would just be dwelling in more trauma.

I still feel that she and I talked about far too much stuff that caused her stress. I will say in hindsight that I would have wished that we could have had more positive talks, and fewer talks about her life's traumas. Also, in hindsight, I see that working through those stresses was integral to her spiritual growth and finding peace in this world. Ultimately, it was my goal to help her find peace with all her issues or trauma. I wouldn't say I was always successful, but I always made an effort.

Knowing that just in our first month, I helped bring peace to her issues with Men helped me know we could heal the past. As much as this process was a healing process for my wife, it was equally as healing for me. I came to terms with many of my emotions, both good and bad expressions. Including a crash course in emotion management, I also learned how to be a caregiver and a healer. Through the healing process, I have found the practitioner is many times healed just as much as the patient. I felt the healing giving me additional strength that I didn't know my body had. That didn't change the fact that even I have limits and I was about to face those limits head-on.

I truly was growing, but I was still yet to face some of my greatest challenges. The upcoming holidays would prove some of the biggest tests of my entire life. It would change me in ways I could not expect. I might even regret my actions if it had not prepared me for even greater tests. My path was not going to be easy.

11
Holiday Troubles

As the Holidays approached, Danielle experienced a new level of recovery and renewed energy. She was walking further up and down the street. She would typically only go a couple of hundred yards to avoid talking to some of the neighbors. Danielle didn't want to create gossip and knew the people to avoid. Encounters typically involved disclosing information about her situation. Danielle wanted to avoid rumors.

Danielle was far more open to the world at showing off her newfound strength. She didn't want to keep discussing the problems she wanted people to see her as strong and improving. Danielle wanted reassurances that she was looking good. Thankfully we saw that improvement with every treatment.

The Curcumin IV continued two to three times a week. After some time, Danielle had come to realize that the slower she did the drip, the less serious the side effects were. It meant that most days she would be stuck at the doctors for three to four hours. I was often working while she was getting her treatments. I usually had little breaks that allowed me to pick her up or drop her off. I was even able to leave during a shift several times to take her home from an IV. It was never a huge challenge since everything was so close. I had a simple three to five-minute drive from home to the doctors or work.

The one benefit of being in Sedona is that everything we needed was less than a mile from the house. My errands could be super quick, and I was able to be a chauffeur for Danielle whenever she needed it. Occasionally our ND would give her a ride, or a friend would give her a ride. I didn't know how to explain it, but I was usually always able to get her to and from the Doctors despite an erratic work schedule. I was working five to six days per week. Which I found necessary to cover our living expenses. My job was just barely covering those, and the slow winter season in Sedona was not helping.

Going into the holiday season the restaurant was unbearably slow. Often, I would try to leave early, if possible, to go home and be with my wife. It was nice to be able to leave, but I really needed the money. The most troubling days I made no money because no one showed up. It was frustrating when I felt like I was wasting my time. The last thing I wanted was to spend time away from a wife who needed me. I had to rethink if the situation at work was still in our best interests.

Years of mismanagement, coupled with bizarre hours, and many cases of bad servers or employees had ruined a local business. I was a witness in several restaurants to what happens long term to restaurants that maintain low standards or employ servers who are terrible at their job. Bad service is a restaurant killer. I could see that I was fighting an uphill battle to keep the restaurant thriving. I've witnessed many slow seasons, but this was the worst winter ever. I didn't know what I should do.

I was not entirely working there for the money. My schedule was ideal, and the flexibility was crucial. The owners also understood and were sympathetic to Danielle's and my situation. My saving grace was regular catering deliveries. I averaged fifteen to twenty-five dollars per hour, depending on which delivery I was making. The regular income helped to keep us from worrying too much.

It was still my first year in Sedona I wasn't aware of the seasonal nature of Sedona. My coworkers informed me that we would get really busy around Thanksgiving and Christmas, but that the rest of the time was going to be slow. It was good to at least have a little heads up because they weren't lying. The restaurant was slower than ever before, using the opportunity to see more of my wife.

In the evenings after work, I would usually spend a few hours with Danielle, just talking. I would usually apply a fresh layer of RSO cannabis mixed with coconut oil to her feet. Truthfully, I needed the effects just as much as she did. However, I was using it for anxiety. I wasn't aware yet that was what I needed it for, but the calming and relaxing effects were perfect for me. I wanted to be that calm, cool, and collected man that my wife married. The additional stresses had made me far more dependent on Medical Marijuana.

Even though I was building up a huge tolerance to the substance, the natural sedative effects that I was receiving was crucial to behaving properly. It's kind of funny when I think about the stigma of the stoner sitting on the couch, acting very relaxed and using a calm puppy dog tone of voice. Crazy enough, that is almost the best kind of demeanor to have with the sick or elderly.

Danielle didn't need me to be the energizer bunny. It was great when we first got together, and we were both healthy and strong. She was just as energetic, loud, fun, and over the top. Danielle did not need those traits now. Instead, she needed cool, calm, and compassionate Brandon. Marijuana was a crucial medicine to help me control my emotions. I would often make time to smoke outside because I would usually sneak a little tobacco into the pipe as well.

Since our wedding, I had kept my tobacco habit a complete secret. I never lied about it, but I also never disclosed I was smoking again. Tobacco, too, had become a tool to manage my anxiety. I could almost calm myself down from anything with just a couple puffs and some deep breaths. I found it to be a devilish medicine because of its addictive properties. Combined with MMJ and Tobacco, I was able to keep my emotional stresses from coming out in front of my wife, most of the time.

However, the holiday season would test my tolerances and my endurance to the max. Going into Thanksgiving week, I was already anticipating working most of the time. I needed to make a good amount of money for the ten days we would be busy at the restaurant. Sadly our busiest day was lining up to be Thanksgiving Day. So I encouraged Danielle to join some friends for Thanksgiving. I didn't want Danielle to spend Thanksgiving alone since I would be working. I wasn't expecting to have to do as much as I ended up doing.

Due to the Holidays, a couple that worked at the Restaurant decided to leave for the holiday — leaving me with covering all the shifts that were left behind. My work ethic has always been impeccable, so I couldn't say no when they desperately needed me. Danielle reassured me that she was doing much better and that it would be okay. I still didn't like it, and neither did she, but we both knew it still had to be done. I couldn't abandon the restaurant, the good person in me, wouldn't allow it. So I ended up biting the bullet.

We were always up around six in the morning. Waking up

early usually gave me over an hour to get ready and prepare breakfast for Danielle and Andora. Somehow even taking the dog for a short walk, I would still make my seven thirty breakfast catering delivery. Because of the lack of staff, I also had to do a lunch delivery every day as well. It was amazing to make one hundred dollars a day plus still be able to go home to check on Danielle. I could never stay long before I had to head back for the next shift.

Every night I was a server, and finally, we had customers coming in. Tourists were in town, and they all loved visiting our restaurant. Some couples had been eating there every year for over ten years. Tourists were easily ninety percent or more of the traffic through our doors. Thankfully, they were spending money and tipping well.

I was making great money for a change, and the financial reward was invigorating for me. I was no longer stressing about not being a provider. I had developed some anxiety about money during the previous few weeks. I didn't want to use Danielle's funds for her treatment because I knew it would stress her out if I did. I was far more equipped to deal with Stress, being I didn't have a life-threatening illness that I was battling inside my body. I didn't share my concerns with her because I didn't want to burden her.

The problem was that months of stress and lack of sleep were starting to leave a mark on me. I wasn't even aware of my mistakes at this point. My objectives were to accomplish everything that Danielle needed, not to worry about myself. Thankfully my natural capacity to have practically limitless energy gave me an upper hand to succeed. However, working ten days straight and being a full-time caregiver was taking a toll on me.

Thanksgiving Thursday was like most days for Danielle and me. Nothing special since her diet restrictions prevented any Thanksgiving feast. We were able to spend the morning together. I didn't have to make a delivery, and I didn't have to work till two p.m. It was the first day in five that I didn't have to wake up and go to work immediately. It was a huge relief and a beautiful morning. We just spent it talking and taking trips between the bedroom and the living room.

Danielle loved being in the living room and looking out the window. The leaves were all beginning to fall, and the colors were magnificent. Fall is a magnificently beautiful time of year in Sedona. While it was significantly colder outside than a month prior, the beauty remained. Danielle was also so proud of how beautiful her house and yard was considering how hard she worked for it.

Before going to work, I dropped Danielle off at her friend's house. Well, they were more than friends and closer to family. The two daughters were former dance students, and she had always been close with their parents as well. From what I understood, Danielle spent many nights at their house when she was having guy problems. She said they helped her with many problems throughout her life. I was happy that she was finally having a little interaction with the outside world. She had pushed so many people out of her life because of the illness, and it made me feel good to see her allow people back in.

My day wasn't as fun or relaxing as hers. Holiday menus tend to throw most kitchens into disarray, but this was something else. The level of madness was insane as the kitchen prepared for hundreds of reservations. Thankfully, the menu was a little easier to prepare than a full dinner menu. Due to the restaurants catering experience, I would have expected to be facing a better situation. This was going to be a big mess by the end of the night.

I had my busiest night ever at the restaurant. I also made more money than I did in three or four nights of work. After six hours of nonstop customers, which eventually filled the entire restaurant twice, my energy levels were depleted. Thankfully, I stuffed myself full of turkey and mashed potatoes for Thanksgiving. We had plenty of leftovers that the restaurant shared with the staff. However, I also ended up working until after eleven at night, which was about two hours later than usual.

Danielle was already texting me around ten o'clock wishing I was home. I would have to say that my efficiency and ability to close the restaurant was second to none. I never wasted a minute at the end of the night, and I was always home as fast as a puff of tobacco and a drive down Inspirational Dr, but never a moment longer. I would feel guilty if I was ever a moment longer, and even the cigarettes made me feel like I was taking away time that I shouldn't. Guilt being something I was carrying too much of surrounding my tobacco addiction. Guilt that was starting to weigh heavily on me.

I was completely exhausted when I arrived home. Danielle wasn't having a particularly good night and was in a bunch of pain.

I quickly ran Andora outside to go potty while I warmed up the bathroom for a shower. Danielle's Thanksgiving adventure out had taken a lot out of her, and she was having a healing crisis. A hot shower was usually the best remedy for Danielle when this happened. We did not see any improvement this night. It was going to be a long night.

The lack of sleep was starting to become an issue. I was becoming far more easily irritable, and this was not a good reaction to have around Danielle. After months of talking about how to behave, me acting irritated or grumpy was a trigger for Danielle. She had ZERO tolerance for it in her state. So in the middle of the night, I made a grave mistake.

Half asleep, I responded in one of the rudest and inconsiderate tones I had ever used toward anyone. Danielle asked me a silly question, and I responded in such an offensive manner that it sent Danielle through the roof. I realized immediately after I fully woke up that I was completely out of line with my response. I immediately apologized, I felt horrible, I felt ashamed, and I didn't know what caused me to behave in such a manner. Danielle was so furious with me that I had to spend almost an hour trying to calm her down. I knew it was my mistake, and I knew I had to make it right. Truthfully, I can't even remember what was said. It just goes to show that it isn't what you say it is how you say it that is important.

I could tell it wasn't going to be easy to make it right. Danielle was not going to be a victim of another person who behaves that way. I pulled my shit together very quickly. It took all my effort to be the person that my wife needed. She demanded it, and I was willing to make it happen. I needed to pull it together for the rest of the Thanksgiving weekend.

Black Friday to the following Monday was even more exhausting than I anticipated. Issues with the restaurant were starting to build, and the amount of work that I was doing was far more than I wanted to be doing with a sick wife. The reward of making a couple of thousand dollars put me slightly at ease. It was a relief to be able to take some financial burdens off my plate. Financial anxiety can be so destructive if left unchecked. I had pushed any money problems into the following month. Assuming I could also be paid on time, which was also a slight issue.

Severe exhaustion was a bigger threat to my stress levels, and I was having far more trouble controlling my frustrations around Danielle. A lack of sleep was also making me far grumpier. I always tried to stuff my problems and put on a happy face. Waiting tables is like being on stage every time you walk up to a table, the better the performance, the better the tips. Now my performance had to be perfect for Danielle, not for tips, but her sake. Failure was not an option. It was going to take every ounce of strength to face my emotional weaknesses.

My desire to assist a drowning restaurant was pulling me down too. After a crazy Thanksgiving at work, I decided it might be best if I look for work at a busier restaurant. I would make twice as much money at just about any other successful restaurant in town. I no longer felt that I had the energy to fix the problems my current establishment faced. I needed a job that didn't require a full commitment to keep the gears turning. I needed a restaurant that was already thriving.

A job hunt was the last thing I wanted to do, but I also knew I had to give it a shot. I needed to change something fast. As much as I didn't want to admit it, I was already failing in Danielle's eyes. My emotions were getting the better of me, and Danielle was usually the person who would suffer. Usage of MMJ and tobacco had increased to the max level. Combined with deep breathing techniques, I was only barely holding myself together.

Maybe both our expectations were too high, but either way, I still wasn't going to admit defeat. I've found there is always a way if we stay vigilant in our actions. Finding a less stressful job was going to solve one of my problems. The other problem of finding a bed would be next. I've never had a problem getting a restaurant job in the past. I have over a decade of high-level serving experience, and I can almost work at any restaurant that I want.

The adventure I set out that first week of December was far from what I expected. I found out quickly that no one was hiring. The winter is too slow in Sedona. Five restaurants told me the same thing. I was devastated. A new job was not going to happen until spring. I took the realization a little hard knowing I would have to endure my existing problems. All my problems were being made worse by sleep deprivation.

I was hoping that over the following weeks I would be able to find a bed. I wasn't sleeping well on the edge of a single bed. I had made the small bed work by adding some pillows between the wall and mattress, providing me with additional support. However, sleeping for months on the edge of the bed had bruised my hip. Since Danielle was having far more regular discomfort than I was, I sucked it up, because I felt bad ever complaining to her. My problems were still insignificant to the problems she was facing, often causing me to overlook my problems.

However, my problems and stresses were starting to pile up. After about three months of non-stop work, I finally started to show signs of serious instability. My behavior started to become less what I wanted and far more erratic and uncontrollable. I really couldn't explain it and just started blaming it on the fact that I was tired. I needed to get a bed so that I could sleep better. I made a promise not to spend any nights away from my wife. Despite the problems that caused, I couldn't break that promise. Her needs were far more important, and I was committed to making sure that I could provide all her needs.

The lack of sleep was making me far more irritable. Truthfully, Danielle rarely irritated me, but some of the topics she wanted to discuss triggered my anger or anxiety. This would be the next challenge that I faced while helping Danielle. For months I had been able to, calmly, discuss almost any topic with Danielle despite certain topics being incredibly upsetting. Now, I was finding it increasingly difficult to manage my emotions regarding specific topics. Her family was definitely a topic we both avoided for that reason alone. Danielle would instantly recognize any tone in my voice that wasn't kind or caring.

Danielle was always trying to work through her family issues, which always would bring up a wave of conscious or unconscious anger inside me. These discussions would often lead to heated emotions coming up for both her and I. Discussing Danielle's family was becoming more and more difficult for me to talk about from a neutral perspective. Every conversation was starting to feed my inner anger towards her family. My frustrations from observing her family's behavior were overruling my better judgment, forcing Danielle to hide her frustrations so that I wouldn't cause a scene.

I never wanted to cause a scene in front of Danielle, but I was finding it difficult to keep it together. Some topics didn't trigger my emotions, while others would hit hard. Danielle could feel incredibly passionately about an issue but still not trigger me. I didn't have anger towards the past as Danielle did. Which, when compared to the family issues, was far less present in our daily life. Community and Parent problems usually caused by inappropriate texts were some of Danielle's biggest nuisances. Combined with her feelings of abandonment, she was having a tough time with the community she spent so much of her life helping.

Danielle felt like so many people she helped during her life were letting her down. I repeat with the highest regard, the initial outpouring of support was great, but the support we needed never continued past the first month. Few know what it means to be there for someone and make sure that person knows that you are there for them. Danielle didn't get this from the people she needed it from, the only support she got in that way was parents wanting to bring their children over. Thankfully people are writing books and articles about how to behave with someone diagnosed with Cancer.

Through the Holidays, Danielle was saddened by the lack of support she received from the community. Danielle was not someone who participated in social media, nor would she have during her ordeal. Danielle valued her privacy. Sadly, it seems that people don't know how to communicate regularly without Facebook or Facebook updates. My wife, who was a constant source of support and strength for so many people, was not getting half the support that she deserved. It triggered the greatest levels of compassion in me. Those conversations made me realize how important my support was to Danielle. Which is why I always tried to hold a positive space for Danielle.

Even with all the fun and beautiful things that we talked about, often something stressful would always arise. It was becoming more and more difficult for me to remain calm. I probably could have used more tobacco, but I still was hiding my habit from Danielle. Many times I would put off using tobacco if there was a possibility that Danielle might find out. The addiction then triggered more anxiety cause me to be more unhinged.

Tobacco did such a great job of calming my nerves, but it was equally causing my nerves to crave it more than ever. On my off day, or sometimes days off, I consumed far less tobacco, which meant more anxiety. Working multiple shifts every day was a great opportunity to feed my tobacco habit. So instead of relaxing on my days off, I was constantly craving nicotine, which resulted in my behavior becoming increasingly more offensive.

If Danielle became offended, I would usually immediately check my attitude. It wouldn't completely fix Danielle's anger towards me, but I would eventually and almost always bring a positive resolution to the situation. I was far from out of control, but I wasn't staying in complete control of my emotions. Danielle was often the victim of these emotional outbursts.

These slips of emotional control were becoming far more common. I was just as frustrated with myself as Danielle was. Both of us were so confused at what to do with my behavior, and I knew I needed to make adaptations. I wasn't going to give up, and it was my duty to overcome my shortcomings, beat my inner demons, and not let my emotions get the better of me. I still had much to learn to be the person my wife needed.

12
Not So Jolly Christmas

Several weeks into December, it was time to do the final check on her surgery. Confirming to Danielle that she had fully healed. Danielle asked her ND to do the preliminary check and make sure the final little hole had healed up. We were all about to be shocked. The tiny hole had not healed, and there was a far more serious problem now. A tube from a previous surgery had slipped down into her vagina. The doctor and Danielle couldn't believe it. Danielle was furious at the situation. Despite having a good attitude about her progress at this point, it was devastating to Danielle's spirit to have another serious situation.

We talked with the ND about our options. Danielle's anger and frustration caused us to look to another doctor to help fix the problem. The discussion had led us to the conclusion that we didn't want to see the surgeon who caused the initial problem. We scheduled an appointment for the following Tuesday to meet with an Oncologist in Flagstaff. It wasn't going to be a very long adventure as Flagstaff is only forty minutes from Sedona.

I made sure to bundle up Danielle in many layers of clothing since we were heading to practically freezing weather. I was fully expecting snow on the ground. The drive would be uneventful as I took a slow and easy drive through Oak Creek Canyon to Flagstaff. We also started to see the signs of the recent snowfall that hit the area several days prior. The top of the Canyon was a beautiful sight to be held, and we both marveled for a moment at the beauty. It felt so good to share such a beautiful moment with my wife. It didn't change how nervous she was about meeting with the new Doctor.

Google maps had led us to a dead end at the main Hospital. I had looked up the wrong office, and the staff informed us that we were not in the right location. I felt bad because we were already running a couple of minutes late. I quickly looked up the right location and made the trip around the block to the Doctors private offices. I walked Danielle to the door of the Office then proceeded to park the car around the corner. I made it just before Danielle was called back. Thankfully we didn't have to wait very long.

It wasn't a very long interaction with the Doctor. To our great disappointment, we were not going to be able to have the doctor perform the surgery, and we should have had the doctor who installed the port also remove it. We had the doctor schedule the appointment with the other Doctor's office right there on the spot. We were going to have to wait another week to have this problem removed. They scheduled Danielle's surgery the day before Christmas Eve. It was a Tuesday, and the one day a week I always had off.

My work schedule was looking like the twelve worst days of Christmas. On the first day of Christmas I would work. On the fifth day of Christmas I would take my wife to her surgery. I was not looking forward to another extended workweek. The added problems of the surgery were making things far harder on me than the month prior. Danielle was furious, almost twenty-four seven leading up to the day of the surgery. The dissatisfaction she had with the medical industry was all that she could discuss. It wasn't healthy, and I wasn't making the situation any easier.

Now I couldn't hide my anger towards the medical establishment. Danielle was constantly triggering my resentment of the for-profit medical industry. It didn't matter what Danielle complained about because I could always find a fault in how the medical field treats illness and disease. My concerns were less about Danielle's situation and more about the general situation people are forced to endure. I couldn't believe how much Danielle was forced to conform to the mainstream model, despite her constant protests.

Danielle was worried about being put under again with anesthetics. Her digestive issues were always of concern, which is also why her diet was strict. Anesthesia was not part of her diet, and a guarantee that constipation issues would be present for a couple of weeks. It was almost impossible to calm this fear within Danielle. The stress of having to make the trip to Phoenix, was building up a massive load of anxiety in both of us.

Our mutual anger and frustrations were building off each other. We were frustrated the doctor installed the port without permission in the first place despite us giving him the authority to do anything necessary to remove her cancer. Danielle hated the port and even more what it stood for. She would regularly joke about the idea of them using a chemo bath on her sensitive body. We both agreed adamantly about how destructive a chemo bath on her insides would have likely been. So it was not easy to see the doctor who also warned us about the treatment in question a month after recommending she start the treatment immediately. Danielle and I were both angry.

I always tried to limit the anger we expressed to each other, to diffuse the emotions that were charging our conversations. However, I couldn't stop Danielle from worrying about her ever-present problems. Especially, not while she would lay awake at night with those concerns running on repeat. I didn't understand what was occurring until it was too late to fix. I was becoming more aware of how ill-prepared I was for the challenges we faced.

I was able to be supportive for the week leading up to the surgery. Despite having another excessive work schedule through Christmas season. I was expecting to work twelve out of the next thirteen days and my only day off being our trip to Phoenix to fix the dislodged tube. I against the needs of the restaurant had reserved the entire day off to help my wife with the endeavor. Christmas Eve the following day would be my longest day with two morning deliveries and a busy night of reservations. Thankfully Christmas was just an overbooked evening shift that started in the afternoon.

Then the unthinkable happened, the surgeon had to cancel and reschedule the surgery the day before we were to go in. His receptionist explained he could only do Christmas Eve, which was impossible for me. The same couple that left during Thanksgiving had also decided to leave for Christmas Vacation too, which left me picking up the slack and meant that we were short two servers.

I couldn't leave them down three servers on the busiest night of the season. It was a super tough decision for me to make, but Danielle also understood the circumstances. I think because of her loyalty to her friend, who owned the restaurant, she didn't push the issue. Danielle and I were frustrated at the couple who left, but there was nothing we could do.

The next earliest appointment was the following Tuesday. We were going to have to wait another week with Danielle worried about still having a tube stuck in her vagina. She was worried even more about a potential infection, and it was becoming a huge stressor. The thought of having a vaginal infection was something that she could not get off her mind. It started to stress me out managing Danielle's concerns.

The following week at work was the most stressful of my entire life. I was working two to three shifts every single day, with only short breaks to run home and handle a pilling list of chores. It was by far the most impressive display of my natural endurance. Somehow, I was still able to make sure to complete everything Danielle needed of me. Accomplishing tasks were easy, but meeting her emotional needs was a far greater challenge. I was becoming emotionally erratic and unable to communicate properly, especially if the topic under discussion was emotionally charged.

Topics like her family started to become almost off-limit topics. I couldn't talk about them without getting upset, and Danielle noticed this fact. I was even useless at this time to address concerns she was having about the Doctor. My frustrations and anger were too strong for me to control. In my moments of weakness or exhaustion, I was making grave mistakes. My responses were not loving and kind but filled with irritation.

A perfect storm to create the worst Christmas's ever. As much as we tried to make it a beautiful morning, my behavior was still a serious issue. The more frequent slips had become almost commonplace as my mental exhaustion took over. I tried to cope and tried everything in my power to maintain a good balance within myself, but I wasn't succeeding, I was failing miserably. Danielle held me accountable for every action, whether I was aware of it or not.

Christmas morning was very tense. Danielle was constantly expecting me to fail, despite my efforts to fix my problems. On top of that, I couldn't excuse myself to smoke some tobacco. No morning delivery meant I couldn't sneak a puff, so my anxiety levels were high. Danielle's problems just antagonized my anxieties to be worse. I tried my best to be the best person I could be that day and didn't do a bad job, but that still didn't undo my past mistakes. She was holding every mistake I made over my head. My failures were pushing us apart.

I hate to say it, but the Christmas season didn't include much in the way of communications from people in Danielle's life. There were those few students that always sent cute and uplifting texts, but the Christmas spirit seemed to skip over Danielle. The community didn't reach out at all, and the anger that Danielle had towards that was huge. After I left for work, she didn't hear from anyone, and I don't believe any of her family even called her on Christmas. Danielle was devastated when I arrived home that night. Danielle felt abandoned, and my behavior was now adding to it.

Usually, I was the one that would ease her abandonment issues, but I was emotionally abandoning her too. I was becoming more distant in an attempt to get myself under control. I figured that if I just did all the tasks, that Danielle would be happy with me. I could perform anything physically, such as cooking, shopping, showers, and a foot rub. No chore was too much for me. Danielle's pain eclipsed my pain, pushing me past any previous limits. I was happy to be of service to my wife, but in my blind pride, I was making a huge mistake. A mistake that had been building for months.

I made it through the weekend and that following Monday at work. It was stressful, but I was also relieved that I could finally have a two-day break from work. I ended up working thirteen days straight without a single day or shift off, picking up two shifts the week prior because of the rescheduled surgery. I was exhausted and expecting a little break from the mayhem. I was not going to be so lucky.

Danielle and I had to wake up at two a.m. to leave by three-fifteen for our trip to Phoenix. We were scheduled for a four-thirty check-in, followed by a five-a.m. surgery. When I woke up from two hours of sleep, I was not in a good mental space and still to this day, don't remember exactly what happened. I remember the consequences clearly, but honestly, I can't recall the exact behavior that triggered them. The one thing I know is that I responded to her in a tone that sent her over the top. I could not speak in a calm tone of voice. Anger, Irritation, and frustration were pouring out of me, and every word that was coming out of my mouth seemed to make Danielle even more furious. I couldn't fix myself this time, and I let my emotions pour out.

I was an emotional wreck. I started yelling in response to accusations showing true emotional immaturity. There was not an ounce of kindness in my tone, all I could do was think of myself. I was everything that I abhor about the people that had upset Danielle.

I was the epitome of bad energy, an angry demon incarnate. All the anger, all the pain, and all the frustration just poured out of me. I was cold, I was cruel, and I couldn't control it. I felt bad, but I also felt right in my behavior. Not to say my behavior was right. I still find that behavior to be very, very wrong, which is why I feel so bad. I was in a state of confusion and shame.

I felt like I was in a blur, a blur that just boiled with anger. I knew I was toxic, and I asked for Danielle to give me space, the problem is I didn't ask nicely. I did it by yelling at Danielle to be quiet, and I'm pretty sure I told her to, "SHUT UP" once or twice. I also sadly remember repeatedly yelling, "LEAVE ME ALONE, AND STOP TALKING TO ME!" I knew we weren't going to get anywhere talking, and we had to drive to Phoenix. However, Danielle was so incredibly mad at me that I still can't express in words how mad she truly was.

The trip passed in almost complete silence. I couldn't talk, I had nothing nice to say, and I knew better than to express myself at that moment. I have known for years that when I get angry, it is toxic. My anger left unchecked is a very destructive force. I've never been physical with anyone, but my words have cut deep wounds. Months of bottled up anger was exploding out of me. I had pushed all my problems aside to focus on Danielle, neglecting any self-care. Little did I know the time bomb that I had become, and the destruction I was instigating.

The check-in at the hospital went smooth, and we moved upstairs quickly. Our trip upstairs took us past the site of our wedding, which did not bring us the feeling it should have. We didn't feel the love that day. I was trying to hold myself together to make up for the shame I felt about behaving so poorly that morning. It never occurred to me that even at that moment, I was making a monumental error.

I later found out how upset Danielle was at me for putting on a fake happy face for the nurses when we got to the hospital. It was just an unconscious behavior from working in restaurants and a great tool I had been using with her, but now that she saw through it. Danielle just saw that I was hiding a bad person. I get why she would feel that way, and she wanted people to see me for the villain I was. However, I was clearly hiding it from everyone else, which enraged her.

Danielle did everything to discuss our problems while we waited for her surgery, but I did everything I could to avoid the conversation. I knew I didn't have the strength to stay calm. My avoidance just made her more upset as she needed to work out the problems we were having. Sadly I couldn't make that a reality, which led to one of the most heartbreaking moments of my story.

The nurses arrived to administer anesthesia before carting Danielle away. Before she went to sleep, she yelled how horrible and terrible I was, saying I was the biggest piece of shit in the world, and I believe it may have gone on for a bit. I understand she needed to vent, and I had gone off the deep end that day. The thing that hurt the most about all of it was that one of the nurses who was present said she was at our wedding and that she felt so sorry for my wife. It hurt because I felt sorry for my wife too.

I couldn't believe my behavior and spent the rest of the afternoon, pulling myself together. I used the time to make a trip to one of the MMJ Dispensaries in the area to get anxiety medication for myself. I was thankfully able to take a couple of tobacco breaks and ate a strong edible brownie, that calmed all my anxiety. The power that MMJ has to calm anxiety when mixed with a little time provided me, a needed emotional reset. I had for the first time in a couple of weeks, a few hours to myself, and by myself.

Despite the work I did on my state of mind, my wife still hadn't changed her tune about me. She was pissed, and I completely understood. I tried to apologize, but I knew there wasn't anything I could say that was going to fix it. I knew this was something I needed to put some serious time and effort into making sure it never happened again. The drive home was super tense, but I did everything in my power to make it as peaceful a ride as possible. I didn't cause any additional problems other than the ones I had already committed.

The rest of the day was not much better because of my need to get some rest. I ended up consuming a copious number of edibles to put myself in a Euphoric state. I felt the need to dramatically alter my consciousness to come to terms with the issues that had been arising in the past month. I have used MMJ and other psychedelics as tools for spiritual and emotional growth in my youth. Getting exceptionally stoned was supposed to get me into that state of mind. After thirteen days of work and the previous twenty-four hours, I needed a break from it all.

Thankfully I did gain some insights into my shortcomings, including new methods I could use to address the situation. Danielle did not view my adventure in a positive outlook. She only saw me change into the different super high Brandon. She didn't see it with compassion or as something that would help me, and she looked at it with all the societal dogma's that go along with drug use. She was furious with me. Danielle didn't see it as a spiritual experience and saw it as me fucking up again.

I have, throughout my life, used the shamanic traditions of medicinal plants to expand my perceptions of the world. Many of the greatest minds of our time have done similar endeavors, and coming from experience, I can understand why. Steve Jobs and other enlightened individuals have attested to the benefits. My wife had never partaken in any substance-induced mind journey. Danielle's preconceptions were combining with her previous anger towards me.

My inability to function at one hundred percent was not putting her at ease. It is why abuse of Marijuana can also be so destructive over long periods. Had I consumed that much regularly, I would have been far less helpful to Danielle, but knowing my tolerances kept me from becoming a stoned couch potato. In no way could I convince her that it was in my best interests to fix my emotional instability. Still, I found insights that night.

In my altered state, I was able to perceive my issues more clearly. I had seen that my level of exhaustion had caused me to overextend myself. I wasn't able to think clearly if my energy fell to low. This realization helped me to understand how important rest was for my mental health. I didn't find the root of the problem, but I saw how I could prevent future problems. I now needed to rebuild the trust I lost with Danielle.

I hadn't realized that Danielle had started isolating us further because of my instability. Leaving her with few people that she could vent her frustrations. She would often vent her frustrations to her sister, which wasn't good for me. Danielle's sister and I never got along because of my outbursts towards her poor behavior. I'm sure she just ate it up that I was acting worse. I'll admit it I had acted that one night to the hospital worse than any single behavior shown from anyone, so they weren't without ammunition.

147

The only other person she could talk to was the ND who had been a long-time girlfriend and trusted colleague. Danielle shared everything with her, and to my surprise, I also had no idea that this was happening. At this time, all the women in Danielle's life were turning against me, and it wasn't looking good.

The truth is that Danielle was being advised by everyone to throw me to the street. Danielle supposedly needed to get me out of there because I was a bad or dangerous person. At the same time, Danielle was always considering who would then pick up my reigns. No one else was stepping up to the plate, and the people informing her what to do weren't offering a legitimate solution.

Danielle knew there wasn't anyone else, and she told me so. I was all she had left, and I had been her rock for so long. Despite my shortcomings, she needed me. I was working to pay the bills and just barely succeeding. I was taking her to practically every doctor appointment and every IV. I was up all night in the shower or on the toilet with her. I would with haste accomplish all of her needs, usually without question. Meeting her emotional needs was my largest failure. At the time, I wish I knew how many people thought of me as a failure.

I have found we often live up to the expectations of the people in our lives. I was having trouble with being a failure, but so many people in my life were projecting that on me. I understand the part I played to put myself in that position, but I found it increasingly more difficult to succeed. My failures were compounding, and it seemed like there was little I could do to change Danielle's perceptions of me. Danielle expected me to fail and was creating situations that continually tested me.

I found the ability to control my anger became almost non-existent. I had to come up with methods to not talk and sit in silence or be allowed to read. I had to find ways to occupy my mind with things that wouldn't cause emotional stress or pain. God knows I was sad, and I was in pain that my wife was sick, but I couldn't show her those emotions. Fear that I would lose control, always went through my mind.

Danielle needed me to get myself under control. I realized that Danielle was not going to tolerate my behavior for much longer. The threat of kicking me out had already been mentioned. If I wanted to stay with my wife, keeping my promise to sleep by her side, I needed to stop being an obstacle. Danielle had enough obstacles to face.

13
Troubling Turmoil

Even with all my issues, I was still far from the biggest concern that Danielle was facing. The third operation had done a real number on her overall health, and we saw serious setbacks. The medical industry was bringing complications from the medications, which destroyed much of the progress we had made. With dwindling support from even the people in her life, it appeared everyone, and everything was failing Danielle. The mountain of stressors never seemed to stop pilling up.

Following the tube removal operation, Danielle's greatest fear manifested. The tube had spent almost three weeks dislodged inside of her vagina. Now, after the surgery, she was faced with an ever-present worry of the possibility of a bacterial infection. Managing that fear was one of my biggest challenges. I was constantly cleaning and making sure that Danielle's space was above and beyond her cleanliness standards. I was constantly washing my hands and using hand sanitizer.

I will admit that some of the rest of the house became messy, mostly due to my lack of time. We had looked into a cleaning service, but it was going to cost over five hundred dollars just for the initial cleaning, which did not fit in the budget. I had the energy to maintain the areas we trafficked, while the rest of the house would just have to wait. I was always sweeping up the floor in our room and the bathroom, to keep the environment spotless. As much energy as I had, I would always use downtime to finish some chores.

I would rarely have more than an hour or so to myself if at all. The time I did have to myself was usually spent reading a comic book. I never was into comics, but this ordeal had inspired me to escape into the colorful fantasy world. I needed a break and getting lost in several comics was a great release for me. However, Danielle did not view it the same way. My increased reading was becoming a problem with Danielle. She didn't want me to take one minute away from her. I couldn't deny her wishes, and this led to me feeling guilty whenever she brought it up.

Danielle had become highly resentful and perpetually angry towards me. She knew that she still needed me, but at the same time, my past behavior was a constant reminder to her that I could become unstable at any time. Danielle was constantly testing me, attempting to push my buttons to the point of blowing up. I knew that if I blew up or lost it again, my next stop was on the street. She had shown her capacity to push people out of her life who did not live up to her standards. Me being an unknown variable, left her feeling way out of control.

Danielle was a control freak in every part of her life. She had always maintained a level of control that even her friends confirmed with me. Danielle could keep hundreds of things straight at a time to manage her house, her business, and her life in ways that few others even show the capacity. Cancer was still the cause of many issues that Danielle couldn't control, and she compensated by controlling all other aspects of her life.

I realized long before this that Danielle was in a way using me to that end. The control that she lost she gained in me. I was there to do her bidding and make sure all her needs were met. While she never took advantage of this kindness, it now became a tool to punish and control me. Danielle knew she didn't have the strength to get mad at me, and the few times she did, it was devastating to her health.

According to Danielle, I had performed unforgivable behavior, and I agreed with her. I was willing to perform my penance. The result was me punishing myself, while also giving Danielle a target to direct her anger. We were starting a pattern that became very difficult to break. For the longest time, I had avoided the anger and frustration that Danielle felt towards the rest of her world. The service I did for her, and the love I provided had protected me from becoming the target of her anger.

Thankfully I wasn't working nearly as much as the holiday season. We were back to a much slower winter season. However, I was still getting more and more stressed with each shift I worked. The problems I had with how the restaurant operated was wearing on me. A decade of restaurant experience at some of the most successful restaurant companies in the west taught me a thing or two about what it takes to run a successful restaurant. All of this combined to make me very angry and resentful every day I went into work.

As much as I tried to leave my work troubles at work, I couldn't deny that they still followed me home. I tried to medicate myself continually into a calm state of mind. I would have to excuse myself for regular breaks to keep myself in balance. My being out of balance had gotten me into this mess in the first place. Not doing what was necessary to keep me sane had taught me a thing or two about self-care — realizing that I needed mental breaks just as much as physical breaks was a new revelation. The issue I ran into was that my solutions were not always Danielle approved.

If I was reading and Danielle didn't want me to, she would make it very known. She would demand that I be present with her every moment. Even if it wasn't me that was bothering her. I was always going to be the one which she took it out on. I tried to prove to her that I could be the person that she needed. Small failures and personal setbacks were still hampering my progress, which led Danielle to trust me less and less. This loss of trust was something I wasn't even aware of at the time.

Danielle didn't have anyone else to help her except me, and her family still hadn't shown up for more than a couple days. We also didn't receive any financial assistance from either of our families. I'm assuming because of our benefactor they didn't feel the need to help financially either. I was personally bothered by this, mostly because I had worked my butt off almost every day to meet our family's needs. Instead, Danielle would tell me her family would complain that I wasn't doing enough.

I knew her family hated me, and because of losing my temper towards them on several occasions, they had a reason. My behavior had cemented a perception in their minds. Although now the perception was starting to manifest as a reality. Had I known so many people were feeding this perception of me, I would have seriously done something about it. I've noticed the more someone expects me to act a certain way, the more difficult it is for me to act the opposite. It might also explain some additional difficulties I had with controlling myself. Danielle needed me under control.

The extra stresses meant Danielle needed me more than ever.

The tensions were building, and more anxiety led to more problems throughout the night. Several showers a night became normal with three or four bathroom breaks too. I became accustomed to waking up every couple of hours. If only I could have returned to a comfortable bed, it might have been different, but I was starting to feel the sleep problems that come with sleeping improperly for months.

I had become increasingly frustrated with her friend, who was paying for treatment. I had several reasons to believe that the friend was using her. Danielle wouldn't believe a word of it and made me feel really bad about it. She had reason to believe that I was concerned about the money. The truth is that it did not matter to me as much as her wellbeing. Danielle did not see my insights with the same intention that I hoped. A comment I made created this perception in Danielle.

I will convey a little background before I share this controversial comment. The friend who was supposed to be helping us, would always come over and get tarot readings from Danielle. Including listening to problems and offering advice like a therapist. In my opinion, Danielle did not have the energy to be of service in that manner. Again, I was the one who would deal with the repercussions. Sadly for Danielle, that meant being up all night in pain, in the shower, and worrying about if she is going to poop before breakfast. Danielle felt obligated to help her friend out because she was helping us.

So needless to say even though the friend was helping us out financially, I also felt she was not helping with the biggest problem, which was Danielle's overall health. Danielle didn't have the strength to be helping others anymore, and she needed to focus on her recovery. I didn't see why she should spend energy on situations that drained her. I saw this, but Danielle refused to see things from my point of view. I only made several inferences until one day, I finally snapped.

I did not understand why Danielle was going so far out of her way to help this friend. Danielle said it was because she helped cover the expenses of treatment. I was appreciative but didn't think we needed to help her out as a result. If what Danielle said was true than even the money, we received was just a tiny fraction of this person's total net worth. I want you to understand my logic because we had received many gifts from the community as well. Many people gave fifty to one-hundred-dollar gift cards to help us out. So according to my logic, I made a rather fair comparison.

I stated, "If one of your students possibly had ten thousand dollars and gave us a hundred dollars, it would be the same percentage as someone worth several million giving us twenty thousand dollars. However, I don't see you giving your students any tarot readings or calling them about their problems." It angered me that my wife could be manipulated by money. Danielle's inconsequential response did not stop me from blurting out in further frustration, "If this person wants to keep getting tarot readings, she better start paying you for your health. She should pay you $100,000 for the services you are providing."

Danielle only heard that I expected her friend to pay us One Hundred Thousand Dollars. She assumed I was looking to get rich quick. I intended for Danielle to put a value on her health. Danielle didn't see the problem that I had observed. Danielle distanced herself from this person out of fear that I would say something inappropriate. I would never have caused a problem considering the importance Danielle put on their relationship. Danielle was truly an amazing friend to people, and I had a hard time telling her that there should be limits.

I was frustrated further by promises that were made but not kept. The friend had commented on our bed and offered to help buy a new one. However, now three weeks later, when nothing was moving forward, I wasn't any bit happier about this person. Danielle told me that she had a lot on her plate and that she didn't want to be pushy and keep asking for things. It didn't matter to me because I desperately needed a bed, and I felt she had forgotten a promise to both of us. Honestly, I don't know how anyone allowed us to sleep in a single bed, in the first place. No one else even offered to help or thought it pertinent to fix — the one thing I needed.

My parents finally did offer their help in making a new bed purchase as a Christmas Present. Initially, they offered to drive my sister's bed, but then it became a moving issue, so they offered to pay for a new one. Woefully the cheapest bed we could find that was organic and didn't have memory foam was sixteen hundred dollars. The bed was about one thousand dollars more than my dad was initially looking at, so Danielle and I decided that since the friend had offered to pay for the mattress that we would use some of the money she already gifted us.

We gave my dad one thousand dollars so he could purchase the organic mattress from Sears, and have it delivered. We even started the process before Christmas, but little did I know that we would have some additional shipping problems. The mattress ended up being returned before it was ever delivered. We then found out that it was unable to be shipped to our house and would need to be picked up. After months of hell, I was ready for a decent night's sleep. It was one ounce of relief in our gloomy lives.

Another bit of relief came to me from an unlikely source, a mainstream nurse. Danielle's frustration with me was at an all-time high, and she couldn't believe my past behavior. Even with all the tricks and techniques, I was using to stay calm; I was still finding it more and more difficult to control my emotions. One of the nurses told us that it was rather common for married couples to fight or blow up during times of illness. She had seen some husbands lose it in the waiting rooms, and some wives go completely crazy on their husbands. It wasn't uncommon, and she made us feel like it was far more common than people are led to believe.

I say that this comment about poor behavior helped because, for the first time in a long time, Danielle had some compassion for my plight. I will always remember this moment because it was also a time in our relationship where I had a reprieve. Danielle no longer held the view that I was just a horrible person. She could now see that I was also a victim of the circumstances we were facing.

The fact that I had held it together for so long made me feel better about myself. I know that it didn't excuse my past behavior, but for the first time in my life, I started to see I wasn't alone. This burden I was carrying was a burden many before me also failed to carry. Now I had to think if people are less prepared than me than I can't imagine the hell they might face. I gained new levels of compassion for just how bad I could have let myself get.

Danielle and I would often talk about what it takes to be there for someone going through the healing or dying process. Danielle had a lot of experience from the AIDS epidemic in the '80s. She said the stigma and the shame associated with the disease forced many to be abandoned by friends and family. Most people ill-prepared for the ugly nature of the disease and how horrific death can be. However, Danielle could be there for anyone and truly be there.

Showing up and being present was her gift to the world. She found it in herself to be there most of all for those that had been completely abandoned by this world.

Every day I tried to live up to her expectations and to be someone she deserves. She would tell me of the behavior that people would show, the anger, the blame, the shame, and the guilt. Friends and Family would abuse the sick people in such selfish and thoughtless ways. Only now did I fully understand the full spectrum of what causes some of these atrocities to happen. It was becoming obvious to me that as a society, we are truly failing many of the sick and dying. I too was guilty of this, and I knew I had to find a solution. I had to do it because Danielle deserved it, she had earned it, and there wasn't anyone else stepping up to the plate to give her what she needed.

I know I wasn't ready for anything that I went through with Danielle. No amount of life experience can truly prepare anyone for the experience we went through. Realizing that others are going through this every day, brought more purpose to my life. I know that few people realize how difficult controlling our emotions can be without proper practice. Volunteering more with the sick and dying would have prepared me better. Spending more time helping my aging grandparents would have helped. I still to this day feel bad about not helping the family more with my Grandparents. A mistake I will never make again.

The abundance of mistakes through this process by myself would not be in vain. I would not allow my emotions to control me. I would show a more proactive approach to maintaining balance. Danielle was not going to make it easy with her expectations for me to fail. I had cracked the dam, and she was testing the integrity. Danielle was testing me at every turn to see if I would lose control. She was having a hard-enough time keeping it together without me adding to the troubles.

14
Breaking Point

After the holidays, Danielle felt like she was losing control of all aspects of her life. Her IV treatments were not showing the same improvement that they once were. Danielle felt the pain start to increase during and after each treatment. Also, she was not showing the steady signs of improvement that she had over the previous several months. The increased discomfort had her scared. She always worried the cancer was spreading and potentially where it could spread to next. Her greatest fears being cancer's that cause horrible and terrible deaths, like liver or brain cancer. So many concerns put too much strain on her body.

I would have to say that looking back; I don't know how I could have possibly eliminated all the stresses that confronted Danielle. Short of doing it all again with all the knowledge I have now. However, without going through what we went through, I wouldn't have all the knowledge I have now. A conundrum that I still wrestle with to this day.

There was still so much working in our favor. I couldn't believe the treatment funding appearing with a perfect job schedule too. While also having two perfect living situations manifest at the perfect time. Even the timing of doctor arrivals, to the perfection of our meeting, and even our wedding day was miraculous. There was honestly so much beauty amidst a sea of troubles.

The new year would bring more undesired troubles and fewer miracles. For the first several weeks of January, Danielle and I were facing truly terrible times. These few weeks would prove to be not only our greatest obstacle but a time I still am grateful to have endured. I for the last and final time reached my breaking point, a point that broke Danielle's spirit and my strength.

It wasn't anything specific that caused me to break again. I had reached the end of my ropes, and nothing could stop my decline.

My behavior was unacceptable, according to Danielle. Despite feeling like I was doing my best. The conflict in our relationship was quickly starting to accelerate. Danielle was increasingly starting to take all her anger and frustrations out on me.

I accepted her wrath as punishment for my past behavior. I felt I deserved it apparently as much as she did. However, the constant punishment was also causing me to become unstable. We became stuck in a vicious cycle that created more instability. Danielle feared I would show my instability just when she needed me the most. She didn't want to live in an environment where she may not have the strength to do something about it. I could not entertain the idea of losing to cancer, creating additional disagreements.

Danielle would express she was dying, which would always trigger my emotional response. I would almost forbid the conversation despite Danielle pleas that she was doing worse. The prolonged struggle finally was the straw that broke the camel's back. I couldn't for one instant accept that my wife was going to die. I knew that all the treatments we were doing were supposed to be curing her, there wasn't a chance that we would fail. Entertaining the idea of losing the battle to cancer was never even a possibility for me. The topic further divided us.

Four months straight, I was holding the space that we would beat that disease. I couldn't imagine the thought of my wife losing to Cancer, and it was a pride issue for me. I had studied curing and treating cancer alternatively for at least six years. I felt proficient in my knowledge, including my hands-on knowledge learned through the Doctors. I thought that without a doubt that I could heal my wife and make her Cancer free. We were going to beat this disease, and I didn't want to hear otherwise.

Danielle no longer agreed with this assumption. Her health wasn't improving. I failed to see the problems subtly worsen. My shortcomings were leaving me shortsighted. The added issues she was developing were causing her more concerns. Danielle was getting worse, and I wasn't doing anything to make the situation better.

Almost two weeks into January, Danielle started taking a real turn for the worst. I wasn't willing to accept her decline, and it was causing increased tension. I was still working six days a week, and the added stress of my being away was not helping the situation. Nothing Danielle or I did was making things better, and Danielle's failing strength was making everything harder for her. The IV's had become unbearable at this point, and the relief given was nothing compared to the healing crisis she would have those nights.

We were sometimes taking three to five showers a night to help with the pain. It would usually just be a temporary relief, and I would always reapply the meds for additional relief. I was finding the medicinal marijuana that we were using was not strong enough to manage the pain that Danielle was feeling. I tried everything and still nothing. Danielle knew her treatments weren't working as well as they should, which was also causing Danielle to lose faith in the treatment. If it wasn't going to make her better, why was she subjecting herself to additional pain or self-torture?

It was about this time that she started having more problems with her bathroom breaks too. Just after the first two weeks of January, Danielle was showing problems in her urinary tract. She was having discomfort mixed with having to pee almost on the hour. It had her very concerned.

To add to concerns, I was expecting my dad for a visit. It was the first time I had seen my Dad since my Birthday in August when he first met my wife. I had known for a couple of days that he was coming up, and Danielle was fine with him visiting for the weekend. We weren't expecting the whole weekend to blow up the way it did, but the timing in a way couldn't have been better.

After one of the hardest treatments that she ever endured and a mess of additional health concerns, Danielle decided that night she needed to go to the hospital. It wasn't an emergency, but it was dire. We decided to have it checked out, during a healing crisis in the middle of the night. I finally admitted that the situation was getting worse. However, I also had to work at seven in the morning.

I couldn't screw over my work, but I also knew I had to take Danielle to a hospital to check on what was happening. Since the situation had been building over time, it wasn't an urgent emergency. However, it was hard to deny the signs. Danielle had taken huge steps backward over the previous several weeks. I was finally starting to accept that things weren't improving, and things were not looking good overall.

I was heartbroken as I went into work that day. I probably cried at least four times, just getting the food together for my early morning delivery. I also had a talk with my manager that brought us both to tears. I knew that there wasn't any way that I was going to be able to work anymore with Danielle's health deteriorating. Thankfully Danielle's friend, who had been helping us out, had also given Danielle another check to pay for further expenses.

I was able to tell my manager that I was done working after that shift. I felt bad having to give such short notice to them, but I also knew that my wife's health was more important. Truthfully, I didn't feel as guilty because I had worked so many extra shifts for the restaurant. I was the one who picked up shifts left and right when other people were unable to work, and now it was my turn to have someone pick up the slack for me. I felt I had earned the right to do what I did, so I did it without looking back.

I tried to contain my emotions at work. Thankfully, it was a delivery, and I didn't have to talk to many people. I fell into a deep state of depression, seeing very little hope on the horizon. I was finally coming to terms that my wife might not win this fight. She had told me for the past week that things weren't looking good, but I didn't listen. I tried to be the positive reassurance in the relationship, but my emotional problems were making that impossible. So now I was left with a blinding realization.

We both needed help, so I made sure that I let my dad know what was going on before he left Tucson. The dire circumstances and our decision to go to the hospital in Flagstaff had inspired both of my parents to make the journey. We were even going to be meeting up with Danielle's close friend and gracious benefactor. She lived in Flagstaff, so it was an easy drive over for a visit. I was relieved to have the additional support, I so desperately needed it. To say it was a bit of a tense ride to Flagstaff would be an understatement.

Being in the hospital, Danielle was relieved to start getting more answers. I was relieved to have additional support. Danielle's friend was the first to arrive, which allowed me to step outside for a quick smoke break. I had to navigate the massive snowbanks, but thankfully, the roads and parking lots were mostly clear for walking and driving. Flagstaff was located high in the mountains, having far more extreme winters compared to Sedona. It was refreshing to step out and also check on my parent's progress.

My parents texted me that they were still several hours away. Their journey was about four hours from start to finish, so I wasn't expecting them to meet us there. I enjoyed a discreet smoke out the side of my car. I needed to be at my best for Danielle, and I finally had an opportunity to reset. Danielle needed me to be calm for the report on her condition.

. I wasn't having an easy time, either with all the emotions flying around. I was at my Breaking point, and it seemed Danielle was too. All of my emotional instability aside, we were both still concerned with Danielle's growing health problems. The hospital had to run tests to figure out the source of the issues. We were accustomed to waiting for results.

Danielle's first concern was a possible vaginal infection from the tube that was dislodged. A urinary infection would be horrible for Danielle. Danielle knew her body, and she knew that her body did not react well to antibiotics. She knew it was going to be even worse with how sick she was. The fears were growing exponentially. The main concern still always being the possibility of constipation with any medications.

Danielle was scheduled for a full-body scan to find out if the cancer was spreading too. Spreading was probably the greatest fear of all but still wasn't the main issue that we were there to address. All of these possibilities and unknowns were stressful on Danielle and me. There wasn't anything that I could do to make her feel better, and her bitterness towards me just made things worse. Danielle was constantly testing me at this point, pushing my triggers in a way to vent her anger on me. I did everything in my power to handle that with grace and ease.

It wasn't easy and thanks to her friend arriving things became much more peaceful. It was such a blessing to have someone there to help us through that day. God knows we needed the support. I was grateful for the miracles that occurred. It certainly was a lucky chance that my dad was already planning a visit that day. Now we were going to have both of my parents to assist us.

My parents arrived in the evening, and after a few introductions and some catching up, my mom decided to take me out to dinner. They could all see the tension between the two of us. We were both having our issues, and thankfully, my dad was there to help Danielle. It was a blessing, and it also allowed me to take a real break.

Danielle and my father had a special connection that I still

161

can't explain. Danielle told me she always had a connection with those in the military because of a past that she still says I'm not allowed to discuss. That part of her life was long behind her by the time we met, but it was still part of who she was. So my dad, being a former Air Force Academy graduate and fighter pilot, was the ideal person to enter Danielle's life.

It was amazing to see my dad step up and immediately start showing Danielle the support she needed. He didn't have a problem throwing me under the bus either, and after about fifteen minutes of everyone reprimanding me for my behavior, I had to excuse myself. I was too tired, too upset, too angry, and too guilty about everything which meant I was ready to break again. I know that I was in the wrong when it came to my behavior, but it was hard having everyone team up against me. My family had plenty of reasons to throw me under the bus.

Due to my mother's excessive drinking, I would, in the past, get very upset with her. I started to have very little tolerance for her behavior. My mother was a grown adult who behaves more like a child while under the influence. Most times we interacted in the past while she was intoxicated, it would end with me blowing up on her. I have, on numerous occasions, had to yell at my mother to "Shut Up," because asking nicely always seemed to go unnoticed. Other family members used my reaction, to my mother's behavior, to crucify me. My anger had dug me into a deep hole.

My family used this past behavior to attack me while confirming to Danielle that I had a problem. This did not help me one bit, but it did bring Danielle some Peace. She finally had some validation, and it wasn't just her saying it. So far, these were the only other people in my life that had ever been hurt by me showing my anger. Now they were all united, and it seemed I was the bad guy.

After all of that my mom took me to dinner, my parents could see I needed a break. That was exactly what I wanted. Truthfully, I hadn't done much in the way of real rest or relaxation in almost two months. Many of the activities, like hiking, biking, or yoga, were on hold while I assisted Danielle. I hadn't done much of anything for myself except reading. Reading was the only escape that I had, and it worked most of the time. Now I had a break without worrying about Danielle's needs, and this would be a first.

My mom and I took a cab since we were both planning on

drinking. She wasn't drunk yet, so it was still safe to be around her. If she had already started drinking, it would have been a lot harder for me to tolerate her behavior. After a couple of beers and a bunch of food, I was ready to head back and see my wife. We grabbed some dinner to go for my dad before heading back to the Hospital. My dad had helped Danielle come to some peace about a lot of what was happening. He offered that logical male perspective in a way that I couldn't. Plus he had spent the past several years helping his mother pass, so he was rather well equipped for the situation.

Our marriage issues were definitely at the forefront of many of the discussions while my parents were present. I knew that because I was still at fault, there wasn't an excuse, I do believe in no excuses. Excuses prevent us from taking proper action, and I was not afraid of taking the proper steps. I believe that in life, it is necessary to make appropriate adjustments, and I was willing to make them. I was committed to not making the same mistakes again, but I was aware I needed help to do this.

The biggest issue that the family helped me address would be the results from the rest of the tests. We had some results come back that day, and it wasn't looking good. The first issue of vaginal infection was confirmed, which sent Danielle into almost a panic attack. First off, she knew she was going to need to do a round of antibiotic treatments, and her health was already taking a quick nosedive. The scans showed an even graver picture.

Thankfully by the time the imaging came back, my parents were present. It was hard to hear the news that the doctor had to share with us. We were devastated to find out that other masses were developing. The scan had found a mass that was starting to develop near the liver. Including other indications that possible tumors may be developing other places. Danielle had truly lost all hope with this news.

The knowledge that Danielle had gained was going to lead to many new decisions she was going to make with her life. I didn't have much say in the matter other than providing her the support she needed. I wasn't just a yes man to Danielle because I was someone who was there to support her best interests in the best ways that I knew how. So to say it wasn't easy to agree with some of her decisions, I knew I still needed to support them. Even the hardest realizations as Danielle started to prepare for death.

Almost immediately, she decided to stop doing the curcumin IV treatment. Treatment was unbearable, and since the treatment hadn't stopped the spread of the disease, there wasn't much point to continuing. Danielle had decided to accept her fate. It was hard on everyone present, and no one was taking it lightly. I could tell her friend was probably the most upset about the decision. Immediately she tried to work with Danielle on solutions. Possibly seeing other doctors or trying other treatments. Danielle wasn't interested in continuing the struggle.

I knew better than to try and get Danielle to change her mind. I learned that lesson long before this day. Supporting her decisions went further than challenging them. Exercising patience would also allow me to question those choices too. Patience was imperative if I had a problem with a choice she was making. It isn't what we want to say but how we say it that is most important. If I gave her a choice versus trying to push my opinion on her, I found far better results. Sometimes she didn't want my opinion or didn't want to do things my way, but sometimes she did. I had to be fine with either outcome. I wish more people acted in this manner.

We were all sharing a moment of emotional turmoil, which brought everyone closer together. The amount of compassion that filled the room was miraculous. The support that we were all showed was invaluable in helping Danielle through such a horrible experience. The Cancer no longer appeared to be something we could beat. We were forced to take a different look at planning the remainder of her life.

After more bad news than we had since our wedding day, it was time for some needed rest. I as usual spent the night at my wife's side. We pulled up a recliner, and I had one of the most comfortable night's sleep, in a hospital chair. I didn't sleep particularly well, but at least I was comfortable. It was the one thing I remember about going to bed that night. Well, that and a beautiful video that my sister had put together.

Even though my sister was over a thousand miles away in Thailand, she still contributed. Her gift was touching in so many ways. My sister found a time that day to put together a beautiful video for Danielle and me. When my mom shared it with us earlier that day, it brought us all to tears. I had completely forgotten that my sister took a bunch of amazing pictures of Danielle and me when they visited for my birthday. It was amazing to see some pictures of how happy we were before all this happened. It was hard to believe that we even had a life like that because it was such a short time, five weeks to be exact. Now life was much different, and a night in the hospital wasn't out of the ordinary.

The next day we woke up to hospice. It was the first time I had ever met with someone regarding the end of life. It scared me a little. The only reason for hospice was to help Danielle make the transition from life to death. Danielle had so many questions for them, and I too had many concerns to go along with her questions. Hospice was going to be another undertaking.

Thanks to Danielle's insurance, we were not limited in any way to the available options. We actually had three companies that worked in the Sedona area to choose. I knew that wasn't going to be an easy choice. Danielle and I would have to vet them thoroughly. It was the same thing we did to every practitioner that came into the picture.

The presence of friends and family made everything a little easier. It helped so I could get more breaks so that I could be the person that Danielle needed. I started to see a positive difference, a little rest and extra medication were having. My emotional health was improving exponentially. I knew after some talking with my dad that I could manage my problems. Eventually, showing Danielle that I can be the better person she needed.

I needed to find a better way to behave under stress, and the answers were manifesting. However, those solutions would be far easier to arrive at back home. We knew it was time to get out of there. Hospitals made Danielle so uneasy and nervous, so the less time she was exposed, the better. We were preparing for a new chapter in our marriage that I could never have foreseen.

15
Finding Light in the Darkness

As we all prepared for the trip back down the canyon, it was imperative that my dad takes Danielle in his car. Our marital issues were at a record high, and we needed a break. My mother would accompany me back in my car. My father's car was a rental, which meant it was going to be a much smoother ride for Danielle. Danielle also needed more fatherly advice.

My dad and I had already talked before he left. It was important to me that we get over the problems that we were having. He was familiar with my angry outbursts in the past and was the best person on the planet to talk to Danielle about it. My mother was the exact opposite. I didn't want my mom talking to my wife at all. She was feeding the problem.

My past outbursts were typically due to my mother's excessive drinking. I am not proud of the number of times I have told my mother to shut her mouth. My failed attempts to avoid hours of obnoxious behavior. I wish I were exaggerating, but that's the truth. The sad truth is that my mother would only remember me telling her to shut up. It's hard not to treat someone, like a misbehaving child when they repeatedly behave that way as an adult.

My dad had seen the repercussions of my behavior and also how it previously alienated me from the family. While that is a completely different issue, it does show just how destructive my anger can ultimately be. By this time, I had learned my lessons with my family. If I didn't want them to upset me with the behavior that they were choosing, I either needed to become fine with my mother's alcoholism or avoid contact. We could continue to maintain a functional relationship in very small doses, such as attending family events or dinners.

It wasn't a huge deal to me that my parents were using my past to help Danielle come to terms with my behavior. The big issue was that I no longer was the person that my mother was talking about with my wife. My mother had no clue who I was at this point. Her memory of my angry outbursts is five years old and clouded by twenty years of drinking. To say her communication with my wife was troublesome would be an understatement.

Thankfully Danielle recognized my mother's behavior and quickly realized why I always said the things I did about her. It isn't that I don't love my mom, I love her very much, but I despise the person that alcohol has forced her to become. It is that person that I knew was very harmful to be in my wife's presence. It became evident on the first opportunity I gave my mom to help Danielle out.

We all knew I needed to start taking more personal time. It was step one to creating a more positive attitude for Danielle. One of the most productive activities that always made me feel better was hiking. I love hiking, and there isn't a time that hiking hasn't made me feel better. The hiking in Sedona is half the reason I moved here, the job offer being the other half. Sedona is a perfect place for me while having a creek nearby makes it almost heavenly.

Since Danielle and I married, I had only been hiking two or three times. I wasn't getting my usual release in nature. Now with some help from my parents, I would have the time to explore. While my dad ran errands, I decided to do a quick two-hour adventure up the Canyon. My mom was supposed to stay with Danielle so that I could take a break, a real break. A break without worries while knowing that my wife was in good hands. Well, that isn't how it went at all.

Within about forty-five minutes, I started receiving messages from my mom, asking when I would return. Instantly I had all the anxiety return. I texted my mother that it would be at least another forty-five minutes. I just arrived at a place to sit down and relax. It was perfect because I had water running on all sides of my huge rock. A brisk sunny day complimented the scenery as the sun poured through the naked trees. I could have sat there for hours, centering my mind. Despite being rushed to go home, there was a huge benefit I felt sitting there for a few minutes.

It was amazing the transformation that I felt from just one trip to the Creek. My former, stronger self had returned, full of emotional strength, and longing to fix the mistakes that had been occurring. I finally was in a mental space that I could be there fully for my wife. Observing the difference in how I reacted to the world was a huge wake-up call. My new awareness was helping so that I could be the person that my wife demanded.

It was also time to sit down with my Dad and Danielle to have a serious conversation. I knew that I had all sides against me. I couldn't blame anyone but myself for my behavior. This knowledge of what I did wrong brought me a lot of shame at the time. I knew I made my mistakes, but I also wanted to start moving past them.

After a talk the previous day with my father about everything that was happening, I knew that I had at least one person in my corner. He understood that the past several months was very difficult. My behavior was not the real problem, although he did say that it needed to stop. The problems were due to me facing complete exhaustion combined with a dying wife. He explained it was something that few people are equipped to deal with, but he could see that I wanted to learn. I also explained to him that she had high standards because of her life experiences.

It was difficult to hear Danielle rub it in that she helped eight other people pass from AIDS. I wanted with all my heart to live up to those expectations, expectations that I feel now might have been far too high for myself under the circumstances. Too much Pride had blinded me to my shortcomings. I had faced impossible odds, but now with proper help, I had no more excuses. I loved my wife so much I would do anything to make her happy.

I could no longer be a source of pain for my wife. It had become clear to me that I was mentally exhausted. Many of the problems I had were because I didn't have any help. I was alone in all of this for so long, and we needed to make some serious changes. It was going to be important that we have someone come over from time to time to give me a physical break. To make sure I didn't have to worry about Danielle, and also to get added support. The other issue was keeping my emotional strength up, and there was a big conversation planned.

It ended up being a couple of days before I had the big sit down with Danielle and my father. I was finally feeling better since I additionally wasn't working. The additional free time was helping dramatically. Taking time for myself was not an issue like it was in the past. After a couple of days but I was finally back to normal, I wasn't irritable, I wasn't agitated, and I wasn't the problem that I had been building for the previous several months. I was me again, and I was ready to take a serious look at the problems.

I will admit it wasn't an easy conversation to have with Danielle and my father. Both of them were just as tired as I was with my behavior. However, one of the first things that I believe shifted my perspective was when both my dad and Danielle said I was an angry person. For so long, I couldn't imagine being an angry person. I was always happy and positive. No one in my life would classify me as angry, except for maybe my family... That was the realization.

I was unmistakably an angry person around my family. However, that was a more recent development as I had a very charmed childhood. I was rarely angry, growing up. Until I hit my early twenties, I was only angry maybe once a year. The rest of the time, I was happy and having fun. For someone to call me an angry person, it would almost feel like they didn't know me at all. This time though I didn't hear it the same, it shot through me like an arrow.

It shattered my world because I could see how angry I was. It was all so true; I was filled with anger. I started thinking about all the topics that make my blood boil. The list included the Mainstream Medical Establishment, my wife's family, GMO's, toxic beds, human trafficking, child abuse, and hundreds of other things that are wrong with our world. I was angry at the Cancer and the fact that the medical industry doesn't want to tell us what caused my wife's cancer. My anger included doctors saying alternative treatments don't work, inferring, those treatments will likely lead to death. I could go on and have done so.

I spent countless hours posting articles or videos related to these topics on Facebook. Other angry people always attacked me, causing entertaining comment conflict. However, I pretended not to be angry about anything, or I would only get angry when someone else behaved inappropriately. Still, I never considered myself angry, despite getting angry from time to time. I knew I struggled with my anger but to classify myself as angry was a brand-new way of thinking.

I'll admit I spent the first twenty years of my life rather oblivious to the problems our world is facing, now that I'm aware I can't deny my anger. It becomes even more infuriating when there is little to no chance for me to personally fix all those problems. I would drive myself crazy if I even spent half my day being angry at everything wrong with the world.

A shift happened in me when I realized that I was angry. I hadn't realized how much my anger had been controlling me versus me controlling my anger. This realization also helped the conversation move forward. My acceptance of my weakness also helped Danielle to open up. My dad said one other thing that I don't know if it helped me as much as it helped Danielle, but either way, it practically fixed our relationship.

For so long, I had been comparing myself to Danielle and the fact that she spent weeks and months caring for people who were dying throughout her life. Danielle's highest calling was caring for people that society discards. It was also such a high standard to live up to. My dad put things into perspective for both of us. He said, "The situations are not the same because Danielle, you didn't love those people as Brandon loves you."

That made both of us think. It wasn't easy for me to watch someone I care about so much go through so much pain and agony. The Surgeon said it best when he said Cancer is a Bitch. It truly was, and after four and a half months of watching the love of my life suffer, it had done a number on me too. Months of witnessing misery in all its forms.

Enduring the suffering of a loved one was even more exhausting than any other experience in my life. Nothing compared to what I faced with Danielle, and honestly, I hope nothing ever does. Danielle and I both grew from our struggles. We both were finding our peace in the sea of turmoil. It was an honor to have an opportunity to experience this with such an amazing person. The walls that had been built were starting to crumble.

Danielle admitted she had changed the will, and she felt ashamed. At the time of our wedding I was going to inherit the house should something happen to Danielle. The issues we were having as a couple and influence from the other people in her life had forced her to rethink her will. Several weeks prior, she had a friend take her over to the lawyer to remove me from the will. She had decided to leave the house to one of her students because she didn't feel that her family would fulfill her wishes for the house. I truthfully wasn't bothered by not getting the house because I didn't want it in the first place.

It was upsetting to find out just how much faith and trust that Danielle had lost in me. No longer did she see me as her husband through sickness and health. I had broken that trust. Considering the problems we were having, I did sympathize, agreeing that I probably should not get the house anyway. When we first drew up the will, we weren't expecting five months later to be in the situation we were facing.

My dad agreed I shouldn't get the house. I didn't have the means to keep up with the repairs, nor was I completely sure if I would want to stay indefinitely in Sedona. It was nice to have a little support from my dad on the issue. It calmed Danielle's fears while resolving many of our issues. My dad also didn't want to be the one to foot the bill for repairs. It was in everyone's best interests that someone else gets the house. My dad was stepping up to be exactly what we needed at that moment, a mediator.

My dad had become a dad to not only me again, but also to my wife. After years of being rather estranged, it was nice to be able to connect with such depth. I still wish the circumstances could have been different, but I've always tried to make the best even from a really bad situation. This really bad situation had brought out the best in my dad. He could see that Danielle and I needed help, and he willingly changed all of his work plans to help us. I don't think that my dad understood what was occurring until he was at the house for a couple of days.

He had observed that Danielle and I were having the most problems because I was a target for her anger. Danielle was incredibly angry and rightfully so. Danielle had more to be angry about than I did, and I hadn't realized that I was a big reflection of her anger. My dad recognized the vicious cycle we were stuck in. My dad's intervention curbed her coaxing me to get angry. It had become a problem that I couldn't do anything about previously.

Her anger towards my behavior would often lead to that very behavior manifesting. My desire to make sure that didn't happen was where my real growth took place. Despite the constant encouragement from Danielle to show that I was a destructively angry person. I wasn't going to be an angry person anymore, and I was making a choice.

The return of my mental strength and the added support were allowing me to endure any stresses. By addressing my anger in a more honest approach, I had, in a way, taken away the power that it once had over me. While it wasn't like my anger just disappeared, it felt like a huge weight had lifted off my shoulders.

During our conversation, I also came clean about my Tobacco addiction. Surprisingly that went over much better than I would have thought. I was expecting Danielle to be upset at the fact that I was smoking since the wedding. To my surprise, she wasn't upset about it at all. It didn't change that I felt bad about hiding it. I never lied to her about it, but I hid it well enough that she never even asked. It was one of the hardest things I had been living with the past several months, and it was so powerful to lift the burden off my chest.

I explained how putting a little tobacco in my pipe when I smoke my medical marijuana would truly reduce the stress or anxiety I was feeling. I also admitted that some of my problems were because I didn't smoke enough nicotine. Certainly, some of my blow-ups were because I was unable to excuse myself for my nicotine fix. I apologized profusely even though it didn't bother Danielle. She was a little concerned that I had successfully hidden it from her but also knew I never lied about it.

After months of trying to figure out ways to cope with the stress, I finally had the upper hand. Even though Danielle didn't believe me yet, I knew I was ready. The following couple of days saw a huge improvement in our relationship. My emotional strength had returned, and I was the person that she needed me to be. It wasn't easy, but I knew I could do it.

I felt stronger, more in control, and a new person altogether. Danielle still wasn't convinced, but she was opening up to it, and I was willing to be patient. Patience was a virtue that I was constantly cultivating during our relationship. I could feel that I was already a better person. Now I had to prove it to Danielle.

The time we spent together involved moving past much of the pain we had both gone through over the past months. I repeatedly apologized for my lack of strength and that I would not allow myself to go to that place again. I knew using the proper tools at my disposal, that I could be the person that she needed. I began to embrace vices that I once considered terrible.

Now that I didn't need to hide the tobacco usage, I was able to keep my cravings in check. I was also able to use nicotine as a tool to calm myself down quickly. I learned fast that if I excused myself before I reached a point of no return, that I could quickly recenter myself. I'll even admit that there was a learning curve.

I knew that if I left myself unchecked that I could fall out of balance. My past had proven that it was not good if I went past my breaking point. It could take several hours to a full day for me to regain my mental strength. I was not going to allow myself to get to that point and using copious amounts of nicotine and THC were my saviors. I was embracing plant medicines on a whole new level.

Danielle and I had both dramatically changed our views about plant medicines. We were changing together again. Our renewed relationship was moving forward. It would be necessary for the challenges we were about to face. My new-found strength would be tested.

16
Sailing through the Hurricane

Our situation had truly taken a turn for the worst. We were no longer expecting a recovery but instead planning for the end of life care. It seemed that all our efforts to beat the disease were made in vain. The reality Danielle and I now faced together was terrifying. Thankfully we weren't going to have to face it alone. My dad had decided to stay for another week as we expected Danielle's family to arrive.

My greatest test would be Danielle's whole family visiting. I knew they didn't like me, but I didn't like them much either. I didn't have many nice things to say about them, and usually just tried to keep my opinions to myself. There was little point getting my kicks out of putting her family down. Especially since I was now just as guilty of causing problems as they were. I had some sympathy for them now. It didn't excuse our behavior, but I had more compassion.

I understood that being so emotionally connected to someone sick or dying is difficult. I made my mistakes, and I had to forgive them for theirs. Danielle demanded that we all be on our best behavior because she wouldn't tolerate anything else. One of her greatest concerns was that I would lose it around her family. She explained more about her fears, saying, I would not be able to control myself around them.

I promised my wife that if they did come, I would not cause a single problem. I promised to be a perfect angel and prove to her that I could be the man she married. I promised I could be the man I knew I had to become. I reassured her and told her that this would be my true test. I would prove to her that despite all the anger, I could remain calm.

This visit was going to be longer than a weekend visit. We were planning on a full week of people showing up to help the crisis we were going through. Many more family members were planning on making this journey to assist us. Danielle's family had decided to make a genuine gesture of love toward Danielle. Her sister and husband, including their two daughters, were coming. Also, Danielle's mom was going to be traveling with them too. Everyone would be flying out in the next couple of days to be with us. It was going to be an occasion.

Danielle had asked my dad to stay, which he did without a second thought. He took several more vacation days to make sure that he could be there for us when the family arrived. I was going to be far more prepared for their arrival this time. So I got to work cleaning. My mom helped for the short time that she was in town, but her time was cut short. She had to head back home for work and was planning on coming back the following weekend.

One issue that we didn't have to worry about was money. Danielle's friend had given us another check so that I would be able to be a full-time caregiver for Danielle, which removed a big stressor from my world, my job. The relief from not working constantly gave me a huge advantage. There was just one problem, Danielle wasn't going to be able to make it into the bank to cash the check, I would have to do it.

It was a large check, and the bank put a hold on it right away. I anticipated this might happen, but the hold only upset Danielle. She sent me back to the bank immediately to take care of it. My dad accompanied me because I was upset by the circumstances. After spending almost an hour at the bank on the phone getting the funds verified, we started moving forward. Next, we needed permission to allow the check to deposit into my account. After verification, we still had to wait twenty-four to forty-eight hours for the funds to be released. The ordeal was beyond frustrating.

Danielle felt apprehension with me having all the money in my account because of our relationship problems. She trusted me, but I hadn't fully regained her unconditional support. I hadn't fully rebuilt the trust she once had in me. I knew I could do it, but I couldn't fail again. I had to be strong for Danielle because it was the only way I could make things right.

Her family arrived different days throughout the week. Everyone came out for as long as they could to help Danielle. I was excited to get more help around the house. Truthfully, I hadn't gotten much rest since we returned. It had still been rather hectic in preparations for their arrival, which caused added stress for Danielle. Much like myself, Danielle feared her family would misbehave too. There was nothing I could do to help that problem, and it was up to her family to address those issues.

Danielle's family arrived without a hitch. Things went well as everyone introduced themselves. Both of our families enjoyed getting to know each other. It helped my situation to have my dad there for support. Our support team was growing every day. We had a lot of people in the house by the end of the first day, and it was a bit overwhelming for Danielle. She wasn't having a particularly good day mostly because the added stress had worn her out. Danielle also became rather irate at the behavior of everyone the first night.

Danielle came out into the living room for most of the evening, but every time she would start to feel tired, she would have to retreat to her room. Most of the time, I was the one who assisted during any moves throughout the house. I would also make sure that wherever she was traveling to, she would be comfortable. The cold weather outside had made it difficult, but I had the woodstove down to a science, I could heat almost the entire house with a well-maintained fire. It made for a cozy house for people to relax.

It became a party the first night as everyone was getting to know each other. Most of the group had started having a few cocktails, considering most of the group was drinkers. The spirits had everyone in high spirits. Danielle was offended that people were laughing, yelling, and partying while she was in the next room, going through excruciating pain. She had already retreated to her room, so I asked everyone to keep it down. We spent most of the evening together while everyone continued socializing.

I wasn't impressed by the initial show of support. However, Danielle's nieces were incredible, and they were her family's saving grace. I found them to be the kindest young ladies who clearly admired Danielle. They behaved more like Danielle than their own mother. Almost immediately after they arrived, they started helping out with the cleaning.

No one wanted to cover the five-hundred-dollar cleaning service, so we had to do it ourselves. Danielle's mom enlisted me for many different projects immediately. The first endeavor was washing all the laundry in the house. Not that difficult until I realized that there was a full mini van's worth of stuff to wash. My dad and I filled twelve high capacity washers at the laundromat before he left to run other errands. After doing several hours of laundry, Danielle was more than eager to have me back at her side.

The house was coming along nicely, and it was amazing the effort and detail that her nieces were putting into the cleaning. I didn't see Danielle's sister help out much, but she did bring her daughters and help, therefore, was provided. I was somewhat relieved. It felt like a different family and had partially restored my faith in them.

As my faith in them returned, so did our need to find some additional solutions. Danielle's family was concerned with our situation and that we didn't have that much support from the community. It was upsetting to everyone that we had been left so much alone, although looking back, Danielle pushed much of the community out to protect herself and even hide me. The people who were showing up now felt too little too late, which is when we all had an interesting thought.

We could go across to the East Coast where her family lived, and they could help. Danielle's sister said that they had a guest wing on their house that we could stay. We also would have her mother to give us rides, and the cousins lived nearby too. It sounded so good. We would have both her sister and husband for back up in the same house. For the times when I needed a break, I could take it. It brought me a huge sense of relief

The next few days involved running a ton of errands while still maintaining my responsibilities to Danielle. I also had to prepare both of us to move across the country, into extreme winter weather. We were heading to a white Philadelphia currently facing a brutal snowstorm. The weather was not going to be our friend, and we needed to prepare.

Thankfully Danielle had enough winter clothes in the laundry I cleaned. However, a lifetime in the desert had not left me ready for a snowy winter. I had to go shopping for clothes and shoes with my mother. Danielle had to make plans for doctors and someone to administer her saline IVs. Her family spent hours helping her find places that would meet her needs. It was an all hands-on deck kind of moment. I did everything that her family asked and more,

I was perfect.

I was keeping my promise to my wife, and I did everything I could to make sure that things went smoothly. I could feel that things were going to be okay. I had some concerns, but since Danielle felt good about it, I was in either way. Danielle's happiness and making sure she was taken care of were my biggest concerns. I couldn't see any downside if Danielle was supporting this decision.

One decision that we couldn't make up our minds about was what to do with Danielle's house. I had decided to pass on inheriting the house, and Danielle was looking at her family to take the house possibly. She did purchase part of the house with some money from an inheritance. Danielle's family felt almost a right to get the house if she were to pass.

Danielle first offered to give the house to her nieces and nephews. They were gracious for the offer. Danielle wished that they would keep the house in memory of her. Danielle didn't want her house sold. Instead, she wanted it to remain a symbol of what she loved. However, that later became an issue as all the young adults wouldn't be able to afford the house. The next option was leaving the house to Danielle's siblings and mother.

The group of them could make the Sedona Vacation house a possibility. She even asked that I get some time in the house after she passed. I wasn't expecting that request, but I also assumed they agreed. Danielle's family simply nodded in agreement. Danielle was ready to move forward with that plan. We had finalized so many decisions in such a short time.

It seemed like the universe was providing the perfect solutions. My mom even came back to town that weekend to help with the move. My dad decided to use his flyer miles to get us tickets that following Tuesday. There wasn't a thing that was telling me that this wasn't a good idea. It seemed like divine timing, and like things were continuing to work out in our favor again.

All of the plans were finally concrete. Danielle's family were going to fly back first, followed by Danielle and me two days later. There wasn't any issue other than getting Danielle physically across the country. A feat all its own if we pulled it off. However, Danielle's health needed to improve for a trip to be successful.

Other than being very busy for a few days, there weren't any problems Danielle was having with her family. Everyone was in such happy spirits because Danielle was going to be joining them all on the East Coast. No one was showing their sadness or disappointment as they did before. It was a beautiful time, and even her mother stepped up to the plate. I was truly impressed by her mother's efforts to help Danielle, one evening, in particular, stood out.

Danielle's mother truly showed Danielle, one of her nieces, and I that she was capable of showing true compassion. The moment had all of us in tears. It was such a simple and beautiful moment to be able to share with my wife, and I also felt it brought some real peace between Danielle and her mother. It was simply a relaxing technique that Danielle's mother showed her, where she just softly brushed Danielle's forearm. She spent almost ten minutes, gently stroking her daughter while speaking with a gentle, kind voice. The moment was unforgettable.

I had lived up to my expectations of myself and exceeded Danielle's expectations. I had proven to her that I could properly interact with her family. I hadn't shown any signs of instability during their stay and never became angry. I had redeemed myself in a small part, but I knew we still had literally a long way to go. It would take every ounce of energy Danielle had to make the day-long journey across the country. It had her worried, and that was causing her health to suffer.

The infection that Danielle had dealt with the previous week had reached the end of the antibiotic round. However, problems with frequent urination and discomfort persisted. Danielle pulled me aside before dinner to tell me that she was having issues and that she would need to go to the ER that night to get it checked out. I understood her concerns because she was worried that she didn't take the proper amount of antibiotics.

The doctor had told us to take the antibiotics one way while the prescription told us another way. The doctor's recommendation was about half the regular prescription, and Danielle decided to take his advice. It was a risk on her part but also if it worked would have been better long term. Now Danielle feared the antibiotics had failed. Which meant she likely needed another round of antibiotics to prevent further issues.

Danielle knew this was not going to be good for her overall health. She decided then that there was no chance she would be traveling in the next couple days, and that we needed to tell the

179

family ASAP. I recommended we wait till after dinner because the information would be easier to handle on a full stomach. Danielle agreed to wait as we were just about to eat.

When Danielle came out of her room to tell the family, she was not looking good. Her presence concerned everyone. I explained that Danielle wanted to share something with the family. Danielle was very emotional when she explained that the infection was still causing problems and that she would have to go to the ER that night. She also explained that there was no way she was traveling and asked if anyone would stay to help.

Her mother was the first and only one to respond. I still to this day can't believe what was said, but to my best recollection she said,

> "That's not possible we all have lives, your sister obviously can't handle it, and everyone else has work or school."

I would have to say that the whole room just sat in silent disbelief at what Danielle's mother had just said. Danielle stormed to our room in a fit of rage. She was more upset than I had seen her ever. In a rush, she prepared for a trip to the ER. The ride there was intense as Danielle poured out her anger towards her mother. Danielle was beyond irate about the insensitivity that her mother had shown. I was more surprised by the silence from everyone else, which made me instantly worried. I was rising to the occasion, but her family was showing they were not ready.

My promise to stay calm was stronger than ever. I had successfully navigated the frustrations of packing and getting ready for the trip. I had done every task requested of me with a smile. It wasn't easy for me to get everything together, but I did it. Now, all that work was a waste, and still, it didn't bother me. I truly had shifted my attitude. No longer would I fly off the rails, I was truly a new man. I could be the calm person she needed to keep her from going nuclear.

At the hospital, we had to wait a few minutes in the ER waiting room. Danielle's nieces and nephews were already waiting for us. The immediate topic of discussion was obviously Danielle's mother. Everyone was completely appalled at Danielle's mother's response. Not one person could even comprehend that someone could say something like that to their daughter. It also appeared that

Danielle's nieces were very upset at the fact that their own mother sat there and said nothing. I was not even close to the angriest person in the room. I expected this behavior while Danielle was devastated.

After processing Danielle's paperwork, they called us into the back. It was another quiet night in the Sedona ER. The nurse, as usual, took all of Danielle's vitals and also did the blood draws. The first task I had was to help her get a urine sample. I, as usual, assisted Danielle in all trips to and from the bathroom. Despite being as weak as she was, she would try to do as much movement herself as possible. Even when she was doing poorly, she showed a strength few possess.

The conversation with the Doctor was one of the most upsetting talks Danielle had with a Medical professional. It started with explaining all the problems that led us to the problems Danielle was currently facing. Danielle and I explained the whole scenario to the doctor from the tube to her most recent antibiotic round. I could tell the doctor was very concerned because he started to ask Danielle some interesting questions.

First, the doctor asked Danielle about the antibiotics she was told to take and the dosage she took. We were told to administer the dosage almost half the recommendation on the bottle, which, according to the ER doctor could leave the body susceptible to infection. Without a complete antibiotic round, a possibility of harmful bacteria overpowering good bacteria is exponentially higher. In Danielle's weakened state, a bacterial infection could be life-threatening.

The doctor's second concern was to find out what infection we might be facing. The doctor called up to Flagstaff because he said that it often took several days for a culture to develop after an initial inspection. We were a bit confused by why Danielle would be prescribed antibiotics before results were available. Danielle became very upset with the doctor until he explained further.

The doctor stated that finding stuff in the urine is often treated as an infection regardless of the cause. I could tell it bothered Danielle, but I was more surprised at the way doctors do their testing and prescribing. The news the doctor delivered next was the most upsetting of the night. The culture in Flagstaff did not show any signs of an infection, and we couldn't believe it.

Danielle lost it completely there in the ER, solely at the incompetence of our Medical Establishment. She couldn't believe that not only was she miss informed on taking the first round of antibiotics, but she was also going to have to take a second one to make sure the first one didn't kill her. Then just to put the icing on the shit cake that they were serving, she never had an infection in the first place. This evening shattered Danielle's spirit.

I did everything to calm Danielle down. Thankfully I was in a good place to be there for her. The efforts I had made for her family had earned more of Danielle's trust. Instead of attacking me and my behavior, her family was now the target of her rage. I didn't even have to convince her because they had dug their own graves as far as I could see it. Danielle's family was the first domino to fall in deciding to stay in Sedona.

The second issue was Danielle started peeing about every thirty minutes. The challenge was making for a miserable or near impossible journey. The trip would require constant movement while being up longer than ever before. We were facing a roughly ten-hour journey through airports with several long car rides before and after. Crossing the country without any help would be very challenging for me, but that didn't concern me. However, Danielle was concerned about my ability to make the adventure without medications. My biggest worry now concerned her family.

The previous several hours showed me that her sister and husband were not going to be helpful during times of crazy stress. Danielle's news about her declining health and inability to travel almost left her sister in a state of shock, hence her mother's wicked response, "your sister obviously can't handle it." Truthfully Danielle's mother was completely right about that one, and I knew that I didn't want to have to depend on someone like that. Still, the comment had Danielle questioning her mother's ability to help.

Before this happened, we decided that Danielle's mother would help give us rides. We needed regular rides to the Doctor's. Not having a car was a logistical nightmare for me, combined with all the added uncertainty of Danielle's declining health. After the comment, Danielle wouldn't force herself into further situations with her mother. I could tell there were other concerns she wasn't sharing with me, but it had become clear she was unwilling to travel.

During this time, we talked to Danielle's nieces and nephew.

182

I found out that they all lived two to three hours from where we were moving. I considered their presence a deciding factor in making my choice to go there for help. They had proven how helpful they could be when they were around. They informed us that they would only be able to visit some weekends. I was glad for their honesty and support.

Even in this moment of crisis, they took Danielle's side, which said a lot. So when I learned even more that they wouldn't be able to help more than a weekend here or there. I didn't want to be left in the hands of the three people that did not show me an ounce of help. My opinion about moving had quickly swung to staying versus pursuing complete uncertainty.

For four and a half months, I had taken care of Danielle without a single bit of help from her family. They barely lifted a finger their first visits, while even causing additional problems. They never helped in ways that improved our lives. Even though Danielle talked to her family every day, she still never received the support she needed. Now they had ruined their second visit in a way I never saw coming.

I can only imagine that this epic situation was ultimately a test. I feel the opportunity to have her family rise to the occasion during Danielle's darkest hour was available. However, they let the possibility slip right through their fingers. While on the other hand, I had succeeded in keeping my promise to Danielle. I had proven to her that I could be civil with her family. At the moment, she needed my complete support.

Danielle and I arrived home late that night. Every healing crisis seemed to become worse and worse, and this night was no different. The news from the hospital and her family had her drowning in stress. I still feel that she was the angriest with the Doctors and their misdiagnosis. Combined with her family, we had a perfect storm. Danielle was emotionally crushed, causing her health to decline rapidly.

The next morning was tough because I almost couldn't change the topic from either the problem with the infection or how her family had behaved. It was all she could think about, and to my benefit, it took all the heat off me. I was thankful to have passed the test.

Danielle was incredibly impressed with my behavior, and

this made her question the doubts she had about me. It wouldn't be until after her family left that she told me that her family was not a huge supporter of me. Danielle was frustrated that they couldn't give me the respect I deserved. I fixed my behavior and proved to her that I could do it. We had brought peace between us, and our relationship blossomed into new frontiers.

She wasn't about to be Peaceful with her family after the constant abuses. Her anger and frustrations were so valid and understandable. I couldn't manage that anger because even trying to stop her, became more upsetting to Danielle. She knew she had a right to be angry at their behavior, and it was up to her family to set things right. I did nothing to help the situation because my mind was made up. Danielle's family had dug their holes just as I once did myself.

Danielle's family did not attempt to fix the situation that had happened the previous day. They still expected Danielle to make the journey, which only upset her further. The push back from her family only solidified her desire to stay in Sedona. Danielle wanted to be in her home, and if she was going to die, she wanted to die in her home. The only reason she considered traveling East was to improve her relationship with her family, but now that ship had sailed.

The withdrawal from supporting her decision to stay in Sedona honestly felt like another fatal blow. Danielle pleaded for her family to stay in one more final attempt to recover the damage done. Danielle's mother met those pleas with another horrifying statement. Taking the only good moment she had with her daughter and throwing it in her face.

I wasn't present for the situation but heard Danielle explain how it made her feel enough times to understand. She explained that her mother threw the relaxing arm brushing technique in her face. The manner which the information was delivered seemed to trigger Danielle. Sadly, that immediately erased the beautiful memory from the night her mother brought us to tears. To taint the only beautiful moment she shared with her mother devastated Danielle.

Crushed and Disheartened by how her family behaved, Danielle went into a dark place. I knew that I had to be the strong one and that my wife needed me more than ever. We were also going to need to find some additional help. We had to come up with some solutions quick because her pain was becoming increasingly unmanageable. I knew I couldn't handle it alone.

17
A Ray of Light in the Darkness

In the aftermath of Danielle's family, there was a lot to discuss. We scrapped the plans of traveling across the country, but we hadn't planned on staying either. The issue we still had with Sedona was that we hadn't received the support we needed. Danielle was now more willing to reach out for help. Her renewed faith in me had reassured her that I wouldn't act a fool. Danielle began to trust me again.

Despite my new strength, I still needed more help. The demands on myself were only getting more intense. Danielle needed more assistance with everything in her life. The showers, bathroom visits, and even walking required constant aid. Danielle still did not like having to depend on others, but a sense of humility had developed now. We reached out for help from the community. The response solved most of our problems.

Problems that were not related to her health were still major priorities. Sadly the visit from her family was not the end of their involvement. So much was left unresolved from her family's visit. Danielle was still in communication with her sister after they left. A desire for peace and cooperation were all that Danielle wanted from her family.

The day after her family left, Danielle received a call from her sister complaining about their visit. Danielle explained that her sister was complaining that a friend didn't introduce themselves when she stopped by specifically to help Danielle. There were ten new people in the house that day, which would have been overwhelming for anyone. However, her severe allergy to Andora was the main reason for a quick visit. The lack of consideration of others was clear. But that wasn't all she had to complain about.

Her sister continued to complain that she was also upset that Danielle had asked her nephew at one point to leave the room. At the time, it didn't seem like a big deal considering that Danielle wanted to talk with my family and me. I don't even remember what we discussed, but it was still Danielle's decision. To have her sister accost her for making that decision was equally as upsetting. Danielle couldn't believe that her sister would call to upset her even further. It was mindboggling to me that her sister would react this way.

I did have at least some understanding to why she was reacting this way, but it still didn't excuse the behavior. The whole family was upset that Danielle had decided not to make the trip across the country. The lack of understanding led to much emotional tension between her family. Everyone was emotionally compromised and showed it. I had similar problems that I ultimately fixed. Their behavior continued without fail.

Since Danielle had lost all faith in her family, she removed them immediately from the will. The discussion about leaving the house to them was not finalized, but now it never would be. Danielle also based her decision off of a statement made the last night we all went to the hospital. She found out from her nieces and nephews that their mom and grandmother were discussing excluding her brother from the will.

Excluding her brother would have made it far easier for them to sell the house after Danielle passed. Danielle couldn't believe the further lies and deceit. Considering that Danielle did not want the house sold were she to pass, this was heartbreaking. On top of that, she hadn't heard from the girl she was first going to leave the house to, not a word. This was someone who was supposed to be a daughter to her but for some reason hadn't reached out. Who could Danielle leave her house to, who would also honor her wishes?

Danielle decided to reach out to the friend who helped us financially. The first thing Danielle shared was how bad the experience ended with her family. She was disgusted by their behavior and also explained the issue we were having with the house. Danielle wished for her legacy to live on and needed someone to take the mantle. In her panic, she laid down a list of desires that would have scared most people. I felt that Danielle was expecting too much from her friend.

First off, her friend was having a seriously hard time talking about Danielle passing. I could tell at the hospital that it was becoming increasingly difficult for her to be present as Danielle made a choice to stop treatment. She even offered to pay for a trip to Europe if Danielle felt that there was a chance. Obviously, if we couldn't make it across the country, Europe was out of the question.

Danielle was also going to be the third close person in her friend's life that was going to pass. Danielle would constantly share with me the struggles her friend had with sudden losses. Danielle had been someone who had helped her through those losses, and now she would lose her too. I completely sympathized because it is always hard to lose someone who is such an important part of your life.

Danielle was a very important person in her friend's lives and someone who was a huge asset for emotional support. For years Danielle had been an honest friend because she was true to herself. Most of all, she never used her friend because of her incredible wealth. Danielle lived a modest lifestyle that she took pride in creating and supporting herself. This trait was one reason that Danielle had become such a trusted confidant.

Danielle and I would discuss the issues that come with being very wealthy. I had watched wealthy people get taken advantage of because someone is trying to get an easy ride. So often people make huge promises, and when the check comes due, they are unable to settle-up. Few people I find are willing to do the work it takes to be successful, and when people are playing with other people's money, they are even less inclined to put in the extra work. Too many people want the free ride, and often at someone else's expense.

We watched as one person tried to take advantage of her kindness by possibly using Danielle to make it happen. Although we never allowed the meeting to take place, the intentions were clear. People are willing to do crazy actions for personal gain. I have a problem when it is at someone else's expense.

It was appalling how people will mistreat someone to take advantage of their money, and Danielle had dozens of stories of this happening to her friend. So when Danielle was approaching her with giving her the house, so that she could fix it up and turn it into a dance school for little girls. Danielle wanted her friend to foot the whole bill. It had Danielle all lit up, and I could tell this was her goal if money weren't an issue. It would have taken me years to save up enough to have the house outfitted and ready to be a full-time dance school. I wish I had the means, but I didn't have that, or the experience needed to make it work on my own.

It was the following day that the full reaction to the circumstances came full circle. I was really worried that Danielle was overstepping her wishes and putting obligations on someone, that couldn't handle the situation. I was entirely correct about this intuition, but I never realized how it might have turned out. The reaction to Danielle's wishes was unexpected.

I knew the weight of Danielle taking a turn for the worse was not going over well with Danielle's friend. I could see it in the frustration she had to get Danielle to pursue additional treatment options. She couldn't accept that Danielle was going into Hospice and would be passing at some point. I could hear the desperation in her pleas to convince Danielle not to give up.

Incredible stress leads people to do things that we wouldn't imagine doing under normal circumstances. This woman had been such a friend to Danielle throughout the entire healing process. She was our financial security and the one who said that she would be there for Danielle to support her in anything she needed. It gave us a sense of security to have that support, especially since I couldn't work while caring for Danielle anymore. Danielle and I depended on that support.

Danielle's dying wish of having her house turned into a dance studio, didn't come back with the reception that Danielle was expecting. To my surprise, Danielle handled the conversation with such grace and ease, even though I could tell she was devastated and hurt by the conversation. The hardest part Danielle had to face was that her friend was unable to be with her through the dying process.

The way it came across was probably not the way it was supposed to be received. However, that didn't change how Danielle felt. Danielle felt that her friend would only continue to be part of her life if she was continuing treatment. On top of that, she made Danielle feel bad about the treatments that she wouldn't continue to take. I found this to be a low blow even from my point of view.

The reason that we had purchased the extra curcumin treatments was that it was on the possible FDA ban list. Our Naturopathic Doctor informed us that it could be made unavailable at any time, considering the improvement we saw right away we didn't want to be left without a successful treatment option. The friend who paid for all the treatments agreed to purchase the maximum amount. Danielle had used most of it, but there was about nine hundred dollars' worth of product that had gone unused. Danielle didn't respond with anything but respect and kindness while on the phone. It was after the call that her true emotions poured out to me.

She first off was devastated that her friend had, in essence, abandoned her only two days after having her family abandon her. It felt like a knockout blow and just put Danielle into a deeper state of depression. Now financial stressed returned. Thankfully we had more than enough for several months at our current expense. How long that would last was now an unknown factor. The unknown was not something that Danielle could control, which worried her.

The other issue that Danielle had a problem with was that her friend made her feel bad about not doing the remaining treatments. To her friend's defense, she was doing everything in her power no matter how desperate to get Danielle to continue treatment. I had done similar behavior before I accepted Danielle's decision to stop treatment. I sympathized with her friend also considering the amount of death she had already experienced, but sadly it still didn't excuse what had occurred.

Danielle was devastated, and we had another huge hit to her morale in less than a week. I did everything in my power to help Danielle not spiral into a deep depression. We would have to talk about those issues to help her move past them. Personally, it was really easy to talk about some topics while others were far more taxing.

Thankfully, I was getting far better at controlling my anger around Danielle and started to recognize it early. Catching myself before I became upset would allow me to excuse myself for a quick smoke. I found the new technique would quickly bring me back to a calm place to continue the discussion. Despite more breaks, I was there more for my wife. I was even able to help Danielle come to terms with her friend abandoning her. Some people are equipped to help those that are dying while others can't handle the emotional stress. I was someone who was unequipped but willing to learn no matter the circumstances, so I had a ton of sympathy.

It was several days later that I lost almost all respect for our former benefactor. Danielle had stopped communicating with her friend because of what occurred. This sudden lack of communication led to a nasty text in response. As much as I would like to explain the detail of the trauma caused because of the respect and gratitude that I have towards the woman who helped us, I won't go into much explanation.

I read the text, and immediately, Danielle could tell something was wrong. I couldn't talk about it, but I told her that there was absolutely no way that I would let her read that text. I spent twenty minutes composing a response to the text, which was not a smooth process. I was beyond livid, my anger was ready to pop, and Danielle wasn't making it any easier for me. After about ten minutes, I had to ask Danielle to be quiet until I finished. I promised I would read her the response but not the original message. Danielle's curiosity was satisfied, giving me the space I needed to compile a proper reply.

When I completed the message and read it back to her, Danielle couldn't believe the response that I had put together. Danielle was so impressed at the words that I articulated. I didn't want to disrespect this person who had helped us so much, but I couldn't let Danielle be disrespected in such a way either. The response was with the highest gratitude and gave truthful reasons to counter the accusations. The message gave Danielle a huge clue to the content of the original message without having to read words that would have cut far deeper.

The way I had handled the situation gave Danielle a lot of confidence in my ability to handle a stressful situation with grace. She was glad that I was not being vindictive or mean in return. I realized that acting that way would have done nothing but bring problems into Danielle's and my life. We had enough problems without creating more.

Danielle was upset, but at least we maintained peace between us. A peace that I would soon ruin again. It wasn't something I did intentionally and was something that Danielle had asked me to do, but the way I did it was the problem that we faced. Danielle wanted me at some point to pay her friend back for the IVs that had gone unused. Danielle did, even though she was upset, feel bad about not using all the IVs. It wasn't something she wanted me to handle right away, but I started brainstorming.

In my quest to do what Danielle wanted, I had come up with a plan. I had decided since we had at least five months of bills covered, that we could spare a little bit from our emergency fund. After several conversations with the ND, who was also mutual friends with our benefactor, I decided to ask her if I could pay for the vials privately. I also wanted to make sure that the treatment was used on one of Danielle's friends. This friend was one of the people that had been there since the beginning, and due to her health problems was unable to see Danielle as often as she wanted. I knew she could benefit from the treatment. I thought I figured it all out.

The ND could pay the friend back secretly because I didn't want her to know it was me right away. Also, Danielle's friend would benefit from the treatments, and everyone would be happy about the situation. I thought it solved all the problems, but I didn't want to tell Danielle right away. I wanted to surprise her. However, the next time she complained about the situation, I told her the truth, but I never expected her response.

First off, the fact that I had done anything without her approval, was the main issue. Then because I had done it with our money, she was even more irate. Danielle didn't care what I had done with the money, she didn't care what the money was being used for, and she didn't care about my intentions either. The only question was if I could get the money back. After Danielle sent a nasty text to the ND, asking for the money back, I quickly went over to her office to pick it up. I apologized for everything and took full responsibility.

This betrayal of trust was not something that our relationship needed. Danielle again lost faith in my capacity to care for her. At this point, I completely regretted the decision I had made. It was an error that I could never have anticipated. I was truly ashamed, and Danielle made sure I paid for that mistake. It was clear that Danielle's concerns about our finances were far more serious than I previously thought.

Thankfully my dad arrived just in time to help with the new issue. It was clear that Danielle was concerned that I would improperly use the funds, I had zero problems with complete transparency. I wasn't trying to hide anything, and even the thing I hid wasn't supposed to be a permanent secret. I wasn't there to cause Danielle problems I was there to help. I would never have made the decision that I made had I understood the consequences. There was no way I would repeat this mistake. Assurance from my father and giving him full access to my bank statements made Danielle feel better.

I could stop making errors, but I also needed to make sure that I didn't burn out again. It was time to enlist a little help from Danielle's close friends. The possible list of individuals wasn't very large, but it was time for us to reach out. My father was a big help in making sure that Danielle took those steps. He could see the problems we were having, and some help was crucial to giving us the best opportunity for success. Too long, I had set myself up for failure, and now was not a time to fail.

Thankfully four women, who Danielle approved of, stepped up right away. They were four of the most intelligent and driven women in town. Danielle easily outshined everyone in tiny little Sedona. Each woman equally admired Danielle for the strength and courage that she had shown her whole life. This respect was why they knew it was important to step up and be there for her in her time of need. Three of them were parents of students or former students. They all understood that young or ill-equipped students were not allowed over because they were committed to helping Danielle.

We decided that the four women would rotate daily visits to relieve me from duty. That way, I could run errands or grab a bite to eat without feeling overly anxious. I noticed that as Danielle's health declined, the concept of leaving her home alone, was increasingly worrisome. Now that I could get a real break, I had more strength than ever. I hadn't realized how much constant stress I had been under until it was gone.

Danielle was finally getting a break from the stress too. The uncertainty of how the end of her life would proceed scared her. She wanted to stay in her house because she loved it so much. The comfort she felt at home was incomparable. Now that she had decided to stay in Sedona and we had the proper support, it was a real possibility. It made me feel good to be able to give her something she desired. Danielle wanted to die on her terms.

We were making some serious progress towards improving the circumstances we faced. Danielle and I even shared a renewed level of intimacy as our relationship improved. It is truly incredible to find beauty and love in places that you wouldn't expect. Never would I have expected that after months of pain and trauma that we could still have such an intimate connection to each other. We always found our ups despite all the downs.

In one moment, we would spend hours in the shower while

constantly reapplying medicines. While in the next moment we could spend time just talking truthfully and honestly about our feelings for each other. Our love was always growing stronger. Even if it appeared to disappear from time to time, it always returned brighter than ever. Love is a powerful force, and I was starting to see the power it was having in our lives. As we let the love in from those in our lives, we saw more help appear.

It was about this time that the universe graced us with one of the most beautiful individuals that I have ever met. It wasn't even the ideal circumstances, but it was highly synchronistic. The day we met this angel was also the day her mother was diagnosed with cancer — obviously a hard day for anyone. To our surprise, when the ND asked if she could bring her in to say hello, we accepted immediately. Danielle had met her previously in passing, but now Grace officially entered our lives. I will refer to her as Grace considering the amount of Grace that she brought into our lives.

Grace was an angel from the moment we met her. She never once mentioned her mother's diagnosis despite us overhearing her talking to the ND. The entire short interaction was very pleasant. By the time we finished chatting, she was offering to help in any way that she could. Danielle and I were blown away by the offer.

This person had shown us what it truly meant to be a positive influence in other people's lives. Not one person had displayed this level of compassion and caring, while on top of that being a practical stranger to both of us. We exchanged information, and she asked if we would include her in the rotation of helpers. Danielle and I approved wholeheartedly.

Grace had shown a level of character and mannerisms that I admired. A selfless giving was outdone only by the calm demeanor she carried in herself. Grace gave herself to Danielle in a way that no other person, including myself, had done. Grace was someone who I knew I was ready to learn from, and the universe was providing me the perfect solution to improve myself.

I found out that Grace acted exactly the way that Danielle wanted. Grace quickly became Danielle's favorite due to the positive impact she would have every time she visited. I admired her demeanor so much that I put every effort into emulating Grace. My whole life, I've observed then emulated people who I admire. I felt I had an opportunity to learn from a master. Grace was a gift from the universe to help Danielle and me.

18
A Hospice of Questions

A big decision for Danielle was deciding which hospice to choose. We had received information about the different options while we were in the hospital in Flagstaff. I had already started doing some additional research before we scheduled appointments. It was important for me to find the best Hospice for Danielle. However, Danielle's high standards and demands would create additional challenges.

Due to her medication sensitivity issues, it would be ideal to find a group that would cater to Danielle's necessities. Hospice was an extension of the Medical Establishment, so the solutions were going to be similar to what the hospitals provided. The traditional approach worried Danielle as she didn't want to rely on prescription medications. To our surprise, we were soon to find out a wealth of new additional information.

The first hospice we interviewed, sent two nurses for the initial appointment. Danielle was tremendously anxious about the meeting, with the whole idea of hospice stressing her to the core. She had a million questions for the ladies who came over. Danielle wanted to be informed about every possible outcome. All questions about her specific disease and how the dying process would proceed. All the questions were difficult to ask, but without those answers, Danielle wouldn't feel at ease.

Some of Danielle's biggest concerns were that she was worried that she might have made the wrong choices. Danielle specifically asked if she chose the correct path of treatment. I couldn't believe the response, and I was amazed by the honesty of the nurse. The nurse told us that considering Danielle's diagnosis of stage 3C ovarian cancer, that she would not have undergone chemo or radiation either.

It was one of those moments that the universe made sure to

remind us that chemo could have possibly killed Danielle faster than she already was. It also reaffirmed that the success rate in late-stage Ovarian Cancer is low. If a hospice nurse were willing to share that choice, then I would have to expect Danielle made the right choice too. The only study I could find showed under a nine percent chance of survival to five years with chemotherapy. Now it was more than just statistics because someone who witnessed the aftermath of chemo confirmed those suspicions.

Danielle was additionally worried about pain management options. This hospice informed us that there weren't any natural options available. They instead used different medications dosages to help with the pain, which means that they could provide micro doses. Hospice gave me the first answer that was legitimate for treating my wife. I believe this is because many people become hypersensitive to medications towards the end of their lives. Their statements did not ease Danielle's concerns.

The most disturbing part to me was that we weren't going to be getting much support from the nurses involved. Hospice informed us that a nurse would only be visiting several times a week, and the visits would be about an hour. While this wasn't as important for our situation since we had extra help, it did make me start to observe the shortcomings of our Hospice system. Had we needed more help, it wasn't going to be provided even under my wife's incredible health insurance plan.

The biggest thing that they reassured us is that if any complications were to arise that we could contact them at any time. They would then send out a nurse to help with any medical situation. The nurse would then stay until the patient stabilized. The service was available 24 hours a day and even on the weekends. It offered some relief but not quite what we had expected. We asked why they didn't come by daily. They said that it wasn't usually until the last weeks of life that they need to send out nurses for continuous care.

They also said that there was a lot of support staff that would also be helping in the Hospice program. I thought it was great that they offered emotional support too. Priests, therapists, and volunteers were all possible options. It wasn't something that particularly appealed to Danielle because she would prefer her privacy. Danielle was not interested in letting many new people into her life. She had already recruited the support she wanted.

Danielle wasn't completely sold on the first organization even though she liked the nurses. Danielle appreciated their honesty, and that gave them a foot up on any competition. Danielle needed trust and confidence before she would make any decision. The trust was there but not quite the confidence. The second option held a more optimistic choice because of the additional services they provided. My research showed this was a more likely candidate.

The second visit happened the day after our first meeting. The first hospice had already prepared us, so now it was finding out the additional information that set them apart. We had three incredible nurses arrive to share the information with us. Danielle again had a great connection with the nurses and even felt the same level of honesty from the nurses. It had everything that we liked about the other hospice, but what set them apart was the added benefit of natural treatments.

I couldn't believe that they offered the options of doing acupuncture, massage work, or spiritual guidance. Then to top it all off, they also offered herbal medications. Shocking news to both Danielle and me because we had never had the medical establishment offer us anything other than traditional synthetic medications. Now we were going to be given a choice. Danielle even opened up a conversation about using Medical Marijuana. They supported the usage of it and even encouraged that Danielle uses other methods of delivery.

Danielle and I were thrilled at the added support and options we were going to have if we choose the second hospice. The nurses were also very professional and promised we would receive very experienced nurses. Danielle wouldn't settle for second best. While it was still a very difficult decision for Danielle to make, it was an obvious choice between the two options. The nurses already won my favor by provided me an opportunity to expand Danielle's medications.

I was thrilled by the prospect. I, for months, had wanted Danielle to start vaping medical marijuana oil. I had in my experience enjoyed the concentrated effect. Often, a small puff would provide the same results as smoking much more from a traditional pipe. The fact that she could get a more concentrated dosage would help provide even more immediate relief. The topical and edible products we were using would take thirty minutes to an hour to kick in. The vaping would provide almost immediate relief. The challenge for me would be to find a product that Danielle could smoke.

Danielle was sensitive to chemicals before we met, and now in her weakened state, she was hypersensitive. I couldn't use most of the products produced on the market because they used chemicals like butane or alcohol to extract the oil. Thankfully I knew there was a process that uses CO_2 to extract the oil, and it makes a far cleaner extract for cancer patients. The other issue was finding something with a high enough level of the proper cannabinoids.

THC the most commonly used cannabinoid on the market because of the psychoactive properties was not what Danielle needed. Danielle wouldn't react very well to large doses of THC. The psychoactive properties would cause too much anxiety and loss of control. Danielle was scared of losing control. The added fear was also due to her improperly dosing herself with a large quantity of Rick Simpson Oil. CBD oil was the best solution for remedying that.

The problem with CBD products is that at the time it was still a developing industry. Few products existed on the market with high CBD concentrations. The demand was not there yet. The local Sedona Dispensary discontinued several strains of high CBD flower because they weren't selling as well. Although most of the concentrates there were produced with chemical solvents. My search proved how few products met the qualifications Danielle needed.

I needed to find a high dosage of CBD strain. Ideally, I wanted a no THC strain, like Charlotte's Web, made in high concentrations without the use of chemical irritants. The best product that I was able to find at a nearby dispensary was a three-part CBD to one-part THC vape in a forty percent concentration. It wasn't quite as strong as I was looking for, but it was made using a CO_2 extraction process. It was a better solution, and I had Hospice to thank.

Luckily Danielle's insurance was also going to cover all expenses when it came to Hospice. It had taken a little financial stress off of us because she also wouldn't be in treatment anymore. It was a small relief to both of us, considering we weren't going to be having to worry about money for a while. With almost five months of funds available, it was looking up. Then another miracle happened.

One of our helpers, the mother of Danielle's prized student Rose, delivered a message from her daughter in Europe. It was a touching message which brought Danielle to tears. The letter also informed Danielle that she was coming to visit. It must have been such a shock to learn about Danielle's declining health. Danielle was, after all, in most of her student's minds indestructible.

It was a huge deal to Danielle that she made the gesture to return from Europe. Danielle was touched and truly looked forward to being able to see Rose before she passed. Rose wasn't scheduled to return for another six months and had coincidentally left for Europe the day I met Danielle. It was a coincidence that I would not disregard.

It was a hard issue for Rose to face since Danielle had been like a second mother to her for a majority of her life. Rose showed real signs of maturity with her letter and her action to visit. The renewed faith also solidified our decision to give the house to Rose. I still didn't have the means to take care of the house, nor did I want the stigma that might have come with inheriting the house after just meeting my wife. We felt it was the best solution for everyone involved.

Which also led to another miracle when Rose's parents offered to pick up the mortgage payments. It was such a blessing we didn't even know how to express our thanks. It was the perfect miracle to help Danielle quit stressing about the money. Although it didn't completely fix the issues, she felt better that we wouldn't have to worry about money for over half a year. Also, the added support from my family and the community was giving her the morale boost she needed.

Danielle was also relieved that she survived the second round of antibiotics. She took the entire regimen as directed by the bottle without any deviation. Constantly Danielle was concerned about her digestive issues, and, the antibiotics had definitely caused irregularities that made Danielle worry more than she needed to. Anything out of the ordinary would be a cause for concern for Danielle. Danielle wanted to know what to expect at all times. The more guidance hospice could provide, the more confidence Danielle could feel moving forward.

The first couple meetings with the head of the hospices didn't answer all the questions Danielle had about going through hospice. She had her basic questions about what to initially expect but didn't know what to expect when things would get closer to the end. Danielle would save the remaining questions for our first nurse. Danielle wanted to discuss everything that she could expect from their time together.

The nurse arrived on time, and I quickly escorted her back to our room. Danielle would often try to take visits in the living room, but the decline of her health topped with the cold winter prevented her from leaving the bed. The nurse proceeded to take the usual health readings and tests that would become regular during every visit. I honestly think Danielle enjoyed that part a little.

Danielle usually was very involved in this process and would always request the results of any tests performed. The knowledge she had about her health, blood pressure, and practically everything going on in her body never stopped growing. Danielle knew her numbers better than the doctors or nurses that visited. The answers Danielle wanted were about the journey she should expect.

We were both unprepared for the answers we would receive. It is still rather difficult to understand why the nurse proceeded to answer the questions the way that she did. I will admit that I was even traumatized by the interaction. The damage done by such simple statements became irreparable.

Danielle had many questions for the nurse, and for a short time, she answered normally. Then Danielle brought up her concerns about using medications at the end of her life. The constipation issues would become a great concern at that point. Danielle explained her problems to the nurse and why she had those fears. Without much thought, the nurse answered Danielle.

The nurse proceeded to tell us, paraphrased, that Danielle could expect a huge possibility of constipation, and that was a big problem that she personally observed. She then proceeded to tell us that there was a possibility of it becoming so backed up that it could burst the intestines inside the person. We were both completely scared, considering that was one of her greatest fears. Death by exploding intestines was now a real likelihood. In no way was Danielle willing to die that way. She became consumed by the fear of this new possibility.

It was after this interaction that I faced some of my first signs of fighting Danielle's fear of death. It wasn't the dying that worried her as much as how horrible getting to the dying was going to be. It was clear that cancer was a horrible way to die, and the nurse had just informed us that it could be even more horrible than we ever imagined. Danielle had zero desire to go through that and, sadly enough suicide became a new hot topic.

I completely opposed any thought of her trying to commit suicide no matter the journey ahead. Despite her pleas to end the suffering, I couldn't entertain the idea. Danielle had such a desire to go to heaven, and I felt that it was my purpose to help her get there successfully. Much of my spiritual studies showed that committing suicide was very traumatic on a soul, which created karma that would remain after death.

My research and showed that people are forced to return to an incarnation with more challenges to clear that karma. The second incarnation is made to prove that they can endure suffering without committing suicide. I believe this because of a wealth of proof from my own research. I may be wrong, or I might be right, but I did everything in my power to convince her suicide wasn't a solution.

My obvious go-to when she started having suicidal thoughts was to remind her about all the children that looked up to her. Repeating if she committed suicide, she would set a horrible example for them. It would also forever tarnish her reputation in town. Between using her fear of gossip and being a real role model for her girls, she would always see through using suicide as a way out. It was clear that we were going to have to face this journey together, no matter how bad it got.

Thankfully we had a different nurse for the next visit. The new nurse was far more concerned about Danielle's new fears. It was clear that the conversation about exploding intestines had truly left a scar on Danielle's psyche that she couldn't move past. The nurse was most of all concerned because she had never heard of something like that happening before. We were both surprised at the response.

The problem was that Danielle didn't believe the new nurse. She said that if it doesn't happen, then why would the other nurse say otherwise. It was clear that we had a big issue, and it was going to be a huge concern until we found a resolution. Danielle had her trust betrayed, which made her incredibly upset. It was easy for me to show Danielle the support she needed considering that I was equally appalled at what occurred.

I still don't know what would cause a nurse to scare my wife with a story that wasn't true. I told the new nurse how strange it was that she told us all that upsetting information. It just seemed like total disclosure was the policy of the first visit and to inform us about what to expect during the following four to eight months. Telling us what to expect seemed reasonable. Now to find out that it wasn't reasonable nor true made me very angry.

Hospice was typically only reserved for patients who have less than six months to live and have completely stopped traditional treatments. We signed up for the end of life care not to torture Danielle to death. I still can't comprehend what would cause another woman to be so cruel for no reason at all. If she did lie, it seemed almost psychopathic to behave in such a manner. Now we had to face the consequences.

Hospice quickly resolved the situation. First, they banned the nurse who made the comments, and I believe she might have been fired too. Also, on top of that, they brought in an amazing new hospice nurse to remedy the situation. The head of hospice informed us that the nurse just recently joined hospice but had many years of Nursing experience. Danielle truly liked this because she knew that the nurse wasn't going to be coming in with an ego. She was fully aware that the nurse was going to be in constant communication with her superiors, which meant Danielle would always be getting second opinions. This was a huge relief to Danielle.

I was so impressed at how they fixed the situation, and on top of that, they sent in the head of the hospice training division. Much of the fear that Danielle had developed was finally put to rest when she appeared. Again, she had never heard of someone's intestines blowing up while in hospice. While it was still always going to be something that lingered in the back of Danielle's mind, it immediately stopped Danielle's threats of suicide. I was relieved, and I believe everyone in Hospice was relieved that Danielle was satisfied.

Danielle being upset was not good for anyone, and most of all, not good for herself. I was constantly trying to help her work through her anger so that it didn't control her. I found that Danielle was good at talking about her problems, assuming I could keep a calm demeanor. I was improving in the mastery of my emotions and very rarely let my emotions control my reactions. It didn't change what I was feeling, but it did start to change how I expressed those feelings.

This change within myself was also helping Danielle bring change in herself. She had started to accept that she was nearing the end of her life, and that forced her to look inside. Danielle realized that there were a lot of unresolved issues that were ever-present in her life. She lived a very traumatic life while also an amazing life. The amazing parts had overshadowed the trauma, but it was now that the trauma was unavoidable. In one lifetime, Danielle achieved many lifetimes of experience.

Danielle's unresolved issues were extensive. The list had developed more through the experiences we faced together. The topics included her family, dying early, treatment choices, not teaching, her students, the constant physical pain, and so many other little issues that she wanted to resolve. I had been able to help a lot with her abandonment issues, male trauma, and her anger. Danielle would tell me that she recognized her anger in my outbursts, but she condemned me for my display of that anger. Thankfully she inspired me to be better.

Many other issues were more important for Danielle to master, and they weren't always issues that I, too, was facing. Despite my lack of life experience, I was very well suited to help her with hers. I could offer her a different and usually more positive perspective about a subject. I have always been good at seeing the good in most things. However, I found in death, that there are many things we decide to address that would have otherwise gone unanswered. Hospice passed on this advice while recommending professionals to assist with those problems.

Hospice had a non-denominational spiritual pastor that they offered to come over and talk with Danielle. We declined initially because it didn't seem necessary. Now it seemed more apparent that Danielle needed additional help. It wasn't easy for her to come to terms with dying. We all lacked the skills Danielle required to find some peace.

It just so happened that the pastor had decided that she didn't want to get a flu shot, which Danielle and I both supported. However, it also meant that the woman was forced to wear a mask during the appointment. I greeted her at the door, but even with the heads up, I found it somewhat unsettling. I had hoped to stay the entire time with Danielle to observe the conversation.

My friend who I asked to pick up a specific medicine in Colorado, was driving back to Tucson. Thankfully I was going to be able to meet him just off the freeway 30 minutes from the house. I told him that since he had done me such favor that I would be happy to make the trip a little easier and meet him. The meet up ended up being timed just perfectly with the visit from the Pastor. There was a little relief that I didn't have to leave Danielle alone. However, this didn't take away all my anxiety about leaving Danielle with someone who we weren't familiar.

I made the drive as fast as I could without speeding and just stopped for a quick minute to say hello to my friend. I didn't even realize until I got back into my car how not present, I was. The entire interaction all I could think about was getting back to my wife. I felt seriously bad that I behaved in such a way towards my friend. It brought awareness of the anxiety I would have, just being away from my wife. I had not observed the reaction before.

This simple awareness had shifted my perspective and to realize there isn't much benefit to be stressing about something I don't have any power over. I should be more present in the moment, and if I have time to get away, I shouldn't be wasting it on worrying. Worrying wasn't doing me any good and too much just became exhausting. The car trip had allowed me to observe that massive increase in anxiety that occurred simply by leaving my wife.

Arriving home, I found Danielle and the Pastor finishing up their time together. Danielle was calm and very relaxed. Thankfully she found some benefit in her conversation, although she didn't discuss it much. Her only comment I recall is that it wasn't quite what she was expecting, and it was weird having her wear a face mask. Danielle had an aversion to anyone with a cold, so it made her feel uneasy. I feel it might have been more productive if we had allowed her to remove the mask, but that never occurred to us.

After the Pastor left, I pulled out the new vape pens I acquired. I now had a more powerful medicine to help manage Danielle's pain. It was such a relief to both of us to be able to get her pain under control again. For so long, the pain had started to spiral out of control. The support from hospice allowed me to try the medicines that we all felt would be more effective. We never stopped the topical or edible medications, which still provided mild relief. However, the increased dosages from the vape pens were having a very positive effect.

Danielle was even starting to sleep more. For a long time, the pain had kept her awake many nights. Danielle wouldn't purposefully take naps, but now I was noticing it happening naturally. I noticed immediately that the higher CO_2 concentration that my friend picked up in Colorado was almost exactly what we needed. It provided a bit more of a head high than Danielle liked, which I knew how to remedy.

In my research, I found that CBD often reduces the psychoactive effects of the THC. We used a combination of high CDB vapes with the high THC vapes. When she took a puff of the more concentrated THC vaporizer, with a puff from the high CBD one, she would see a more balanced effect. I would also use a CBD tincture to supplement if that didn't work. This new mixture was almost miraculous in how well it managed her symptoms.

I still wish that it didn't take Hospice to give Danielle the go-ahead to try smoking vaporizers. It is proving to me again that our Medical Marijuana Industry still has a lot of room for growth in producing effective medications for Cancer patients. I believe this is also why the Medical Industry has attacked many who are doing just that. The lack of support from pharmaceutical companies has stifled the progress that Danielle and I needed. Times are, thankfully changing.

It was finally nice to get some real support from what I considered the Mainstream Medical Establishment. It was rare to get advice that was truly helpful and to have another practitioner who fully supported my point of view. I had felt that much of my knowledge was still second-hand information when compared to the opinion of doctors or nurses. I knew I was right, and I would often need a medical professional to confirm my stance for Danielle to accept it as fact.

She did this with everyone around her, which is why I constantly had to learn to withhold my opinions or manage the way I would share them. If it was important, I could ask the medical professional if my idea was valid. A simple question could open up discussions on topics that I wanted to talk about seriously. I found this more productive than ever trying to force my opinion on Danielle. In my opinion, she put far too much faith into our mainstream doctors despite their repeated displays of ignorance.

I found that many of the opinions I held from my studies were confirmed. However, I also found many were more complicated. It was a big learning process for me, and it always felt like the universe was working to help me understand. Every single challenge we faced led to different opportunities for growth.

Each time I would stay strong, I found the universe would provide the perfect solution. While each time I would fail, I was given the perfect opportunity to rise again. As I saw it, the only way to stop finding miracles was to give up completely. It wasn't something I could explain, but even as we neared the end with Danielle, the miracles just continued to spread.

19
Miracles Everywhere

The last several months were full of miracles, some beautiful and some necessary. While it wasn't at all easy, life was always providing little reassurances. If it weren't for those little boosts to our morale, we might have faced far more dire circumstances. I am forever grateful to all the little ways that life made the unbelievable happen. Sometimes those unbelievable things happened so that we could have another important experience.

I felt one of my biggest miracles was getting a new bed. It had taken until my dad arrived the second time to handle the situation completely. Even with everything that had prevented us from getting the bed, it had finally materialized. It was the perfect timing because that was my final solution. It was becoming far more challenging to stay strong without a proper place to sleep. Now I could get the sleep I desperately needed.

Danielle and I immediately slept far better than the tiny single bed we had used for months. Being the thoughtful husband, I gave Danielle most of the bed since her comfort had been my highest priority. Now, looking back, I should have taken a little more concern in my wellbeing, but life allowed me to learn. I had found that life was constantly challenging me emotionally to the core. For several years before meeting Danielle, I suppose I was working on mastering my emotions. Now I had the perfect opportunity to perfect my emotional weaknesses.

It felt like the universe drove fate to give me this unusual life experience. I had the chance to address the full spectrum of emotions that Danielle and I were going through. It wasn't easy navigating some of the heavier emotions of guilt, shame, anger, or grief. However, I realized quickly that I needed to learn. I've always embraced the learning that comes with life experience. Life can feel full of miracles as we embrace the infinite possibilities of what can manifest.

Which also led to one of the biggest miracles that I could imagine. For months I had truly become upset with Danielle's family. I even played nice when Danielle asked me to, even while the entire time they were undermining me. Her family actively tried to break Danielle and me up, without stepping up to fill my shoes. It didn't matter to them what I had sacrificed for their loved one. I had redeemed my mistakes with Danielle, but they failed to see that truth.

Danielle's family only dwelled on my past mistakes while actively continuing to make their own. I remained patient but still ever so aware of the continued problems. I was becoming increasingly upset, especially after the last visit. Every conversation just fed that anger in me. Even Danielle could see the problems with her family never changed and never improved. I could see the agitation coming to a head and her realization that things were not going to shift.

I view it as a miracle because of how it manifested and the benefits we received. I doubt Danielle's family would agree since I believe it was the last time she ever spoke to them. Some miracles work out in our favor, while others may seem tragic from another perspective. I can't deny the tragedy of the miracle, but it was still a miracle to me.

The miracle happened on a typical afternoon while the nurse was visiting Danielle. Danielle answered a call from her sister over speakerphone. We all could clearly hear her sister crying into the phone hysterically before Danielle turned the call to private. She was yelling into the phone about a dream that she had about Danielle. In the biggest case of irony, the dream was a nightmare about never being able to talk to Danielle again. Danielle lost it on her sister almost immediately. I was upset and reached out for the phone.

Danielle handed the phone to me after a few choice words. I immediately left the room and proceeded to reprimand her sister for the last time. I returned and apologized for the outburst, but instead, Danielle and the nurse commended me for the way I handled myself. Danielle wasn't up for dealing with their behavior anymore. She decided to stop all further communications after that phone call. If Danielle was finally done talking with them, then I was finished too.

Danielle also decided that afternoon that she was done taking phone calls entirely. The phone calls were already causing her headaches, and we constantly had to keep electro-magnetic devices out of the room. I couldn't have my phone in the room or the Wi-Fi on, except for brief intervals. She had already reduced her phone calls down to mostly necessary calls to hospice. Hospice would call several times a week to check on Danielle.

She would say just enough to convey what she needed as I held the phone next to her on speakerphone. Danielle would then say, "I'm finished speaking to them," signaling to me to move the phone away to finish the conversation. Often this was because she would feel discomfort from using the electronic device. I never felt like she was rude. Her family couldn't understand this, and she was done trying to make them.

No more family meant much less stress invading our space. However, Danielle's family was not going to be fine with being cut off completely. My anger towards her family made me unable and unwilling to provide a healthy line of communication. Danielle and I decided to ask the ladies who were helping us to communicate on our behalf. They all agreed to help, even accepting the conditions Danielle had with sharing certain information.

At this point, Danielle told hospice to stop sharing any information with her family. Danielle was rightfully angry, but I felt she went a little far to make them suffer. It was clear that their behavior had resulted in almost a complete shutdown from Danielle. She was tired of them, and after seeing my transformation, it was eye-opening to her situation. Her family just continued their poor behavior while I had shown a great capacity to change.

Danielle desperately wanted to change her relationship with her family. She was dealing with problems over and over to have a breakthrough potentially. It was always an uphill battle for Danielle. I found some people are just naturally toxic and removing them from your life is the healthiest thing that can happen. After almost five months, Danielle finally stopped trying to win favor with her mother. Including exerting energy to deal with her sister's emotional baggage. This complete turnaround was still troubling to Danielle.

It wasn't a miracle like most miracles, but it also removed a constant stressor from Danielle's life. She finally had an opportunity to come to peace with the reality of her situation. Danielle realized that the peace she was looking for was not going to be found in the people she expected. Danielle acknowledged that her mother was never going to be the mother she wanted and found acceptance in issues that would never be resolved. Danielle had to come to peace that there would never be peace between her and her mother.

It was crushing for Danielle but also at the same time freeing. By no longer needing the validation or having the need to connect with this person, she was liberated. I could see that decision empowered Danielle which made me feel good too. I didn't feel good that her family had failed her, but I did feel good to have such toxic people out of our circle of influence. Having four incredible women handle Danielle's family issues was one of the most miraculous events that I could have imagined — topped with the irony of the dream which caused it all in the first place.

The next miracle was far more uplifting for both of us. Since the decision had been made to leave the house to Rose, she had also planned a trip back to visit Danielle before she passed. It wasn't something she had to do, but it was something she did anyway. She planned on coming out for several weeks before heading back to Europe. Danielle and I were both surprised and impressed by the gesture. Nothing could prepare me for how impressive Rose would act.

Danielle was that she was truly a mentor and a parental figure to so many children in the community, and Rose was no different. Rose was one of the most dedicated students and on top of that, the only girl to ever co-teach with Danielle. It was almost like meeting Danielle's adult daughter. Rose held a special place in Danielle's heart which was why she was so excited to see her.

As much as I felt no one could compare to our connection that Danielle and I shared, I quickly also realized that nothing compared to the relationship that Rose and Danielle had. When Rose arrived, it was a small miracle, because there had been some recent attacks at airports in Europe and Rose thankfully avoided most of the problems. We were happy she made it back safely.

The first meeting between Rose and Danielle was a bit more emotional than I think either of them expected. It was very hard to realize that they were going to be saying goodbye. Neither of them was truly prepared for the interaction. It was a bit taxing on Danielle, but nothing compared to some of the more draining visitors she had in the past. I feel the joy of seeing Rose offset any stress that occurred.

To my surprise, Rose would show herself to be even stronger emotionally than anyone I witnessed. It was amazing to see how keen this young woman was. It was also nice to have a bunch of extra help around the house. Almost immediately, Rose got to work on cleaning up Danielle's dance studio. She was doing some serious organizing from me using it as a storage place. Anything we didn't need we put in the Studio, which after five months created a huge mess.

I would often take Rose away from cleaning to sit with Danielle. I never wanted to leave Danielle alone, so even if I were cooking, I would get Rose. The only time I left Danielle alone was early in the morning. I still went most days to pick up her gluten-free waffle from the Vegetarian Restaurant around the corner. It was the small joys that Danielle appreciated, and having Rose visit was one of her biggest joys.

Even Danielle was super impressed at how much Rose showed true control of her emotions. Rose wasn't coming in and dumping her obvious sadness on Danielle. She even mentioned that she would usually cry the whole drive home, which truly impressed me. Danielle had been such an amazing teacher because it showed. Truly, I couldn't have been prouder to have married someone who helped raise such an amazing individual.

Not in all the time Danielle was sick did anyone help out to the degree that Rose did. It was a miracle to have the love from one of her students fill her house if even for a brief time. Danielle found a level of peace in the support that Rose showed her and to not worry about some of the things she couldn't control. It was beautiful the connection they shared. Rose knew Danielle in a way that I hadn't developed yet.

I felt that Rose's family was on top of that, one of the biggest miracles that could have happened. With the situation that we were in, it was clear that paying the mortgage and all the other bills were going to be a problem. With a mortgage, the money we had left over would have lasted us about three to five months. Thanks to Rose's parents, we didn't have to worry about making mortgage payments. Considering we were leaving their daughter the house, it was a super blessing that they came forward and offered to help more. I also found out that they were picking up other miscellaneous bills, which were even more appreciated.

I couldn't believe the kindness of all the people that were helping Danielle. Considering for almost four months, we were left to fend for ourselves, and now to be graced with more help than ever before. Even hospice was a blessing as their kindness and support was a reassurance to me. Their compassion towards Danielle's sickness and medication sensitivities was extraordinary. It truly felt that even with what was occurring that the miracles were still showing up regularly in our lives.

My whole life was feeling like a miracle since Danielle, and I first met. We never really talked about it much, but it was miraculous that we met when we did, and how we did. It was a miracle that we were married right before her surgery. It was a miracle that I found a job at the end of the street with schedule flexibility. It was a miracle that I lasted four months before failing. It was a miracle that my dad showed up when he did, and it was a miracle that I found the strength to be the husband my wife needed.

It's hard to believe that even during the toughest times, we could manifest a miracle. It seemed to work better if we asked for help. I still believe a huge miracle that just so happened to cross our paths was also when Danielle and I were at one of the lowest points in treating her symptoms. We were having huge difficulties managing the pain that was caused by her cancer. The concerns with using prescription medications were also at a record high. Danielle wanted a solution that wasn't going to cause further problems.

It had been decided by the hospice doctor, that we should start attempting to use micro doses of the pain medications that the nurses could provide. Due to the fear of possible constipation and the still lingering fear of her insides blowing up, Danielle did not want pain meds. That changed when her pain surpassed her fear of constipation. We decided to start with the weakest medication with the fewest side effects.

We started with Tramadol in quarter doses, and we did see immediate relief. Danielle had developed a pain in her mouth and teeth that was practically unbearable. The new medication was helping as we increased the dosage. Over the following week, we continued to take advantage of the medication without any side effects. However, Tramadol was becoming less and less effective at managing the pain.

The tramadol was not handling the pain she was enduring. Danielle discontinued taking her medications completely. Danielle felt there was little point to continue if there wasn't any relief. That ended leading us to our next problem of how we could manage the pain. The risks with stronger medications came more troubling side effects. Danielle was at a point that she had to face her fears.

The unbearable pain led to Danielle finally succumb to the doctor's recommendations about trying the morphine. We were using the least toxic version and were told to only start with one-tenth the full dosage. Which after the first twenty-four hours, we could work up to a quarter of a dosage. We administered the first micro dose with ease. We waited a short time for the relief to kick in. At which point, the unthinkable happened, Danielle started to throw up. Thankfully Danielle was able to keep her vomiting under control.

The morphine failed us and left Danielle with twenty-four hours of misery from the side effects. We had the nurses present for much of this time because of the complications that were arising. It was incredibly traumatic for Danielle, and at that point, we were starting to get the implications that the doctors and nurses did not have any other solutions.   Sadly, I was correct in my assumptions, and the head hospice doctor informed he had nothing else to help with the Pain. Hospice had truly failed my wife.

It was just another case of the toxic chemicals that our medical industry tries to pass off as safe medication. After years of studying the long-term dangers of most medications, including a sleeping pill that I used to take.   I found out there are some very serious side effects from the pill's doctors push.   The pill I was taking caused memory loss and amnesia. I found that out after accidentally taking one in the morning with my vitamins. Six months after the incident, I finally recalled the day I forgot. It frightened me even though I had already stopped the medication.

Danielle had this experience over a dozen times with the different medications that doctors attempted to give us.   It wasn't a solution if the problems became worse than the condition the drugs were meant to fix. For her entire life, she had faced this dilemma, and now it was one of her biggest fears to have that nightmare come true. This broke Danielle's remaining will to live.

Devastated and without hope, Danielle immediately became desperate for solutions. Since Hospice had said that there was nothing they could do Danielle resorted to thinking outside of the box. The conversation that ensued still gives me the creeps. Danielle had already shown signs of being suicidal but still unable to follow through. I even hid all the knives in the house as a precaution. It wasn't easy to face the fact that she wanted her life to end, but it wasn't much of a life considering the misery she was experiencing.

With everything that was happening, it forced the conversation of how to end her life. The first most logical option was looking into the right to die states. Several states in our country allow a pill that would end my wife's life. The process to be approved usually takes months. Additionally, none of those states were nearby, and it would take time to get everything approved. This was not ideal because Danielle wanted to end her life immediately.

As much as Danielle was willing to end her life, I warned her of the ramifications of taking her life. First off, there would be zero chance of not having the cops involved. It would be a huge spectacle, and there would be no way to avoid rumors. The pain she would cause to her students could never be undone. Everyone's perceptions of her would-be forever tainted, and it wasn't something she ultimately wanted to do, which led her to bring up being smothered.

I was upset by this request because I first off didn't want to take another person's life. Second, it was my wife, and that was even more difficult to imagine. Danielle even informed me that it could take between five and ten minutes to complete the act. The ordeal would be filled with struggle, followed by a lot of grief and trauma. I couldn't imagine going through something so horrific.

It was a terrible idea in every possibility. Truthfully, I wouldn't consider it as long as it sounded worse than what we were going through. I told Danielle I wouldn't discuss it further. I was worn out from such talk and needed to take a break. There was no possible way I was going to allow Danielle to commit suicide. That night I prayed for a miracle.

I didn't know what was going to happen, but I asked the universe to provide us another answer. I didn't know if there was another answer, but all I knew is that I wasn't willing to participate in anything we had just discussed. I didn't want Danielle to end her own life, and I didn't want to end it either. I wanted an answer that didn't involve such a horrific end to Danielle's life, and we needed a miracle.

The next day we were scheduled to have a new nurse come in to help Danielle. The universe must have heard my call because the wisdom she had to share was invaluable. First off, Danielle and the nurse connected fast. Danielle brought up that she was doing miserable and was wishing she could end all the pain. To my surprise, off the record, the nurse told us that she had wished her mother stopped eating the last couple of months of her life.

We were both a bit dumbfounded at the response, and it wasn't something we had ever considered. The nurse proceeded to tell us that her mother's passing would have been far easier if she had stopped eating. However, the nurse also recommended that Danielle continue drinking so that she didn't get backed up. Danielle was almost on board right away, and before the nurse even left had sworn off food.

The next visit that day was a couple of hours later and wasn't a typical visit either. Due to the recent complications with Danielle, hospice had sent out the director of training who we had met when we signed up. Danielle liked this woman and was glad to see her again. It wasn't very long into the visit that Danielle brought up the idea of not eating. I was a bit surprised that Danielle brought it up considering the audience, but it ended up being the best thing she could have done.

The director proceeded to tell us that if Danielle was going to decide to stop eating that she should also stop drinking too. We were even more shocked by that response, and a bit confused. She told us that in Arizona, choosing to stop eating and drinking was the only legal way for someone to end their life. It was their choice, and if she made that choice, then no one could force her to eat. The director told us that she taught a class about it over the weekend. It was mind-blowing to have this information fall into our lap.

The Director explained to us that the reason she should also stop drinking is that her body could potentially linger for several months on just water. The lack of movement had put her body into something more like a coma state versus a healthy body that needs lots of energy. The lack of metabolism could mean that she could linger for months on just water. If she stopped drinking water too, she would only last about one or two weeks. Considering how much pain she had to endure, two weeks was far more appealing than two months.

Before the Director even left, Danielle had sworn off both food and water. The decision put the power back in her hands. She no longer had to fear a horrible, long, painful, and traumatic death from cancer. She had control of her life, and it was empowering to Danielle. She had the will power to do it, and I supported her in whichever decision would bring the best outcome. Little did I know just how much of a better choice it was.

Considering that most days only had one or two visitors per day, it was rather unusual to have a third visitor. However, the third visit would complete a holy trinity of messages. We were destined to have a third person come in to give us one more vital piece of information. The third visitor just happened to be one of the incredible volunteers. She wasn't a doctor or a nurse, but she did have one amazing father. According to her father, in a study that he performed, he found that choosing to stop eating and drinking was the most humane way for a person to die.

She stated that compared to all the different ways that people die, that choosing to stop eating and drinking was the least traumatic. He even compared it to the medical industry's morphine-induced coma death. It even reassured Danielle because it was even more humane than the pill from the states that have right to die program. The most interesting aspect I discovered was that most people that receive the right to die pill, never actually use it. The peace of mind gained often allows people to approach death without fear.

Danielle was going to be the ultimate test because as much as it was a far more peaceful death, it also involved having a strong will. The nurses told us that they had never actually witnessed someone successfully making it more than several days before the desire to eat and drink would kick in. Danielle was going to prove that it wasn't going to be a problem. Her desire to end the pain was far stronger than her desire to live in pain. She still had a desire to live, but only if the disease could go away too.

As if the answer we received wasn't already a huge miracle, the results would be even more miraculous. A perfect trifecta of people arrived to provide an answer that gave Danielle hope. That hope would not be lost as we would see profound changes. The pain that Danielle was feeling in her mouth almost disappeared within the first twenty-four hours of her decision to stop eating and drinking. A total shift happened, and for the last two weeks, we were in for one of the most amazing yet difficult experiences of my life.

20
Touching the Other Side

The beauty that came through Danielle after the pain left her body was obvious to everyone. I can't explain the clarity that developed in Danielle. It truly was the most amazing miracle to have my wife return to me. Months of pain had clouded her mind, but now, she was free. That freedom brought us closer together, closer than we had ever been before. It was difficult knowing that our time was limited and not everyone could handle it.

It was particularly tough on our main nurse. She was new to Hospice and had developed a strong connection with Danielle. I know it weighed hard on her to watch Danielle go through the constant struggles. I could tell that her reaction had shifted after Danielle decided to make her final decision. She even stopped her visits, passing the duty of caring for Danielle to a senior hospice nurse. I thought this was understandable considering the experience we were about to face. It was going to be difficult for everyone who supported Danielle in her decision.

It was complicated even more by the extraordinary experiences that we would all go through with her at the end of her life. Though the nurses usually just nodded and humored Danielle when she discussed what she was going through or experiencing. Danielle would often confer her experiences about talking to angels while also sharing indisputably divine information. It was profound to be able to observe so much of it.

I could tell that the words struck many people, but few truly embraced the information she started channeling. We live in a culture that supports spirituality, but few of us truly experience spiritual encounters. Danielle was starting to embrace the messages she would receive. She had many people that had previously passed coming to visit her. I could tell when Danielle felt someone in the room, and when I didn't, Andora would.

Andora was often a big signal when spirits were present in the room. We would laugh watching Andora's intriguing reactions. Andora would often start looking around the room as if something was floating around. If it became too overwhelming or Danielle would say there were lots of angels present, Andora would often leave the room. It was interesting to watch but nothing compared to the experience we had with the angels themselves. One experience before our nurse left had all present blown away.

The occurrence happened not long before her decision to stop eating and drinking. She had some concerns with her health that she wanted to discuss with our nurse. It just so happened the nurse was delayed several hours. Danielle told me it was likely due to someone passing. I didn't know and accepted her opinion.

When the nurse finally arrived late in the afternoon, Danielle told her that she knew why she was late. The nurse smiled at Danielle but said nothing. Danielle then told her it was because someone passed. The nurse nodded in approval but offered no comment. The appointment proceeded as normal with the nurse checking Danielle vitals. We knew it was unethical to share patient information.

Danielle continued by stating, "it was a woman who passed and that she was likely in her mid-80's." The nurse now looked surprised but still responded with no comment. No one was prepared for the following statement. Danielle said, "the woman passed with her mother and sister by her side." Finally, the nurse sat down in the chair in utter disbelief. She just responded, "How do you know this?"

Danielle responded without hesitation that the angels were telling her. We were all completely left in disbelief at the message that had come through Danielle. It wasn't going to be the last time either. It was always fascinating to hear the messages and observe each unique response. Danielle was always given a free space to explore and share those experiences while I was around.

In my life's journey, I have had many interesting experiences with those that have passed. It was not unusual, for me, to hear about the topics that Danielle was experiencing. Considering one of the blogs that I follow is about a woman who channels her late husband. A husband who before he passed was channeling spirits too. Channeling is something people can do where a spirit will share information through the person as if they were a conduit for delivering the message. I could tell that Danielle was a channel for messages from the other side.

Which is why when she asked me one evening, "Who is Sophie," it left me speechless. The reason being is that Sophie was my childhood dog who passed away only a year prior. After her passing, she started visiting me as a giant white polar bear. I never told Danielle, but she had been regularly appearing to me while she was sick. Most of the experiences were regarding clearing dark energies which Danielle never wanted to hear about.

I've had numerous experiences of her being one of my animal spirit guides. This time was a bit different because Danielle explained to me that she was coming to her as a beautiful Angel. Considering that Sophie was one of my most recent spirit guides, it was so powerful to have her visiting my wife too. It made me truly embrace the fact that there is more to this world than just this life. I couldn't deny the synchronicity of my closest guardian angel also appearing to my wife.

Another interesting thing that Danielle started channeling before her passing was strange enough Lakota, the ancient native American language. She would genuinely speak in tongues, with such beauty and grace. She explained this wasn't the first time she spoke in Lakota, but now she was better. She spoke it effortlessly. She couldn't even believe how incredible it sounded.

It was more magical when we would do it together. I admit that I never tried speaking in tongue before Danielle put me on the spot. I was nervous, but I knew it made her happy when I embraced it. I noticed the more I embraced it, the easier the sounds would flow. When I was anxious or tired, I couldn't relax enough to let the words emerge. I loved this unexplainable, unique experience that Danielle and I shared. However, she would also share her Lakota with many of the visitors. She was changing lives without even trying.

Some of the information was genuinely prophetic. Danielle spent much of her last few weeks sharing the information she was receiving. She did a lot of writing, including making sure to pass messages on to her friends and students. She wrote many letters to her students and the important people in her life, and it was amazing the power she had regained in herself. Still, the most interesting visits were when Danielle would call people out on their dreams or

221

nightmares.

She was so good that she had the uninitiated doing Tarot cards to understand their dreams. While common practice for many in Sedona, it wasn't something these professional women were accustomed to doing. Danielle would give answers and knowledge that had everyone believing. Regardless of the belief in Tarot or having prior dogmas, Danielle was showing a side that few people had experienced. It still didn't compare to the experiences we shared alone.

Her dream recalls and recall of other experiences grew every day. She was gaining deep insight into her life's purpose. The messages she would receive were more than just an active imagination. Including one dream that even left me in a state of shock. I was woken up in the middle of the night to Danielle in a complete panic, and it was almost chilling the way she was shaken up. I don't think that I could have ever imagined what it was that set her off. When I asked her what was wrong, she gave me an answer that still haunts me a little.

Danielle proceeded to tell me that in a past life, she was a Nazi Commander who was closely connected to Hitler. I wasn't alarmed by that until she told me that, in my past life, I was a Jewish woman that she had gang-raped and murdered me. This news had a physical reaction that I still recall in vivid detail almost a year and a half later. I couldn't deny that I was having a unique reaction to this news.

Immediately I felt chills go through my entire body, I couldn't explain it, but I felt all the pain and discomfort that came with an experience like that. Little did I know, but the imagery of the incident would also return that evening. Talk about trauma, and to know that in a past life this event may have happened haunted us. Still, nothing could truly calm the anxiety that Danielle felt about being a Nazi War Criminal. It also allowed us to delve into the idea of why she might have lived her current life the way she did.

Danielle had practically lived the exact opposite life of being a war criminal. In reality, she spent most of her life putting criminals behind bars. The local Sedona police department credits her for over thirty-six arrests. She even taught anti-bullying, which is the exact opposite of what occurred in our past life. If looked at from the grand perspective of balancing Karma, she seemed to have succeeded. The added support of my forgiveness helped free her from the pain she carried. Forgiveness was the most powerful aspect of her moving past the trauma.

The mutual remembrance of Nazi Germany was only to be our first realization of past lives. Danielle told me that several years prior, she was given a past life reading. During the reading, she was informed that in the early 1900s, she was a madam. Sadly her life ended abruptly when a jealous lover killed her. Some Drunk had pushed her off a cliff in Jerome.

At that exact moment an immediate chill run down my back and a feeling of embarrassment mixed with shame. I blurted out, I'm sorry, but I believe that I pushed you off the cliff. We both felt the truth in the statement. It also explains my aversion to alcoholism in this life. Shocked, we also recalled another past life we had already coincidentally discussed.

Danielle once had told me that she was the child of Isadora Duncan, one of the women who founded modern dance in the early 1920s. It explained Danielle's desire to dance in this lifetime, and it also made me recall what I had learned about how Isadora Duncan lost not just one child but both of her children in a car accident. I realized that in that life, we were likely brother and sister when we both died together. It was clear to me that we had a close connection to be with each other at the end of our lives.

The clarity I was gaining about the infiniteness of our lives across time and space was becoming more fact instead of theory for me. It is one thing to study the idea of past lives; it is completely different actually to experience and learn from our own past lives. I had embraced these past lives, and each one had a huge impact on the purpose my life ended up taking this time around. It was clear that my frustrations from my mother's drinking were a much deeper issue. If I had murdered someone in a past life because of alcohol, it would explain why people who can't handle their alcohol upset me.

I wish that it hadn't taken until the end of my wife's life to understand her life's purpose. I could be the support she needed because I embraced understanding our past lives. Clearly her life as a Nazi War Criminal had subconsciously driven her to make this world a far better place, even though she didn't know it. However, I could also see a thread of abuse that she endured that from a soul's perspective would balance the trauma she caused in her previous life. The soul experience she had this life was not complete without one final piece of the puzzle. Her atonement also involved me and the forgiveness she needed.

I allowed her to realize that despite her past crimes that forgiveness is the real answer. It was so difficult for her to find forgiveness in the murder of millions of people and being an instrumental part in making that happen. I was able to help her understand that we could overcome those lives where we didn't live with love or compassion. Lives we succumbed to the temptations that exist on earth. This world is a school for soul development, and our souls have sometimes been on these paths for a long time.

While we incarnated in these bodies, we can burn off the Karma accumulated in past lives. From my observations and experiences, I found that much of the purpose in life comes from overcoming Karmic debt. Many people are stuck in the same patterns causing similar problems to arise constantly. Each encounter is an opportunity to grow out of the reoccurring problem. However, as an American society, we deny the idea of Karma and don't even entertain ideas like past lives.

My studies of people touching the other side revealed many miraculous stories. My favorite being past lives that have led to real murder arrests. One man admitted to the murder after being accused by a child who explained her past life murder in perfect detail. Healings have occurred that defied science after past life healing. It was clear that some lives carried more trauma than others. Danielle was processing loads of new Karma from the memories she received.

I did everything in my power to convince her that she resolved those lifetimes. I even told her that the pain she had endured must offset some of the karma from being a Nazi. I had to remind her about all the good she did with her life, whenever the issue would arise. The peace she found came from realizing that she had balanced the Karma with her current life. She eventually saw cancer as something that was burning off her Karma too.

It all surprisingly made sense to me. I felt a strong connection to the other side, and with my wife, that ability was growing daily. We started having many experiences with spirits along the journey. Danielle always embraced the good energies while I felt the orgonite kept away less desirable spirits. It was magical. However, one night, Danielle and I would face another level of evil.

The most powerful paranormal event to occur between Danielle and me happened late into one evening. I would guess that it was about ten or eleven p.m. when Danielle and I both heard a loud *POP*. It wasn't until the second one that Danielle said, "do you hear those gunshots?" I immediately ran to the backroom only to hear two more gunshots. Danielle told me to lock all the doors and turn off the lights. I proceeded to keep a close watch on the yard surrounding the house, watching for any possible movement.

Both Danielle and I were in a state of panic and couldn't imagine what had transpired. After making a personal call to the Local Police Sergeant on Danielle's phone to report the incident, we finally settled in for the evening. I went into an interesting space while sitting in the chair at the foot of the bed. I still can't explain it but what came to me still haunts me to this day. I witnessed darkness that I could never have imagined.

My experience was something I still wish I could forget completely. In my mind's eye, I witnessed something horrific. It felt like I was looking through another man's eyes. Except that man went around his house shooting both of his sleeping children before turning the gun on his wife and then killing himself. It wasn't something I have ever imagined, and it was truly graphic and grotesque. I knew that I couldn't share this experience with Danielle. It was far too much for her to handle. Especially at night, when her health was far less stable.

The problem was Danielle wanted to know what I was doing in my mediation. I told her that I couldn't share it with her, but that I cleared the bad vibes from whatever it was. Then the unthinkable happened. She then proceeded to tell me exactly what I observed. She asked, did some guy go through and kill his children and wife. Talk about something I couldn't make up because I never said a word. It freaked me out and made me believe that what we both felt may have genuinely occurred. I didn't know what to do about it, but it was highly traumatic for me to get another confirmation.

After several hours of discussion, it became completely clear that I was not emotionally stable to be there for Danielle. The image of the murder had made me unsettled, and it truly felt like I was there watching it. By four o'clock in the morning, I had reached a true breaking point, and I finally recognized it, but at four in the morning, I didn't know what else to do. It finally occurred to me that I should call someone for help. I didn't feel that most of the women would understand the unique experience. The only person that came to mind was Grace.

Thankfully Grace had been such a supportive individual, sending texts every couple of days offering her help. This constant support helped me feel comfortable to call her at four a.m. to help me out. She also was very spiritual, which put me at ease after such a bizarre scenario. I was even more relieved to find that she could be over in 30 minutes. The kindness and compassion that she arrived with, really helped put both Danielle and me at ease.

I took a mental break immediately with Grace's arrival. Danielle was becoming increasingly bothered by my inability to control my emotions. Little did I know something so horrific could be so draining to both of us. Neither of us had the strength to recover from what we felt. Thankfully an angel stepped into our life at the perfect time to provide the added strength we needed. I still have no idea what happened that night. It is still a total mystery considering we never had any confirmation of something so horrific happening in Sedona.

I don't know the entire purpose of why that happened, whether I was listening to Danielle's worst nightmare before she even told me, or if it did happen and wasn't made public. Either way, it did help us understand the deeper psychic connection we shared. A connection that I promised wasn't going anywhere even after she passed. I felt that I was developing greater skills to communicate with spirits, but Danielle was worried we would lose the connection.

My life had interestingly enough, been practically designed to give me the tools to accomplish the task of helping my wife cross over to the other side. I was not truly prepared, but no one ever is. It is impossible to prepare for the unknown, but if we keep moving forward, I found the universe will provide the answers. These answers can come in in countless ways to create infinite possibilities.

We were living in a time of infinite possibilities, and I still had one wish. I wasn't willing to give up on Danielle because I still expected her to get better. Then something happened that would create a turning point for me. For so long, I held an attitude that we would beat this disease. It was not easy to let go of that notion. I constantly prayed for a miracle. I did energy clearing to help Danielle, but it never seemed to solve the problems.

It was during an energy clearing that something miraculous happened. It felt like a normal energy clearing, but after I was finished something different happened. Several angels appeared to me and asked how I found the spirits that I cleared. I told them that I found their names in a comic book, and that took me to them. I felt the angels laugh on the inside. I told them that many spirits hide their names in comic books to feed off the fear associated with that name. They seemed satisfied with my response.

Since I felt like I had performed such a miraculous deed, I thought that I should ask for a favor from the angels. I knew that I needed a miracle, and I asked if there was anything that we could do to make my wife better. Then the completely unexpected occurred, I don't even know how to explain it, but I felt my wife's energy step forward in that place. She appeared to me as a beautiful angel in her most elegant form.

A presence that I had felt many times before, but never before had this energy communicated to me in the spirit realm. Danielle's presence was right there before me, and she just reassured me, this is what has to happen. I almost immediately returned to my body after she gave me the news. I awoke from the experience in a state of shock.

Lying there in bed, it took a little time to wrap my head around what had occurred. I had promised not to share my energy clearing work with Danielle, and I kept my word. Despite wanting to discuss it with her, I felt it would cause more problems. It was hard to accept that my wife was not going to beat the disease. It was devastating yet in a way, reassuring too. In a way, she had to make me accept the new reality. My wife was going to die.

21
Crossing Over

The final two weeks of Danielle's life were full of more than just miracles and spiritual experiences. It was a very memorable and positive experience. The disappearance of the pain gave us an almost sublime time together. The support from the community was paramount in helping to create a stress-free environment. In this place of peace and love, Danielle would channel divine energy. Danielle continued having startling realizations. I believe the first big one was about having a supportive community.

It was clear to Danielle that not all people were capable of being present for someone who was dying. It wasn't easy for some people, and their behavior would result in less than ideal actions. After many people failed us, Danielle came up with a solution. "The Inner Circle," as she called it, would be one of Danielle's most important contributions to helping others in the future. The combination of and "Inner and Outer Circle" would provide greater benefit to everyone.

It was a system that she developed to assist a community in giving the proper support to people who were sick or dying. The inner circle would consist of several individuals who were committed to upholding the goals of the person needing assistance. It does not work when people are divided about how they should behave or help. The person in need is always the one who suffers when there is conflict.

Regardless of differing opinions, it was extremely important to be united in the cause. Which means that once a line of treatment is chosen all people, regardless of personal beliefs, need to support the patient's decision. Support is what truly unifies the inner circle in a common goal. We didn't have support like this until we enlisted the help of Danielle's friends. The people Danielle choose to be close to her met her inner circle requirements.

The Inner Circle was meant to be the direct line of communication between the outside world and the individual. It would be used to reduce as much stress and provide as much support as necessary. Danielle was very proud of her revelations explaining how imperative it was that I share her idea. She stated that it was important to have individuals who were emotionally strong in the inner circle. Those who were less in control of their emotions would need a different role.

Danielle assigned the "Outer Circle" to people who were less capable emotionally. This was an ideal place to put people who wanted to help but don't have the time or energy. Many people fall into this category. Due to the stresses that society has burdened people with, many people lack the ability or available time to continually participate in the dying process. Not to say that many couldn't find the time. Instead, our experience showed that most people are already at their limits.

I was a perfect example of how getting overwhelmed causes destructive emotional reactions. I think it is honestly easier for people who aren't extremely close to an individual to behave appropriately. In a society that does not recognize emotional strength nor teach emotional strength in any congruency, we can't expect people to be experts. Danielle and I both recognized a huge failure that our society made when people are terminal or near death.

Too long, I went without any direct experience, and the small experiences I did have before my wife, were with Grandparents who lived at a distance. I felt that I had failed my family a bit by not offering my help more. It made me feel bad, that as families, we often forget the amount of stress that comes with watching someone you love die. The longer that families deal with the problems, the longer the stresses build.

In six months of dealing with the illness, both Danielle and I were exhausted. I couldn't imagine people that deal with years of treatments and all the side effects that come with Chemotherapy. I had witnessed that reality almost daily working in the Medical Marijuana Dispensary. I could see the stress between couples and the relief that many found in Medical Marijuana. It was even more difficult to hear stories from others who told of more failures.

The Hospice nurses and volunteers all confirmed my fears that many people don't receive "healthy" support from their family at the end of their life. We were gifted with five incredible women who were instrumental in helping with making the final weeks as easy as possible. I was getting more help from the ladies every day. It was a group effort to help support Danielle and also to help carry out her final wishes. It would be a challenge for all of us.

I still don't know how Danielle did it, but after the pain stopped, she planned all of her funeral arrangements. It was an incredible feat to watch as she accepted what was going to happen. It was clear to Danielle that she wanted her memorial service to be something special. She had difficulty deciding on which direction she wanted to go. After much thought, she elected to have two separate services.

The reason she wanted two is to have one specifically for the adults and another for the children. The adults needed to have a safe space to express their feelings. Danielle didn't want them to hold back at her service. There were things that Danielle wanted all of us to say as adults, without any hesitation. Danielle wanted to protect her students from anything that may be upsetting.

Danielle knew it is not easy to let go if you are worried about offending young children. Danielle made it imperative that only high school age and up would be allowed at the adult service. Danielle wanted people to let it all out, to be emotional and share. We had shared so many strong feelings about everything with each other, so she knew right away that I wanted to speak at her service. It was clear that there were some serious things that I wanted to discuss in my eulogy, and Danielle knew that.

It was important to both Danielle and I that I comment about supporting. In a town like Sedona, where people pride themselves on acting with love and light, we rarely saw it. Far too often, we were victims of a "more enlightened ego." These people think they are helping, but they are too self-absorbed to discover how they can, in reality, help. Instead, we had people who were "enlightened," telling us what was best without any concern for Danielle's choices.

I've been there too, especially when it comes to thinking I know what is right. My spiritual quests have led me to many profound answers that have changed the way I live my life. I even tried to force other people in my life to adopt these principles as I knew it would improve their lives. However, in the process of helping, I was ending up with the opposite result. For years I was completely unaware of why I was causing this to happen, despite my best intentions.

Now I understand my mistakes and why I failed so many times. My experiences were individual and unique. No matter how much we try to follow in another's path, it still always becomes our own. Just because I have read the information that would work for me, it doesn't mean it works for everyone. Danielle taught me that lesson over and over.

I learned this early and couldn't force my treatments on my wife. Sadly, even spiritual workers fail at service to others even though I expected otherwise. The amount of Ego that spiritual workers display is offensive at best. I see it in the condescending nature that most use to identify people that are "low vibration." The attacks and disrespect create separation among people who would otherwise be interested in spiritual growth. If we only encouraged each other, the possibilities are limitless.

I've met some people that can read thoughts. A powerful life-changing experience, to say the least. I consider all of my thoughts before I think them because who knows who is listening. I have even met others that can read past lives and even talk to animals. The number of people I've met that break the conventional mold is in the hundreds. Each one is living life in their unique way. These differences are not wrong because every person has their truth. Even ignorance lives in its false reality, but it doesn't make that reality any less real.

In my experience when it comes to living in a reality that many spiritual guru's live in, what is correct for one guru may not be the same for another. Many live in different perceptions of reality. It isn't an easy concept to grasp for many individuals since we are taught otherwise in schools. The power of belief is challenging even ideas like aging and fitness. There is even a scientific revolution happening in epigenetics that is proving all of this true.

I learned about a society in Africa that lives in a completely different paradigm than the rest of the world. In this African culture, they believe that the longer you run, the more skilled a runner you become. According to this community, the older men are stronger runners. The idea challenges our conventional model that we are less capable as we age. When science went to check this phenomenon, they found that the elderly African runners were physically equal to elite young runners from America. I've reconsidered beliefs because of these discoveries.

I was truly a witness to the power of belief being active in our day to day lives. I also realized that the power of our belief is far more complicated than I could have imagined. The subconscious plays such a vital role in our beliefs and how our reality unfolds. I watched as my deepest desires and needs constantly manifested in ways that still boggle my mind. In good and bad ways, the constant strangeness still fit into my belief structure. Danielle's beliefs were different than mine creating a far different experience.

I watch as my wife's beliefs were attacked and questioned by people who thought they were helping. Few people in the world tried to comprehend Danielle's situation or sensitivities. She faced a lack of support from family, from doctors, and supposed friends. This reinforcement led to Danielle permanently questioning her treatment from start to finish. This belief pattern was entirely subconscious because she rarely mentioned it around me. It was in her last days that she pulled someone aside and truly asked if she should have tried the chemotherapy.

I thankfully didn't find out until after my wife's passing, as I don't think there was anything I could do to fix it at that point. If I had addressed it from the beginning, we might have stood a chance. After months of her family questioning her treatment options, it became negative reinforcement. However, I believe the idea was cemented in stone by the doctors we were forced to visit. That part upset me the most.

Every doctor by law is required to remind Danielle that she would die if she didn't choose to undergo treatment. If belief is power, then I believe the doctors convinced Danielle she was going to die. I found she put a lot of faith in what they had to say. I even had to approve any of my recommendations with the Doctors. Danielle put Doctors on a pedestal above even common sense.

It was tough to face that reality because it seems criminal to sentence someone to death. Again I mention the Placebo and Nocebo effect as perfect examples of why belief can be so powerful. If doctors didn't believe in the power of belief, then why would all medications need to pass the placebo test? From my perspective, I had plenty of reasons and people I trusted to reinforced Danielle's decision. I thought we had removed that doubt, but I failed in my efforts. The doctors, in cooperation with Danielle's family, had truly set her up for disaster.

We did everything to make my wife better, and everything we did for some reason failed. It was a huge hit to my ego, especially considering all the research I did on the topic. I did not doubt as I had stated before that the dozen treatment choices we made were all potential cures for her cancer. My research showed that the IV and changing the diet were enough to cure cancer. We were doing light treatment, alpha-lipoic acid, mud baths, and it all failed Danielle.

The reason I find that none of Danielle's treatments truly worked is that she ultimately doubted all of them. Her friend had confirmed the doubt she still had. Strong subconscious doubt had been there all along. Danielle never told me, and honestly, if she did, I wasn't willing to listen to such nonsense. I thought we had already ruled out chemotherapy as an option. I wouldn't say I was completely surprised to discover this, but the confirmations were infuriating. Which is why supporting a treatment choice is so important.

Thanks to the women who were helping many of the feelings that Danielle worried about sharing with me were easily shared. It was this added help that brought a huge level of peace to our relationship. We no longer were faced with many of the stresses we had before. Now that Danielle wasn't in constant pain, her demeanor was radiant. She was back to her usual loving and compassionate self. It was amazing getting my wife back even if for a short time. For so long, our struggle had slowly eliminated much of the beauty that we once shared.

This time allowed us both to talk again and get very deep in our conversations. With the added information that Danielle was downloading from the other side, it made for interesting dialogue. I found our discussions about the angels that were visiting her the most interesting. She told me about several women who passed that were coming to visit her. There was an entourage of angels that seemed to be following Danielle through the process. I didn't mind the extra help.

One of my least favorite topics was about me and what would happen to me. It was clear that Danielle didn't want me just to be thrown on the street. Danielle realized that had she left the house to her family that they would have most likely kicked me out of the house immediately. I still didn't want the house, but I also didn't want to have to move immediately either. I wanted some time to cope with all the feelings I wasn't dealing with at the time. I was suppressing a lot of emotions to be of service to Danielle.

Danielle had asked the parents of Rose if it would be a problem if I get six months in the house. They agreed that would be fine. It was even more than I could ask for, but I knew I would need several months regardless. I was not making any plans beyond Danielle. However, Danielle had some guidelines for me to follow after she passed.

Which often led to the next big topic of discussion. Danielle demanded that I never have anyone in the house of a romantic nature. I agreed and would tell Danielle that I couldn't see myself moving on if I ever did for a minimum of a year. Out of principle and the fact that she was my wife, she deserved respect. Even though we had only been together seven months, I still felt out of respect that Danielle deserved that because she was my wife.

Danielle always had a hard time believing that I would wait. Considering that many of the examples of widowers she knew about, moved on within a month or two. That idea was appalling to me, considering that I know it would take me longer than that to come to terms with my own emotions. It wouldn't be fair to someone else if I still were hung up on my wife, it also wouldn't be fair to my wife to fill that void with something that needs time to heal. It was clear that Danielle didn't understand that I was going to need time, but I knew that already.

I had already been single for the year before meeting Danielle, which gave her a little reassurance. Even though the issue came up often, it rarely offended me. There were times that she would get stuck in a pattern of accusations, but I would usually put those quickly to rest. I never questioned my devotion to her, and it was unbreakable. Thankfully, I was not the only one to rise to the occasion.

Danielle's friends were the ones that rose to the occasion, exactly when it was needed. At nearly two weeks without food or water, Danielle was becoming visibly weaker but still holding on strong mentally. We all had to help her move to and from the bathroom holding her up on the toilet and in the shower. I was always needed for showers since it was too difficult to hold her up without being in the shower too. I wore a swimsuit, so I didn't scare the ladies.

The showers had become a necessity because Danielle was nearing two full weeks without food and water. Incidentally, the lack of movement had created a low requirement for energy. We felt that is why her body was lasting longer than expected. After a little research, we decided that we could do a hot-cold treatment in the shower to get her heart rate up. We found this would help her use more energy even though she was too weak to move on her own.

The first couple of showers were very intense, considering I was the one who was holding her under a dripping shower. I could do the shower myself but found it much easier to do with help from the ladies. With Danielle becoming weaker, I had to do all the work to move her. Her frail body was becoming easier to carry as she continued to wither. She trusted me with all her heart when she needed my help.

It was that trust and strength that helped both of us find the courage to face what was ahead. The new way of life was an adjustment. Danielle found it hard not having more things in the day to look forward to, her meal schedule and water schedule were huge parts of her day. Now those routines were gone, and she hated having idle hands. Danielle compensated by taking more control in her immediate life.

Constant demands were common. There was very little that Danielle wanted us to do except wait on her hand and foot. We all did everything we could to ease her discomfort. I spent hours with a warm damp rag brushing it gently across her skin. Not enough to hydrate just enough to keep her comfortable. We did the same with ice cubes to keep her lips moist. Danielle appreciated the constant attention we were giving her. She deserved it after all the pain she endured.

Danielle wanted all her pain to stop long before she quit eating and drinking. Although her body was shutting down naturally, it was still uncomfortable to endure. Constantly feeling the desire to eat and drink must be so challenging, although Danielle did it with such grace and ease. Danielle had an unbreakable will, and when she set her mind to something, she did it to completion — eventually leading to a problem developing.

During a shower, the intensity from the hot-cold therapy had

235

caused Danielle to lose consciousness. We weren't aware of it as we were holding her up, and she usually kept her head down. It was an experience that would change Danielle's expectations. For some reason, she felt the stress of the shower would help her pass sooner. I didn't understand this idea at first, but if it made her feel better than I was willing to give it a try. She immediately began demanding four to six showers a day.

Since it was nearing day sixteen, we were all surprised that Danielle was not facing imminent death. The nurse even explained that she was holding on, explaining it was now up to Danielle to allow herself to transition. This unwavering motivation to live was truly part of Danielle. She was a fighter, and never gave up on a fight. I began reminding her that it was okay to go. She didn't have to hold on for any of us, and we wanted her suffering to be over too.

None of us wanted Danielle to go, but after seeing the pain she was enduring, we understood why it was important to support the current plan of action. None of us wanted to lose Danielle, but the truth is the disease had taken her from us long before she decided to end her life. Surprisingly this action also returned her to us briefly. It was almost harder for the ladies to watch this return only to be followed by a very rapid decline.

Following day sixteen, we were not dealing with the same Danielle. After more than two weeks of no water, we were left with a mind that could think of nothing else. The desire for water drove her every desire. She would constantly tell us how sweet water was, how much she just wanted to put an ice cube on her lips. How she just wanted to lick a wet rag or take another shower. There was no relief for her if we were to respect her wishes.

We had all realized that the showers were doing nothing but keeping her hydrated. Everyone decided that we should discontinue the practice. We ended up making the situation worse because Danielle still thought the showers could help end her suffering. She saw the shower as her solution. Holding this boundary would be my ultimate test. For over a month, I had maintained the calm composure that Danielle needed. Now it all came down to these last few days.

Danielle started a constant barrage of either asking for some ice or being in the shower. It wasn't easy for me to sit there for hours just telling her that it wasn't time for a shower. Even more challenging was telling her she would have to wait for another ice cube. The ice cube would just be used on her lips to prevent dry cracking. However, ice would become a constant source of water if I left it with her. She didn't want to drink any of it. For the first two weeks, she even spat out any water that got in her mouth.

Now her normal reactions were being overridden by reactions of survival. Since she wasn't ready to die subconsciously, it makes sense that her subconscious mind would put up such a fight. Her will to survive was only prolonging her suffering. As much as she wanted her suffering to stop, she also secretly just wished she could live a happy, healthy life. She struggled with this the entire time she was sick, and the people in her life at the end were instrumental in making sure the end of her life was everything she deserved.

Now I was only getting maybe a one or two-hour break before Danielle would throw a tantrum to have me back in the room. It was difficult at times for me to ignore the cries for my return. However, I understood that sleep and rest were equally important for me to function properly. Danielle wanted total control, but if I left, she lost that control. Danielle would spend hours asking where I was, which made things a bit more challenging for myself. The women did a great job at making sure that I would get some rest no matter what. I will always be grateful for their efforts.

Eighteen days of Danielle's powerful presence had worn out most of the women involved. Several of the women worked in rotations to keep an extra hand around the house. We would all rotate sleep schedules to keep ourselves rested. It was not easy with Danielle crying for showers or me. They did their best to keep her calm, but she was becoming more and more difficult to manage. She attempted to drag herself to the shower on several occasions. However, I was the only one who could easily put her back into bed.

I could see that Rose's mom was becoming exhausted. Danielle's behavior was starting to become overwhelming for all of us. The teamwork helped us all maintain our sanity. Days of little to no sleep were having a more dramatic impact on our volunteers. I completely understood that some of them needed to take some time away. However, I wasn't expecting what happened next.

Several women commented on my endurance through everything we had gone through. They told me how impressed they were that I was able to handle this situation for so long. After months of going through hell, it was nice to have a little validation that we really were going through hell. This was the first time I felt appreciated for everything that I had done for Danielle. I'll admit it felt unbelievably amazing. Not once had someone recognized me for all the hard work I had done for my amazing wife.

Amazing was something that everyone present with Danielle felt. There could be amazing sadness or amazing joy, but either way is extraordinary. Danielle had truly manifested the people and tools that she needed to make a successful transition from this world to the other. She brought in people that at perfect times provided tools for growth. Which still blows my mind when I think about how Grace showed up in our lives. Amazing that we met the day her mother was diagnosed with Cancer. I had no idea the amount of learning that I would gain from observing her.

It was Grace's demeanor that I tried every day to emulate. Next to Danielle, she would be my greatest teacher, without even knowing she was teaching me. As much as I learned from her, I feel she learned so much from Danielle. There were so many insights Danielle shared that I felt were going to help Grace with caring for her mother.

Grace even put off seeing her mother because of a promise to Danielle. Grace stayed several weeks longer than she was expecting because she felt it necessary to keep showing Danielle support. This selfless act of support did not go unnoticed by Danielle, and her love and compassion towards this almost stranger grew to new heights. Danielle truly loved Grace for the person that she was, and it was her honor to share with Grace a bit of wisdom. This wisdom was to support her mother fully even if she doesn't support her mother's plan of treatment.

We had faced the opposite problem with Danielle's family, and she didn't want to see the same problem happen between her and her mother. I feel the universe rewards us sometimes for doing things for others. I think my wife was a big gift in that aspect. Grace had already been the greatest gift to manifest at the end of Danielle's life. Which is why what happened next wasn't a complete surprise.

Grace came over that day as my relief, which after another night of not sleeping was necessary. Surprisingly I wasn't particularly tired at this point and decided to read some comics to get my mind off things. I also was getting some needed nutrition which usually involved a bag of popcorn and a bowl of cereal. Danielle wasn't crying out for my return, which is one reason I loved when Grace visited. They had a special connection that would forever be sealed in history.

After only thirty minutes, Grace asked me to come into the room. There was a tone in her voice that expressed a sense of urgency. I could tell that she was concerned, and she commented that Danielle's breathing was starting to change. I observed the change, noting that her breathing was becoming slower and shallower. We both knew what that meant.

I knelt on one side of Danielle, while Grace knelt on the other. I am still grateful that it was Grace that was present with us as Danielle and I were facing this moment. I couldn't help but cry, and it was clear that I was saying my final goodbyes to my wife. As I looked into her eyes, I just reminded her again, and again, "It is okay to go." I also told her she was loved, and there is a beautiful place waiting for her. It was a miracle to see her acknowledge me at that moment and almost give her goodbye too.

Grace and I sat there for what felt like just a moment now, yet it felt almost timeless. We sat there for possibly an hour, but I can't be sure. We remembered she asked us to log the time of her death. Danielle had asked because she wanted someone to do the star chart on it. It still is a grand event that we could be present for this star child as she returned to the Stars from which we all came. Breath after breath I just waited with her.

The breaths became slower and longer in between, and it didn't look like she was suffering at all. Although, I could see a fear in her eyes that slowly faded as she continued to gasp for air. I then witnessed acceptance as she allowed herself to fade with her last breaths. It seemed like an eternity between her breaths as they continued to slow. The final breath being a surprise to both Grace and I as we weren't expecting another. I could feel her presence in the room even after her final breath, it was sad and beautiful all at the same time. The moment we shared was indescribable.

We didn't wait long to let the rest of the group know. They all arrived promptly, and I asked if we could, according to Grace, let Danielle stay for six hours before we move her. It was supposed to help the spirit let go of the body during that time. It also gave us all a space to mourn together. We were all relieved to have helped

Danielle through her ordeal. I had spent so much time being a care-taker it was strange to have it all stop. It was very emotional, and as much as I wanted to escape the outside world, we had to let the world know.

22
It Doesn't End There

I called my dad first to let him know what had happened. It was the hardest phone call I've ever made. I kept the conversation short and to the point. However, the big favor I asked him to do was call my sister. I told him I would call mom after we hung up. Since my mom hadn't been out in about a month, it was a bit of a shock to hear that Danielle had passed. I quickly ended that conversation to avoid being triggered by questions. I only wanted to make it a point to call the people in my life who deserved to know.

Sadly, I felt that Danielle's family also deserved to know, but I also wanted to respect Danielle's final wishes. Danielle had made it her final wish to ban her family from knowing when she passed. The reasoning behind the decision was her family had offended every lady that we asked to communicate on our behalf. They were all so upset by her family's comments that they all stopped talking to them after only several weeks.

One lady even informed us that they were trying to get the police involved as one of the volunteers was friends with the chief of police. The police chief's response to her family was, "Do you really believe that Danielle is doing anything against her will?" Which if you knew Danielle, that was the truth. Danielle was upset that her family was causing so many problems, which led to her deciding to ban them from her life permanently.

The ladies and I decided at the house that day that we would inform her family when we announce it to Sedona. We were waiting several days for personal reasons to share the big announcement. I did feel wrong not telling them, but after their behavior, it was still a bit gratifying. They even spent days trying to call the cops, and the mortuaries in town trying to figure out what happened. I find it most interesting that I never once had to speak to a police officer despite their efforts.

241

The people around us showed Danielle and I the support that she had earned in the community. They knew Danielle only made her own decisions, and no one could force her otherwise. Everyone knew that her family was toxic and that despite their pleas, were never going to get what they wanted. I thankfully had five women who could attest to the situation being as I describe, which is why I believe the police never checked on us. Otherwise, I may have had to face the problems head-on.

I'll admit that my unresolved anger towards her family's behavior has been helped in the writing of this book. It is how I decided to deal with my anger around the subject, by telling the truth it helps me admit my mistakes too. I have far more compassion towards them now than when Danielle first passed. I have found forgiveness for making those same mistakes. If I can find forgiveness for myself, then I can also forgive them. Jesus said something that describes her family perfectly. "Forgive them, for they know not what they do," and in that forgiveness, I have found peace.

I'll also admit I was far less nervous about the service not having to worry about seeing her family. It was obvious that she was angry with them before she passed. However, the real reason she banned her family from her funeral was to give me a safe space to mourn. Danielle didn't want me going postal on her family because of their behavior. She wanted her funeral to be perfect.

Thankfully there wasn't much we had to do when it came to planning Danielle's funeral. Danielle had planned every detail down to the songs she wanted to be played. The only part we had to decide was which weekend we would have both of her services. I left it up to the ladies as it didn't matter to me when it happened. It was their help that made the whole process effortless for me. I didn't even have to call the funeral home because someone else took care of that.

The funeral home arrived that evening to fulfill Danielle's wishes of being extremely discrete. She didn't want her death to be a public spectacle. She only wanted the people involved with her final weeks to be allowed over. It was a time Danielle designated as a mourning space for those involved. She knew that we would all need it. I asked as a favor that the funeral home not cremate Danielle for at least three days. My reasons being a bit more complicated than a simple explanation could provide.

242

In my research about Near Death Experiences, I had read about people who died and after several days, awoke in the morgue to the complete surprise of the mortician. I had also met a woman who was declared dead for several days before coming back with a new huge life purpose. I felt it wasn't too much to ask to give Danielle that possibility, and due to my Catholic upbringing, I figured three days was a good bet. Jesus arose in three days after dying on the cross, and if my wife had any chance of coming back, I wanted to give it to her. The funeral home gave me four days, making me happy and surprisingly hopeful.

In the week that followed we all helped in planning the two funeral services. We had decided to hold the first service at the Sedona Creative Life Center. Which in Sedona synchronicity is the one place that Danielle and I spent the most time before she got sick. The chapel overlooked the gazebo we used to enjoy only seven months prior. How fitting that it would also be the place of our final goodbyes.

I wanted a couple of days away from Sedona and made an adventure down to Tucson to escape the world. I wasn't quite ready to face anyone and wasn't really in a place to talk about it with anyone. The interesting thing was that I was also stepping into my parent's world. A world that I had avoided for some time because of the stresses that had occurred in the past. I was hoping that this would be a safe space for me to stay for a couple of days. I was wrong.

After arriving in town, we decided to have a family dinner that evening. We all decided to go out to my favorite restaurant, Basil's. I was planning on a nice dinner where my family was there to support me after my loss. It didn't seem like a lot to ask, but for my mother, it was too much to ask. The truth is my mother, and I do not mix well when she drinks.

I thought I had a safe place to vent some of my frustrations about everything I went through. I let them know how overwhelming it was working non-stop and taking care of Danielle. I told them that we didn't receive much support from the community until it was too late. I didn't even go on for very long before my mother did something that I couldn't imagine.

My mother, in her guilt, decided to make me feel bad about not asking for help. I wasn't about to have her project her guilt back on me. It was her guilt that she felt for not offering to help. The

243

entire time Danielle was sick, my mom never once offered to visit. I lost my composure immediately after she defended her comments. I went into attack mode, telling her she needs to stop immediately, stating "You need to stop making me feel guilty and instead apologize for not helping."

My mom persisted, saying that I still should have asked for help. I then reiterated, "you should apologize or say nothing at all. I will not feel bad about something that makes you feel guilty." In no way was I going to allow my mother to make me feel bad after everything I just went through. If she felt that bad about what I went through, then, she should have done nothing but apologize. Instead of understanding where I was coming from the drunken fool kept defending her position.

I am not proud of how I behaved next. My mother was being so offensive that I stood up from the table and yelled, "Shut the Fuck Up or Apologize." She then apologized, not to me, but towards both my dad and grandfather for my behavior. I excused myself from the table asked my dad to get my food to go. I was livid, and after all the emotional crap I had been through I was not about to deal with my mom projecting her guilt on me.

Guilt that could have been avoided if she had simply offered to help us. If my mother had been there for her son and dying daughter-in-law, maybe she wouldn't have felt so guilty. The problem is she couldn't own that guilt due to her alcoholism. However, she also brought some serious awareness to the PTSD that I was suffering. I discovered that night, and it would be a struggle to manage feelings if I became triggered.

When my father returned that night, I lost it on him about her behavior, and I told him that if I have one more problem with my mom that I will make sure that she is banned from Danielle's funeral too. Danielle had already banned her family because of horrible behavior, and my mother was no different. She made me feel bad, just because she felt bad, all in a ploy to make herself feel better. Unimaginable, but again I forgive her because she honestly, knows not what she does.

Due to my complete lack of motivation to get back to Sedona, I spent several days isolated playing old video games at my parent's house. I kept away from my mother and helped to plan the services with the ladies. Even though the planning of the services

244

was not something I was looking forward to, I didn't realize just how much help I was going to get. It was a huge relief to come back to Sedona where love and support were booming.

I felt more at home in Sedona with people who were capable of showing compassion. The women who helped sympathized with the plight I had faced and knowing how sensitive I was to everything. The compassion I felt being back home with people who truly knew how to care made me feel worlds better. Something about Sedona is just special, and I could feel my wife's presence ever stronger now that I was back.

The first sign that I noticed immediately was Danielle taking control of my music playlists. Entirely new songs began to play that normally wouldn't. I also found song lyrics would answer questions running through my head. I would be brought to tears as a song would answer the thought I was having. It was almost like my playlist was reading my thoughts and communicating with me. On top of that, it started playing a bunch of songs that Danielle liked, instead of most of the songs that I would normally hear before her passing.

In the quiet of her house, I could feel her presence everywhere. It was crazy to sit in the yard because every thought about Danielle would have an accompanying butterfly. There were constant signs that her presence was ever more powerful now that she shifted to the next life. It was becoming ever clearer that Danielle wasn't gone but with us more than ever.

I even shared the Orgonite pyramids that were in Danielle's room with the Ladies who helped. I explained the purpose of Orgonite. One of which is to help remedy nightmares, which warranted a retort about Night Terrors. Surprisingly enough, one of the ladies had experienced a lifetime of night terrors. She explained that she would wake up feeling that something bad was in the room with her. It was frightening and would mess with her sleep. I told her there was a chance that the orgonite could help.

A week later, I would find out that her night terrors stopped and instead she had a more interesting experience. She said normally she wouldn't have shared the experience, but I was open to otherworldly experiences. Reluctantly she explained that she wasn't feeling the bad spirits anymore, but instead, she was having positive spirits visit now. It surprised me to hear that Danielle came to her and had an audible conversation. I credit the orgonite for creating that miracle.

In the weeks following, I would have other people tell me about her visiting them in their dreams. While I have never been great at remembering my dreams, it was a big goal of mine to become better. Knowing that Danielle contacted others through dreams, gave me a huge incentive to remember my dreams. A life-time of telling myself that I don't remember my dreams had created a mental block. I researched how I could start remembering my dreams more.

I began with journaling to make sure that I would build a habit of remembering my dreams. Using intention, I would say, "tonight I'm going to remember my dreams." I did several oth-er tricks to help with my dream recall, and almost immediately, it started working. I will never forget the first vivid dream I had with Danielle. It was almost as if time had gone back several months and we had a conversation just like before she took a turn for the worst. It was such a comforting experience.

As I sat there with my wife, I could feel her presence just like I once had. We talked a little, but I kept bringing up her treatment and what we needed to do. I felt like I had all the answers this time, but she just kept changing the subject. She didn't get upset with me for being stubborn either. Danielle was so peaceful and reassuring towards me. While I don't recall much of what we talked about, I do know that it was amazing until the moment I awoke.

I awoke to the feeling that what I had experienced had just happened. No dream in my life had ever felt so real. I thought in my world that Danielle was still alive. I knew I finished speaking with her, but now all of a sudden, I was in a different reality, one where Danielle was no longer present. It was crushing having to confront that realization again. However, I eventually gained a deeper under-standing of the connection we still shared.

I felt special to be able to connect with her on the other side. It also made sense why she didn't want to talk about treatment as she didn't need it any longer. Another sign that Danielle wasn't gone she just had moved to a better place. No longer confined to her body, she would start to visit many people in their dreams. All of Sedona was now her home.

As the Services approached nearly two weeks after her

passing, we were all a bit anxious. Danielle had planned the entire children's program from start to finish. It was to be her final performance, a performance that her students would fulfill to the highest perfection. I started training with Danielle's students for the children's service. It was amazing to watch Rose, who returned a second time from Europe, put on the show. I saw so much of Danielle in the way she carried herself.

Each student possessed a special dance quality that Danielle had cultivated. No two students were the same, each having a unique beauty in their artform. Compared to many dance schools which breed conformity, Danielle wanted her students to embrace their uniqueness. It was amazing to see the impact that my wife left on the world. She was more than just my best friend and wife because she was a teacher to all. She wasn't about to stop teaching even from the other side.

It was incredible to learn even more about the girls in the week leading up to the service. It was amazing to find that every single student, even the ones I didn't know that well, were little reflections of Danielle. She was a role model, and the impact of her teachings could be seen in their actions. Danielle shared herself with the world, a gift that impacted many lives. Knowing that I could be there for such an amazing person was genuinely a gift for me.

I know many of the girls felt bad about not being able to see Danielle before her passing. A decision that Danielle made with the highest regard for her students. Isolation was not something that went over well with many of the girls, and we knew it would be a huge trauma to the community. We made sure to reach out to all the guidance counselors to make them aware of the situation. Danielle was very concerned with the wellbeing of her students, and they needed to receive love and support to help them through it all. It crushed Danielle that she didn't have the strength in her final days to have visitors.

Danielle had truly left an impact on this world. She changed lives and helped more people than I could ever count. The spider web of her influence has spread all over this planet, and people are truly better because they knew her. I am a better person because I knew her. The strength she taught me was something I was going to need more than ever. I had no idea just how emotional I was until

I had to write my Eulogy. Typing it up brought up some tears, but I wrote it without an emotional hiccup. It seemed too easy until I tried reading it out loud.

It was clear that I was going to have a little more trouble discussing my emotions than I previously thought. I wasn't going to hold anything back, and I wanted to express many feelings to the community. I also wanted to share a little history with the community about how Danielle and I met. That meeting that eventually led to us getting married in the hospital in Scottsdale. It was going to be a huge emotional speech and my first speech under the circumstances.

The only people that I wanted at the funeral were my parents, considering they were the only ones actually to meet Danielle. It also happened that my Grandfather was going to join, as he lived just forty minutes north of my parents in Tucson. My sister couldn't make it because she was in Thailand, and I didn't want her to ruin her new job. My parents told her it was going to be recorded so she could watch it after.

The anticipation began building as the service approached, and I finished my speech. It relieved me that a couple of my close friends were going to be coming up from Tucson to support me as well. I was going to need all the support I could muster to make my wife proud. It was important for me to show Danielle as much respect in death as I did while she was alive. Just because she left us physically, that didn't mean I was blind to her presence everywhere. I decided to rent a black suit to look my best for her. Danielle deserved the best.

I felt her presence on the day of the service, more than ever before. I made sure that I was cleaned up and looking sharp. The adult service was late Saturday afternoon at the Creative Life Center in Sedona. It was a fantastic little space with huge vaulted ceilings with seating for about eighty people. We hoped that it would be large enough. Thankfully, there weren't going to be masses of children to take up seats.

I suppose I should have expected to be sitting in the front, as my family and I were ushered to a reserved front row. The energy in the place was starting to pick up as people trickled in. My anticipation was building as I waited for the ceremony to start. I was put at ease before the ceremony began when the Pastor stopped by to have a few words. Danielle had asked that she perform the service before her death. Now I understood why. She was truly a magical woman.

The pastor we ended up using was a Rabbi, who also danced with Danielle for years. Danielle also felt a huge connection with the Rabbi and honestly the Jewish faith. I received some helpful advice from the Jewish community. I found relief in the culture because of how they appreciate and respect the departed.

The one tradition I decided to uphold was Kriah, which is the ancient practice of tearing clothes as an expression of grief and anger in the face of death. I was gifted a little thread of fabric that I was supposed to wear for seven days. I would then tear a little bit every day for the following week as a sign of remembrance. I liked the idea, and it was even more interesting to find out the tradition started with ripping one's clothing a little every day. The thread is a less destructive tradition of ripping clothes. Despite the Jewish influence, Danielle had not included any traditional ceremonies in her service.

We had some beautiful music that was played over the sound system as people arrived. There were some familiar faces, but I didn't recognize most of the attendees. It still blows my mind how many people showed up. We ended up with a full house. It was becoming a very intimate setting with more coming in as we were prepared to start. The Rabbi was ready to perform the less traditional service that Danielle had planned.

We decided that I would be the second speaker as I didn't have the nerve to go first. I realized it was going to be a challenge expressing my thoughts to everyone. Thankfully the Rabbi opened up with a beautiful introduction, I could already see tears in the audience. The first speaker was one of the volunteers. Truthfully, I don't remember any of her speech as I was so nervous about talking next. After a brief introduction from the Rabbi, I approached the podium.

As I got on stage, it became ten times harder to contain the sadness that I was feeling. I could feel all the sadness that everyone was sending me at that moment, having lost my wife in such a horrible set of circumstances. I could feel all their pain, and it made mine even more powerful than ever. I started crying almost immediately after I started reading.

I couldn't contain the tears, and with all the strength I had,

I persisted. I spoke through the tears, and I delivered my message. I said everything necessary. I even made sure to cover the topics that Danielle wanted me to cover. Danielle had several points that she told me to discuss. They were topics I was already interested in discussing, but she made it a requirement. I was happy to oblige.

The main topic was calling out the spiritual community for their lack of support. Stated that simply sending positive thoughts for a couple of minutes a day is hardly putting the effort in to be of service to others. I also stated how abandoned Danielle felt by the community. We need to support the sick and dying with loving, ego-free action. We need to show up, with hands of service to make their situation better. Each person's definition of better is going to be different, so please find out.

It was important to me that I share supporting treatment no matter what your opinion is. There were other people, including her family that Danielle banned from coming to her service because they couldn't respect her choices. Narcy was number one on Danielle's ban list next to her family. Narcy was not banned for my benefit but because she had hurt Danielle so bad.

Narcy's behavior while visiting, followed by the rumors after that, were unforgivable. However, Narcy tried to get the ruling overturned before the service. Since she decided to lie instead of admitting to her faults, she was double banned by me. Narcy begged to be allowed to go to the service. One of the volunteers was working as a go-between between her and I. After hearing Narcy's side of the story from my friend, I was even more upset. Narcy's response was even more infuriating because she contradicted herself only proving her lies. Danielle's friend agreed with my assessment and didn't pursue the topic further.

Since Danielle had experienced an overwhelming lack of support for her treatment options from her family, doctors, and other visitors, I had to speak up. Circumstances demanded it. I was sure that the treatment we choose would have cured Danielle several times over. Something had prevented the treatments from working. When I looked in hindsight at the opinions, she received from people around her about her treatment, it made me mad.

Again I was taken back to the Placebo and Nocebo effect. I wasn't sure if I wanted to mention the topics directly or indirectly in my speech to the community. I found the Opinions about treatment options can become even more diverse when you get into the Sedona natural cure community. Even spiritual people just wanted to push their treatment options versus support Danielle's choices. It was honestly just as bad as the medical establishment except for one thing they usually weren't pushing poisons.

I've personally read about fifty different Cancer treatment options that work for some people while being completely ineffective for other people. There is not a universal cure to cancer, and in my experiences with the disease, it was far more complicated than I previously imagined. How many different choices could have Danielle made? The choices are so numerous that it does require support to make that decision stick.

Support was the biggest message I wanted to deliver. I think it shocked most of the crowd when I stated the reason her family wasn't present was that they failed to support Danielle. I still think the stress from her family was the biggest contributor to preventing Danielle from having a full recovery. Their failure to support Danielle caused me more stress than I can even express in this book. It isn't my goal to attack her family but raise awareness. They are an example of how not to behave. Instead, we must practice forgiveness for their ignorance.

The lesson I learned is that family and doctor support is incredibly important to giving a patient the best chance at beating a disease. Since I at times behaved worse than Danielle's family, I won't be a hypocrite. However, I learned from my mistakes, and I hope that others can learn from those mistakes too.

I've learned so many people are stuck in similar circumstances. It is becoming a greater problem in our culture, forcing millions of people into a reality with cancer. Sadly we are watching a problem grow radically without anyone helping address the real problems people face. If we aren't going to address these problems, then they will continue to persist. I intended to bring serious awareness to these problems in just a couple of paragraphs, while also telling everyone how amazing Danielle was.

Since most people already knew how amazing she was, it wasn't a huge part of my speech. I knew that everyone else would be telling about the years they spent with Danielle, the experiences she had shared. I still find that the most common theme was that Danielle was everyone's best friend. So many people viewed Danielle as one of their closest friends and biggest influences. It was touching to hear from several former students about how Danielle positively impacted their lives.

I was in tears most of the service. The dance performance from the Rabbi was spectacular. It was a perfect expression of what Danielle stood for. I couldn't have asked for a better experience to remember Danielle. It was obvious to me that Danielle meant so much to the community and had left an impact that no one could replace. We were all aware that we had lost something very special in this world. It was a beautiful experience.

We shared in some delightful appetizers that were donated by one of Danielle's friends. She ran a catering company in town and immediately volunteered her services. It made for a beautiful experience with televisions playing images of Danielle and her students. I appreciated everyone who came and had a pleasant experience overall. The support everyone showed was spectacular. I wouldn't be so lucky the next day.

I was even more anxious about the next service. Danielle wanted me to perform my first dance ever for a very large audience. Little did I know, but my wife's funeral was exactly one year after my grandmother's passing, and I was slightly surprised my grandfather even came, considering he never met my wife. I sympathized with his situation, but he also decided that he wanted to go home, which meant my whole family would miss the second service.

My parents decided to leave Sedona that morning and not wait several more hours to attend my wife's final performance. It was devastating, and I still don't understand how parents could do something so cold. My sister was even more surprised to hear that happened. My grandfather could have waited in the hotel if he didn't want to attend. However, I still arrived early to help prepare for the big day.

We had a lot of support from her students on the day of her service. We had reserved the local charter school for the performance. I was familiar with the location because Danielle had taken me to visit her students on several occasions. She had decided it was the perfect location for the children's service. Danielle had planned enough performances to provide everyone with all the guidance they needed.

The big day was going to be a final performance for Danielle's students but the first performance for me. Danielle made sure that I would dance in the second service. We even decided together which song I would dance. Surprisingly the perfect song ended up being Justin Beeber, seriously. I almost regretted mentioning it as an option, until I saw her joyous reaction. I was willing to dance to anything if it made Danielle happy.

The song was called "Where are U now," which surprisingly really resonated with the fact that she was gone. The first verse ends with, "When you broke down I didn't leave ya; I was by your side; So where are you now that I need ya?" I was meant to dance to that song at her service. It was the perfect song to display my talents and show respect to Danielle. The song comforted me because I felt I knew the answer to the last question. Only one song I brought a deeper connection from Danielle.

There was only one song Danielle played repeatedly. It always made me cry because I always could picture Danielle dancing to it, and at the same time, it would remind us we were both in over our heads. Matt Kearney wrote the chorus to "All I need" for our story, and it always hit home...

Guess we both know we're in over our heads
We got nowhere to go and no home that's left
If everything we've got is slipping away
I meant what I said when I said until my dying day
I'm holding on to you, holding on to me
Maybe it's all gone black but you're all I see
You're all I see

It just so happened that right before I was supposed to Dance at Danielle's service, this song ended up playing two times in a row. Rose tried to change it several times. Afterward, she said there wasn't anything she could do to change it. Danielle wanted to hear our song twice before she watched me dance.

Watching the student performances, I sat there listening to both songs, feeling tears filling in my eyes. Despite not having my family, I was supported by friends of Danielle on each side. Thankfully, I had two separate parent and student combos who offered to join me. The younger student was always a riot when we would meet. I appreciated the mental break that only a child could provide. She helped a lot of my adult worries fade away. Cutting the tension, I felt when she asked if she could dance too. I just smiled and thanked her for the offer before proceeding to the stage.

I danced with all the energy I had for about three minutes. The irony of that is that Danielle was the first dance instructor to teach me to slow down. Danielle taught me pacing, but I guess I needed a little more coaching. My endurance was a lot to be desired too, considering that I found it very difficult to dance after Danielle's passing. I expected I wasn't going to be ready for a full song. That didn't stop me from giving it 110% of what I had available. When I realized I wasn't going to be able to finish the whole song, I did the unexpected.

I grabbed my little friend from her seat and asked her to join me. Having a supporting dancer helped push me for the last minute. I was even more grateful to have her carry the last minute of the song as I couldn't dance another inch. I left everything I was feeling on the dance floor. I found, at that moment, the power dance had to release my pent-up emotions. There was nothing that compared to how calm I felt after recovering. However, it would take two more performances for me to catch my breath.

After the performances, we had another catered reception. The restaurant I previously worked for volunteered to cater the event. I asked if my former employer would do the Children's service, while another friend did the Adult service. It was incredible that we were so fortunate enough to have the support. Contributions from everyone made for another incredible ceremony. We made the best out of the unfortunate circumstances we all faced.

As strange as it was not to have my family at the children's service, I always felt supported. Everyone was kind and compassionate towards me. It was nice to connect with some of the parents. Many shared some of the positive stories they had with Danielle. I was as cheery as I could be under the circumstances. While truthfully Andora had the most fun. I didn't feel it appropriate to bring Andora to the Adult service, but I couldn't keep her from the children.

Andora had a fantastic time wandering around the schoolyard after the performance. She was a perfect angel through the performance as well. Considering it was far from her first performance, it was great to have her little presence. The students loved having

Andora running around, and she often had a crowd of children following her. I could feel the love Andora brought to everyone, including most of all myself. A little bundle of Angelic Love.

23
Messages from the Ethers

The first month after Danielle's passing was a time that I filled with many distractions. I started to binge-watch everything that I had missed on Netflix over the past year. I even reactivated my Amazon Prime and Audible audiobook memberships. I then spent hours playing video games while listening to interesting audiobooks. I wasn't ready to face everything all at once, and I needed to take breaks from my thoughts. I used electronic media as a means to cope.

My favorite was mixing video games with audiobooks. It made me feel like I was accomplishing more than just sitting around. Since I only listen to Non-Fiction, it helped me expand my mind into topics that were interesting to me. The combination was perfect at preventing me from thinking about anything else. I wasn't ready to think about anything else yet. No one could help me because I had to wait until I was ready. For the time being, I was adjusting to an entirely new life.

Thankfully I wasn't alone in this new life. Danielle's "baby" Andora Wells Luxemburg St. Clair Strabala joined the adventure. She was a blessing in more ways than one. First, she kept me motivated after losing Danielle. She became my daily inspiration because she wouldn't let me sit around all day. Andora forced me to go on adventures with her.

My first purchase for her was a chest harness that would allow me to strap her to my chest. I was hoping that I would be able to take Andora on my pedal street bike. Surprisingly, her front paws fit perfectly on the handlebars while she could balance her hind feet on the frame. I quickly built a front footpad and padded the frame so she would be comfortable during a ride. It was so successful that Andora stopped wanting to go on walks instead she would sit by my bike. She would look at me saying, "I'll wait for you to put your harness on."

I discovered quickly that she enjoyed going everywhere with me. I was relieved to have a little ball of love that wanted to do everything with me. I couldn't have asked for a better companion to help my depression. The support I received was invaluable, which is why I had to make it official.

I had to get Andora her emotional support dog card. Thankfully I knew all the doctors in town, so I made an appointment to get a prescription. I found it nearly impossible to be depressed while Andora was around. Everyone would stop to smile or laugh while she was strapped to my chest. The bike rides always produced hilarious reactions from motorists. The joy that she would bring people was contagious.

We would often ride out to a trailhead and then hike up a mountain where she would run around for twenty to thirty minutes. It was highly therapeutic for me to get out into nature with Andora. I don't know what I would have done without Andora's constant companionship. She could cheer me up, no matter how sad or depressed I would become. The love we shared was the one thing that kept me from slipping into any prolonged state of depression.

Danielle was also going to be helping me through the grieving process more that I could imagine. My openness to contacting those that have passed was something that I expected to start right away. It didn't happen quite as I was anticipating. It would be sometime before I started to center myself. This centering would make me more capable of contacting her in the afterlife. It didn't stop her from sending me messages, and some of the messages were so incredible that I now know death is not the end.

I continued to suppress many emotions after Danielle's passing. I was still using tobacco and medical marijuana to prevent dealing with my anxiety. I hadn't recognized it yet, but my PTSD was still very present. It was far too exhausting to try and process so many unresolved emotions. It was a daily practice to work on my emotions so I could open up to those emotions again. I now realized time was the only solution, and Danielle had thankfully given me that.

Danielle had requested that I be allowed to live in the house for six months. Rose's parents never once made that an issue, because they were amazing. I also had just enough money left over after paying for the cremation expenses, to survive for at least three to four months. I wasn't ready to work the first few months after Danielle's passing. It was important to me that I start to connect with my wife. I didn't want more distractions or stress to be in my life. I needed peace with no worries.

After about a month of avoiding my spiritual self, I started to meditate again. It wasn't easy for me, considering I still had so many unresolved questions. The thoughts that would arise would often trigger anger or regret. As I addressed these emotions, I began to operate with more clarity. It was right away that I started noticing strange synchronicities.

The experiences were extremely far out with a basis in science fiction versus science fact. I started having bizarre coincidences involving time travel, reincarnation, and past lives. Each time something would expose itself as a possibility, it would provide additional coincidences to support each topic. The time travel was still one of the more interesting messages from Danielle.

All of a sudden, there was a multitude of sources that I was following from the Gaia TV network, in addition to some audiobooks. The books and documentaries were describing ideas I had observed in fictional movies. However, the new information had facts to support the theories. I discovered that remote viewers claim to be able to visit the past and have shown surprising accuracy. Then we get into secret space programs and wormholes, and it becomes a real possibility. It opened a new realm of possibilities for me.

It was a plethora of Time Travel, and for several weeks I couldn't escape it. I started to believe that maybe something would happen that would cause me to go back in time. The possibility of seeing her again was all I could consider. I found many stories about random portals appearing that cause people to stop or travel in time. Stories of fairy rings go back centuries. I started to prepare my backpack for any situation that could send me into the past.

One of the biggest synchronicities came on a trip to Vegas with some friends. It was the first time I had left Sedona since Danielle passed. Several of us had rented a room for the weekend. There was a dance festival that they invited me to, which seemed appealing. I wasn't expecting Danielle to send her first message five minutes after we arrived at the hotel.

I had recently found a theme song from a movie about time

travel. The movie had been out for years, and I never once had heard the song from the end of the movie. The song was about going back in time to be with someone they love. It was crazy synchronistic to hear the song played over the speakers at the Casino we were staying. Danielle would often play songs to send messages to me, and this one of the most significant.

Even though I never traveled in time to see Danielle, I felt everything happened for a reason. The hope I gained while thinking I could see my wife again was priceless. That hope might have been the only thing preventing me from spiraling into a deep depression. I started to see more and more the influence Danielle was having in my life. She always seemed to have my back.

Danielle delivered messages in many ways. A personal favorite was little messages she would send as I cleaned up the house. One day I found a card that said, "nothing is more the child of art than a garden." -Sir Walter Scott. That day I had started work on cleaning the backyard to plant a beautiful heart garden. The added inspiration that just fell into my lap gave me a message that she was with me. Danielle knew how to send me messages, and the more I paid attention, the more profound the messages would be.

I didn't talk or communicate with many people over the first six months after Danielle's passing. The daily trips to the water store or grocery store were all the socializing that I needed. Andora would usually attract attention, forcing me to interact with people. If someone recognized us, I would usually reaffirm that Danielle is still very much with us. Many of these interactions would tell me about their own personal messages that Danielle sent.

Many people who knew Danielle had received messages in their dreams. Some were quite interesting personal messages that she delivered. It was always great to know that I wasn't the only one having crazy experiences. Since most of my paranormal experiences happened while I was completely alone, it was exciting to know I was not completely crazy. The signs I witnessed defied any scientific explanation.

Every time I was looking for a confirmation, I would have a butterfly or hummingbird appear. I had this occur more times than I can count. A more memorable experience happened as I was sending my friend a message about the butterfly synchronicities. Just as I was typing that statement on my phone, a butterfly flew in front of my face. The butterfly flew directly in between my phone and my face, which has never happened to me in my life. It all seemed crazy, but it seemed crazier to deny what I was experiencing.

I found peace sitting outside finding unique experiences with wildlife. Never before had I noticed all sorts of birds and butterfly's doing things that just brought a smile to my face. It's like they knew exactly how to cheer me up. I've even heard of many other people having similar experiences, not even associated with Danielle. These experiences were the most beneficial to my grieving process.

There were several people in town that I had developed casual relationships with for conversation. These people helped discuss some of the more metaphysical topics that many people find bizarre. As much as I don't mind sharing those stories, I also understand that many of them can be a bit farfetched, especially when approached from a traditional world view. Some wouldn't see the coincidences the same way that I do, and therefore wouldn't get the same messages that I receive. When I finally had someone appear in my life that I could talk about anything with I was super excited.

It was funny because this person was one of the first people I worked with when I started back working part-time after three months. I didn't get to know her at that time, and because of my orgonite business, I didn't have to stay working at the restaurant. It had been several months since I had seen her. She was now living two houses up with a group of people.

The house always had people rotating in and out, so it wasn't unusual to see a new face. I was often outside greeting anyone who walked up or down the street. I had met or introduced myself to most of the people who lived on the street because of Andora. Since I spent a few hours a day gardening, it wasn't unusual to see several people a day making trips up and down the street. I eventually got to know the new roommate, and we connected immediately on a spiritual level.

I found her fascinating because she had worked as a spiritual guide for several years. She did things like tarot readings but also did deep spiritual work for her friends and family. Due to our connection on spiritual topics, I opened up to her about everything that had happened with my wife. There wasn't a single experience that she found bizarre or untrue. She showed honest support by sharing similar experiences from her life.

This also let her open up about some of her past trauma's, one of the most recent being the loss of her brother. I felt super comfortable around her because of this issue. She had told me how upset it made her that her brother's fiancé moved on to be with someone else after a couple of weeks. From I Love you with one person to I love you with another person in under a month. I couldn't believe it.

I told her that I find it disrespectful not to show a time of morning for a significant other. In my opinion, I felt that waiting a year to move on from a spouse is probably very healthy. It is unlikely that someone who loses the love of their life would be in a place to move on in any less time. People need time to readjust to their lives. Rediscover themselves and move on properly.

I also felt I still had stuff to deal with, regarding losing my wife. I know it wouldn't be fair for me to be in another relationship yet. I really felt like that conversation with my new friend created a safe space for me to mourn my wife. The year was an easy commitment to keep. I had promised my wife a year of mourning, which I intended to keep with all my heart.

It was shortly after we started to hang out that I had an experience with Danielle. It was a rather unusual dream and, in that dream, she gave me something. At the time it really didn't make sense, because she gave me some blue spiritual armor. I didn't think much about it other than I really enjoyed feeling my wife's presence in that moment. The armor didn't mean anything significant nor did it lead to any other experiences over the following weeks. I just wrote it off and never considered it again.

It felt like I had truly developed a strong friendship which was all I expected out of the relationship. I didn't feel that even though I was hanging out with a girl that it would be construed as anything other than friends. I wasn't attracted to the person, and she was not my type. When compared with my wife there wasn't any comparison, and I say that because Danielle was that incredible. Our sharing was really helping to come to terms with some of the pain that the past several years had caused both of us. Loss, struggles, and pain were similar experiences we shared.

I even decided that since in another month or two I might be needing to find a roommate; I made the offer. It was about this time that she started bringing some of the drama from her house down to my house. It was mostly just her venting about the behavior that some of the roommates had such as dirty comments or inappropriate behavior. I knew a couple of the guys, so it didn't surprise me. This kind of fed my anger towards the behavior that men show towards women. It is the lack of respect that bothers me, if all parties are fine with crude behavior then I am fine with it. The problem is that many people force that behavior on people who don't approve.

This was the start of her pushing my buttons to distance myself from that house. It took about a week, but she convinced me that she had to get out of there and created a situation that really seemed plausible. After only a week of her living at the house I started to notice that something was up. There were little things that I noticed but didn't put together.

First off, she was making a lot of promises and not fulfilling any of them. I figured I would be patient and just see what happened, no need to worry. Until she said something bizarre and completely out of the blue about our friendship being just friends. It was odd that she made that statement. As strange as the statement was, I still didn't worry one bit.

It was then that she came home one night and told me that my friend from two houses up was spreading rumors that we were dating. I almost lost it right there, not only did he know my wife, but after our trip to Vegas, I thought he knew that I was truly waiting a year. Not to mention that I thought he knew me better than dating someone like the person I was now roommates. I assumed he knew it would never be anything other than that. I had to wait almost three hours for my friend to get home.

By the time my friend arrived home, my new roommate had already gone to sleep several hours before her typical bedtime. I could tell she was a bit frightened by my anger, and I figured she was trying to give me my space. It was a quick trip up to their house as I stormed through the gate and immediately started accosting my friend in front of five other roommates. Almost twenty seconds into my rant, the entire group had to stop me. All four people almost in unison told me that my new roommate was the one telling everyone in the house those things.

I immediately stopped my rant and asked for them to continue immediately. I was completely shocked at what was occurring as everyone told me the numerous things that this girl had told them. On top of that, I also found out that the spiritual reading that she did in private to connect with my wife was now public knowledge. Every single person in the house knew about her doing the reading, and even more appalling was that she even shared the details. For a spiritual worker, this was such a violation of trust that I couldn't believe that I had even allowed such a dark person into my space.

It also made me realize that all the signs I was getting about dark magik weren't about the other people in Sedona but was about her. During the time she appeared, my life was littered with signs about magik or dark spiritual practices. It was much like the signs about time travel. This time it involved someone that had manifested into my life.

I discovered that she had been practicing dark rituals that were meant to win me over. I knew that despite my normal intuitions that I was drawn to her in weird ways. Since I have great self-control, I always discontinued the thoughts the moment I recognized them. Either way, I had no intention of acting on these strange feelings. The promise to Danielle meant more to me than any temporary moment of gratification.

It wasn't until after this group disclosure that I started to see the whole picture. I began to see the elaborate lies that had been used to deceive me. I was pissed, I was angry, and I was ready to kick this person out of my wife's house. Everyone was sympathetic to my situation and were equally appalled. I thanked them for letting me know the truth. However, I would have to wait until the next morning to speak with her.

She asked me almost immediately if I had talked with the neighbor. I told her that I did and that it didn't go well. I then stated, "I'm going to ask you a question, and I recommend that you don't answer that question right away, and you think about it." She acknowledged this statement, and I proceeded to ask, "What is going on here? and I need you to tell the whole truth, and I mean all of it."

She looked at me like she didn't know what I was talking about. I was honestly surprised after six people filled me in on the other side of the story. They had nothing to gain by lying to me and even told the same stories. She was fighting an uphill battle to convince me she was not a liar. I could tell she was lying again by playing dumb to what had happened. I could finally see through her crap. I told her that it wasn't best if we talk about it right away, so

I asked again, "Are you sure that you want to talk about this?" She nodded affirmatively.

I then lost it on her, full well knowing that I allowed her to let me cool down, or for her to come clean. Either of which needed to happen for me to communicate productively. I didn't want to communicate with her productively, and I was happy to end the friendship. I had to call her out first on all her lies, on the fact that she shared private information with people I didn't approve. She betrayed my trust and on top of that hadn't done one thing at the house that she promised she was going to do since she moved in. It was embarrassing that never once fessed up to one of her lies, continuing to pile more lies on top of it.

The conversation ended with me recommending that if what everyone at the other house said was lies that she should confront them and get them to tell me the truth. It seemed the most logical solution because if there was simply a misunderstanding than she could remedy the situation. I didn't see her for the next five hours. At which point she returned to tell me that she spoke to the neighbor. Explaining he was unable to communicate, and I later found out that the only interaction they had that day was her flipping him off when he drove past the house. Considering the only answer she had for me was a garbage answer, and even worse a complete lie, I lost it one last time.

This time I didn't hold anything back, I told her, "Get the Fuck out of my wife's house." After all the disrespect that she showed my late wife in her house, I wouldn't tolerate her for another minute. It was unforgivable, it was disgusting, and I wasn't going to stand for it. I exploded into a fit of rage that had her unable to speak or get a word out, and I told her to take everything she owned and leave. She told me her ride was on the way. I told her, "That's great, then take all your stuff to the street. I don't want you inside Danielle's house one minute longer."

I proceeded to tell her that it was best that we do not speak, ever again. It may take weeks or months before I will be able to talk to her without becoming extremely upset. The damage that she did with her choices were something that I couldn't believe even happened to me. To have someone come into my space and disrespect me in such a way was hard to believe. Now I was also faced with the regret of not controlling my anger.

I did initially feel bad about how much I had yelled at this person. Despite being rightfully upset, it didn't mean that I had the right to assault this person verbally. I felt that I had restrained myself just before it became outright abuse. Once I said the things I needed to say, I was done. There was no need to keep rubbing it in, because I was ruthless. However, considering the crime, I still felt like she deserved worse. It was not my decision what her punishment would be. I would leave that up to the universe.

Sitting on the porch pondering about if I became too angry, I had a hummingbird fly a few feet in front of my face. It did nothing but take my mind off of what I was thinking. A few hours later, I was sitting in the same spot still having the same regret. Just like before a hummingbird flew directly in front of my face, this repeated sign of reassurance gave me some peace that maybe I did do the right thing. The second confirmation from the hummingbird helped me realize Danielle was sending me a message. It wouldn't be till a couple of days later that it would start making sense to me.

It all started with my recalling the experience with the blue armor. Danielle had given me the blue armor just before I met my former potential roommate. I didn't notice it until I looked back on our friendship and saw that I never wanted to touch her. I had a strange subconscious aversion to touching her.

When we would share deeply emotional experiences, I did not want to hug her like I would with most people. I would hug any of my friends if they were feeling down, but I didn't want to hug her. It happened on a completely subconscious level. I had zero awareness that I was behaving that way until hindsight. Now finding out that she was using dark magik while lying and manipulating me it all came together.

Danielle somehow knew I was in a bad situation. She gave me something that would protect me during this period of growth. The blue armor must have been a gift she gave me to repel the energy used against me. There was no other explanation for my aversion to this person. I have never knowingly avoided anyone in that way before.

On top of that, because of the hummingbird, I realized that the explosion of anger wasn't just my anger but also Danielle's. She was expressing her anger through me, and this person needed to understand how she upset Danielle. That understanding helped me feel a little less responsible for the actions that I had done. I knew I was sensitive, but I didn't think that I was that in tune with Danielle. The rage I felt was on a whole different level.

Even in my worst emotional breakdown, I had never gotten that angry in my entire life. However, I remembered that Danielle told me how she used to blow up on people who were being stupid or dangerous. Her students and friends confirmed these stories. I had done the same thing she did in many other instances. I had to accept the experience for what it was, much of the guilt melted away.

I found out shortly after this that I was not going to be needing a roommate. The family had finally closed on the transfer of ownership and was preparing to remodel the house. It had a lot of issues that needed to be addressed before they wanted their daughter living there. The house inspections turned up more problems than we had initially anticipated. The walls in several rooms had black mold, and the wiring throughout the entire house needed to be replaced. The work required that the whole house be emptied.

After finding out that I was going to have to move out of the house, I decided to create a yard sale. I will admit that it felt weird going through my wife's stuff. She was a bit of a packrat, so her house was full of all kinds of interesting things. She never bought new things and was a huge thrift store shopper, which was what most of her house contained. There wasn't much that I found I wanted to keep. I also asked Rose if there was anything she wanted to keep, and there weren't many things she wanted either.

I mostly kept some of her art, including a headless Buddha. My favorite was a classic piece of history containing all the original newspaper articles from the JFK assignation. Danielle also left me one of her stained-glass windows, which was the only thing that she said was worth any value. I will cherish the piece of art for the rest of my life. Out of a full household of stuff, there was only a small handful of things that I wanted to keep.

It still felt strange selling her stuff, so I decided to donate her personal items to the local women's shelter thrift store. No space for storage was unused and there was so much to sift through. It was a monumental task. I didn't ask for help because it was a task that I felt obligated to perform. I made sure that I kept most of her writings and photos because I felt those memories should be preserved. On top of that, I really found the whole experience therapeutic. However, I still had a lingering doubt about if I was doing the right thing.

It was the first day of the yard sale that I met a woman with whom I shared a piece of orgonite. We ended up discussing the topic of medication sensitivities and I told her that Orgonite was helpful against EMF sensitivities. Other than mentioning Danielle's passing and her experience with medication sensitives, we didn't talk about Danielle any further. The woman was sad to hear, but I think I brought her more comfort to confirm the reality of those sensitivities.

That night the woman went home and had an experience that she had to share with me. The following day she returned to tell me all about her experience. However, I wasn't working the yard sale due to friends that were visiting for the day. My friend and neighbor from two houses up were watching my sale for me when she arrived. She told him that she was there to tell me about her experience. She explained that a woman had appeared to her and started dancing while she was holding my orgonite.

After sharing it with him, he mentioned that my wife was a Dance teacher and pointed to the dance studio. The little old woman lost it right there. My friend told me that she freaked out for a good ten minutes before finally settling down. She, in all the years living in Sedona, never had a Sedona experience. This was her first metaphysical Sedona experience, and one of the most powerful messages I would receive from my wife.

It just so happened that when the woman went home that night, my wife decided to pass on further messages to her. She was told to come back to the yard sale and pass those messages to me. When she showed up Sunday, I was shutting down the yard sale for the weekend. I wasn't anticipating any more people showing up, but she showed up at the perfect moment, and we took a seat.

I could tell that she was a bit overwhelmed by the situation that had happened. I was informed about what had happened the previous day and let her know. She explained to me that there, even more, that happened, but she didn't want to, "Freak me out." Her apprehension was cute, and after explaining some of the crazy experiences that Danielle and I experienced, she relaxed a lot.

She proceeded to tell me that my wife had appeared to her,

267

describing Danielle perfectly. Then Danielle told her, to give me a message. It was a message that I would find so powerfully perfect. She told me that my wife was happy that I was moving her stuff and getting rid of it. The woman explained this was because it was helping my wife let go from this plane of existence. It meant the yard sale was the right course of action.

I couldn't believe this message because it also answered the only question that I was thinking for over a week. "Is it okay for me to be getting rid of Danielle's things? Especially in a yard sale." While I did donate most of her personal things, I didn't have the means to move a ton of stuff, and selling it made the most sense. I could use the money, and it made the difficult work far more rewarding. I ended up making just enough money to survive the full six months without having to stress about money. It was synchronicity at its best.

The second most significant event happened during my first Thanksgiving alone. I was invited to join my dad's side of the family for Thanksgiving Dinner in Los Angeles. My uncle invited my dad, grandfather, and I to join his family. My mom was visiting her mom for the holiday. It was nice to connect with extended family for the first time in several years.

The trip went trouble free for the first twenty-four hours. until a guy outing to the local naval retiree bar and restaurant. It was a beautiful yet dated place right on the ocean. I was surprised to find that they wouldn't allow emotional support animals. Andora was with me, and the greeter told me she had to be a service dog to enter the establishment. I didn't argue realizing it was a cool California day by the ocean. I left Andora in the shade with the windows cracked.

Just before we ate our food, I got a call from my roommate who I lived with when I met Danielle. She called to let me know that Danielle was visiting her regularly in her dreams and that she was in a beautiful place surrounded by love. It was great to hear from my former roommate and even better to get a message from my wife. It seemed a bit odd as I have never had a phone call or message happen like that again.

Almost immediately after I returned from my call, my Grandfather, who had always been a huge skeptic of everything I did, said, "if your orgonite works, then why did your wife die." I was so taken back by the comment that I just responded with explaining how orgonite works. I explained the concept of cymatics and the difference it will make in many people's lives. I don't need proof anymore, considering I've personally heard hundreds of testimonials.

My grandfather wasn't even listening to the proof. He continued his skepticism to a fault. He failed to listen to a word I was saying and telling me I had to be wrong. I was becoming increasingly upset by his level of ignorance. The truth is I still regret not saying, "the reason my wife died was because of shitty family, behaving exactly like you are right now." Since both my dad and uncle just sat there without saying a thing, knowing full well that there is some science and truth to what I do, I felt abandoned.

I finally had enough of my grandfather's ignorance and blew my top. I stood up from the table and told him to "shut up," and I believe I might have called him an "ignorant old fuck." Honestly, I'm surprised I made is several minutes with him considering that is exactly how he behaved. I yelled my anger as I rushed off the patio to the parking lot.

I immediately went to grab Andora out of the car. It was ironic that the one place that I wasn't allowed to bring my therapy dog was also the one place that I would need her most. However, before I could even reach the car, I had an epiphany. I couldn't believe what had just happened and the likeliness of my wife delivering a message minutes before that interaction. My anger drained from my body like I had sprung a leak. My wife shattered my world and nothing but wonder and awe remained.

It was also clear that my grandfather did not have any respect for me. The possibility of me controlling myself under the circumstances would have been slim to none without Danielle. Especially when I considered he was the reason my family didn't go to my wife's second funeral service, a service which I performed. I would have been a raging ball of fury without a reassuring pat on the back from Danielle. She knew family could behave so horribly.

Thanks to an incredible need to pee after leaving the bar, I didn't end up saying much on the way home. However, when my grandfather got into the car, I immediately asked him to not talk to me. Even though he was trying to make an apology I wasn't ready to listen to it, I told him that he lost the privilege to speak to me after saying what he did about my wife. He didn't want to be silenced and felt he had the right to talk. The car quickly came to a total silence after I told him to "seriously shut the fuck up."

If it weren't for the talk, I had with my aunt and uncle that night, I don't know how I would have felt about my family. First off, I felt my dad and uncle had practically condoned their father's behavior. Second, I already felt enough guilt about not beating the disease to have a grumpy old man blame me for not beating it. It was cruel, yet I still found success in my failure in controlling my anger. I failed to control my outburst, but with Danielle's help, I didn't allow everyone else to suffer. No one would have known how mad I was that night despite sitting next to him at dinner.

It wasn't until after everyone left that I was able to open up to my aunt. My uncle ended up getting upset back at me to get me to stop unloading my anger towards my grandfather. He yelled at me that he did say something to my grandfather. To his surprise, I thanked him. Little did he know, but all I wanted was someone to stand up to my grandfather. I left the table, and I didn't hear my uncle reprimand my grandfather. How could I have known that occurred?

This opening of communication ended up, leading to a huge release for me. For too long, I was unable to share my feelings with family, due to drinking or inability to communicate. It was interesting to talk about the fact that my entire dad's side of the family has a problem communicating their feelings. This inability to share or embrace emotions was one reason I couldn't turn to my father for emotional support.

This realization about my family and the growing that occurred was beautiful. While I don't know if my grandfather will ever change, I know at least his children have been forced to change. We all agreed that the Strabala boy's all having girls was a great way to bring balance to force. Seven out of nine of my cousins are girls. Life finds a way.

Danielle also seems to find a way. There are times that her presence is undeniable. I feel her at all dance events and have had people express feeling her too. I have had people say they feel her energy dancing with me as I twist and twirl around the dance floor. In my most profound experience I was attending an inner dance meditation class.

The facilitator played the song "In the Arms of an Angel." I immediately felt her presence flow through, over, and around me. I fell to my knees as tears began pouring down my face. After a minute, I laid back down on my mat. Only moments later I felt Danielle directly over me. I felt her pull me out of my body as she forced me to dance with her. I had the most incredible out of body experience of my life.

Several friends commented on the feelings they felt during that song. I could tell that others recognized her presence without knowing the reason why. One of my close friends was present, and she explained that it felt like water entered the room. Danielle was a water sign, so the connection was strong. Three years later and I have never had an experience like that again.

Every Danielle experience I have had brings me new levels of appreciation. The most recent being an event that occurred on the third anniversary of her passing. For over a year, I had started hosting a free ecstatic dance on the rocks every Tuesday evening. This year it just so happened that her third anniversary landed on a Tuesday too. I was excited to pay respects to her with my dance.

The night started as most nights did. Usually, several people would arrive early to help me get the dance started. After thirty to forty minutes, I had about seven or eight of us dancing around my speakers. It was a special day, and I was happy to have my dance family with me. For nearly two and a half years, I have been enjoying the ecstatic dance community in Sedona. I appreciate the no talking and no drinking rules of the events.

With my free dancing on the rocks, I am far less worried about enforcing the rules. My only intention is to encourage people to dance. We set up just off one of the major trails in Sedona. It is a perfect flat space to dance, drum, and watch the full moon rise. I invite all the hikers to join us for some dancing. Most people smile or laugh, but I do have quite a few people who will join us for at least a song or two.

On the day of my wife's anniversary, I was in for a magical occurrence. It must have been around halfway through my playlist that a group of moms with their children walked down the mountain. As usual, I invited them all to join us, and this group accepted with smiles. The children practically ran down, while their mothers tried to keep up. There must have been six to seven kids that all of a sudden just showed up to dance. I couldn't believe the synchronicity.

Most days, I was lucky if there were any children to join the dance. Usually, it is just a bunch of goofy adults expressing dance with amazing freedom. Ecstatic dance has no right or wrong creating freedom to express oneself in unique ways. Some people jump around like animals, others crawl or roll around on the ground. Children seem to express the most freedom in my experience.

The youngest children started dancing immediately with their mothers. I smiled at all of them and thanked them for joining us. There was an older boy in the group that was a bit skeptical of the whole experience. He spent a few minutes observing the adults acting just as foolish as the children he was with. Then he stopped worrying about what everyone would think and started dancing.

The boy inspired the whole group to unleash their dance. We had almost twenty of us dancing around on the rocks, and the energy was electric. It was one of the largest groups I had to date. I was almost in tears as I realized that Danielle must have loved having so many children dancing. I pulled two of my close friends aside to explain to them the situation. They almost cried too.

Then to make it even more about Danielle, two more children joined the fun. This was truly a special moment for me to experience on her anniversary. The magic she shared with me on those days was undeniable. She played the song "Good to be Alive Today" for the first time for me on the second anniversary of her passing. I put on a random playlist, and that song came on at the perfect time, in the perfect moment to make me know she is still there.

Even in death, Danielle is giving me the strength to overcome my weaknesses and control my emotions. She does this by giving me strength through messages or helping me feel her presence. I feel her everywhere now, and I know she is always looking out for me from the new place that she now calls home. A home that we will all one-day return.

I know that Danielle and I will be reunited, whether it is in this life or the next, it will happen. Our lives have been intertwined for longer than we can even imagine. The lives we lived showed me that connection would likely carry into the future. I have no idea what the future will hold, as nothing in this story worked out the way I expected.

I never expected to lose my wife because the alternative

treatments failed. I never expected to face the problems we faced. I don't think there is any part of this book that I could have predicted. My expectations were thrown out the window the moment I got married. I expected things to work out and for Danielle to still be with me.

It is ironic how my expectations were still achieved. It did all work out in the end, and Danielle is still clearly with me. She has proven herself to be an incredible dance guardian angel who has blessed Sedona with Dance. After Danielle's passing, we had two days of Ecstatic Dance a month in Sedona. While now, we have two to four Ecstatic Dances a week. Dance is the one medicine in my life that has proven that I can express anger in a positive way, but I need to leave it all on the dance floor. Danielle passed that message to me from the ethers, as it was not a skill she mastered in this life.

She gave me the best chance possible to get myself back on my feet and thrive. I may have had to take a few steps backward with Danielle to move forward to the man I am today. That change is a gift from Danielle that I will forever cherish. Danielle allowed me to rise to the occasion. She allowed me to forgive myself and become a better man. The lessons she taught me will forever live in these pages. Now I have the privilege of sharing that knowledge with the world, and I thank you for joining me on this journey.

24
Andora's Afterthoughts

It is hard to believe that it has been four years since Danielle passed. It has been the most exciting time of my life since that endeavor. I don't know how I would have managed had the support not appeared. Although the support didn't always come in ways that I expected, I could have never expected the largest form of support to arrive in a little 6-pound bundle of love. Andora, Danielle's little white Pomeranian, would leave her most significant mark on me, and now I'm honored to share some of those experiences.

The amount of joy and happiness that Andora brought into my life was invaluable. I couldn't have managed the grief and anger successfully without her. The companionship was great, but it was her constant happiness that kept me happy too. It was practically impossible to be sad around such a cute and loveable dog. She always knew how to cheer me up. Andora was indeed a gifted therapy dog.

It would be Andora that would finish the grand chapter of my life in writing my book only four days after my first book release party. It was just shy of a 4-year journey to complete the book, which was an honestly monumental task in itself. The voyage, riddled with small and big challenges, also happened with supernatural coincidences. However, in a final act of Sedona Synchronicity, the unbelievable and unthinkable occurred.

My book release party was the day before Valentine's Day, Feb '20. I felt the date was another synchronicity as my story was a love story although not like any most people expect. I was so happy to share the book with the community as I had spent so many years working on it. Finally, the completion of a considerable part of my life was coming to a close. I could see that as those doors closed, many new doors were beginning to open.

I was heading into my first weekend back at Art Shows after taking the winter off to finish my book. Andora would always come to all my shows with me. It was a pleasure and joy to have her sitting in her chair, smiling at everyone. She was incredible at luring people to the booth for attention, as she never seemed to get enough attention. I anticipate that she did a rather good job of increasing my sales by doing that. However, Andora truly loved being at the Art Shows with me, and I would make sure to spoil her for her successes.

I would set up her double chair princess throne with her purple princess pillow on one side and a comfy blanket on the other. During the hot months, she would even get ice packs under the blankets. I will admit that Andora was indeed a spoiled dog. However, she was always such a perfect angel, so I felt she earned it. She was so perfect that she would cheer up anyone who came to visit, and she had many friends at the art show who would come visit her. Andora loved every minute of it.

Personally, I was so excited to be able to display and share my book at the shows, finally. Mostly I was excited to share copies with my family of vendors. They had likely heard the most about my progress over the previous three years. That group alone probably purchased or traded me for more books than I sold at my book release party. It also ended up being one of the best weekends I've had as an orgonite art Vendor. That was until Sunday night as I was packing up the show to go home.

As I was packing up my car in the middle of the parking lot, Andora started to have an allergy attack. Many of the trees were pollinating, and she tends to have some respiratory issues when there is poor air quality. Fire smoke is the most irritating to her sensitive little Pomeranian throat. I had spent one evening a year earlier with her coughing the whole night because of local fires. Usually, Andora would have a cough or two during allergy season, but this evening would be different.

Andora went into a cough attack without any of her prescription medicines available. I had some CBD and throat herbs I was giving her all day, but it didn't seem to handle this most recent attack. I didn't have the Benadryl or the Oxy-Something the doctor gave us. It was practically the worst time for me to have this occur as I could have run to the store to grab the Benadryl if I wasn't in a rush to pack up and move my car. By the time I finished, I quickly hopped in the car for a quick eight-minute ride home, but we would have the cough continue most of the way. I started to have a real moment with her in the car.

I wanted to help her, but I felt so bad that I couldn't get it under control. I cried out for help and practically started crying. We thankfully made it home as my anxiety was through the roof. I hadn't had a moment like that in quite some time, and it was mostly

275

due to Andora's calm demeanor. Now that she wasn't calm and happy, it was throwing me off my game. Thankfully it would all change quickly after we made it to my room.

I quickly pulled out the medication from under the sink and began dosing her with the Benadryl first. By the time I gave her the 3rd dose, she was already showing signs of the cough stopping. I gave her a dose of the OXY medicine the doctor gave her for this specific instance. Thankfully, after 20 minutes, everything was back to normal. I was so relieved, and we set in for the night.

The next morning I gave Andora her supplements and some Benadryl when we woke up. We had to go on an errand that morning, and I figured she would be okay for the journey. Andora went everywhere with me, and I would never leave her at home. Otherwise, I would potentially face her wrath, something I never did after she got Danielle and me. A story I didn't get into much detail previously in the story.

It just so happened that when Danielle and I first got together, it made Andora very jealous. Apparently, Andora wasn't pleased with me at the time since we were not paying enough attention to her. The first outburst came with her taking a poo on my side of the bed. After rubbing her face in it, I put her in time out. She seemed to have gotten the message because the next thing she did was pee on my side of the bed and poo'd next to my side of the bed. Again she had her face rubbed in the pee, and yet again was put in time out. What happened next blew me away.

The following days we noticed that Andora started bleeding out of her little bottom. These incidents sent Danielle into a big concern as it worsened. We immediately scheduled an appointment with the VET. After a short time with Andora, the VET told us that they couldn't seem to find a problem. They explained to us that it appeared to be psychological! I couldn't believe it, and neither could Danielle. So we went home to figure out our next step.

We sat Andora down in her chair and proceeded to have a conversation with her. We explained that we were sorry that she felt ignored. We would make sure to give her much more attention, and that is exactly what we did. I was surprised to find the issues we were having with Andora disappeared immediately. Which eventually built the strong relationship that Andora and I carried through the process of losing Danielle.

Since Danielle's passing, Andora went everywhere with me. I always made sure to bring her usual needs in my bag, including the Benedryl this time. However, in this adventure, Andora would have another cough attack at the worst possible time. It would be about 20 minutes for me to get home to her OXY medicine. That always seemed to work no matter what, but I just didn't think that we would need it that morning. Plus, it was red liquid and would always get everywhere, so I just didn't think to bring it on a quick journey.

I got home that morning and gave her a few doses of the medication, which again helped immediately. That afternoon she ended up napping, and we went for our usual sunset walk after she woke up. The next 24 hours went smoothly. I was preparing for Ecstatic Dance that Tuesday and was super excited to do some dancing that day.

A romantic interest of mine was also going to be attending that evening. We had only met a week prior, but things were going well, inspiring me to make an extra special playlist. After our morning walk, I ended up giving Andora a couple of additional doses of Benadryl as she coughed several times on the hike. Nothing terrible but I just didn't want to let her keep aggravating her sensitive throat. After my shower, I realized that I might have given her too much medicine.

The best way to explain it was that she almost appeared drunk. I felt terrible about over-medicating her, so I kept checking on her constantly. She seemed fine as she was still giving kisses and smiling ear to ear. Like I said, the best way to explain it was she appeared drunk. I wasn't much concerned as the coughing issue was something we had dealt with in the past. It was just unlucky synchronicity to have the attacks occur when they did, but now everything seemed okay.

I ended up picking up an Angel on the side of the road that day, walking to the dance. It was perfect that I ended up picking up Gabriel, who was able to watch Andora as I put my pack together. She was still having a drunk moment, and that was all I could think was the problem. Considering she had a good run earlier that morning.

This would be the first time ever that Andora was not able to hike up to the dance spot on Cathedral Rock in two years of hosting Ecstatic Dance. I made the best of it, and for the first time I carried her up, little did I know how grateful I would be for that moment I was able to share.

At the dance, Andora just sat in her chair, smiling on her pillow just like she always does. She brought smiles to many faces just sitting there and even had several hikers say hello. Two people also commented that she appeared drunk, and I said I might have given her too much Benadryl. By the end of the dance, things were a little different. I was expecting her to be better, but she wasn't feeling like running around like usual.

I walked Andora down the mountain, holding her again, realizing that her breathing was becoming a little more shallow. It was a bit concerning, but sadly there wasn't anything I could do that late into the evening, so we went home. I gave her a little more medicine hoping that it might calm her down as she was just sitting up breathing. It almost seemed like she didn't want to lay down and close her eyes, but I couldn't explain it.

I kept petting her and saying hi to her every 15 to 20 minutes. I started to realize that I would likely need to take her to the Vet in the morning if this shallow breathing continued. I looked back from the computer, noticing that she had found a spot she found more comfortable, and I went and bundled her up. She just stayed there and seemed very content and didn't seem like she was suffering, just a bit uncomfortable, and now looking back, she was likely a little scared.

It truly was an honor to be by her side as she passed to the beyond quietly without my knowing. As I looked back, realizing that she had stopped breathing, I immediately rushed to pick her up. I cried out for her as I wanted her to come back to me. It was such a shock to me. A shock that I was not prepared for in the least. I continued to cry with her in my arms as thankfully, I was also home alone.

In another bought of Synchronicity, my romantic partner who had only manifested in my life a week prior would also manifest this evening. I called her in tears explaining the situation, and she, without missing a beat, offered to come over to be with me. I accepted the offer and thanked her for that. After that call, I knew I needed to call someone else. I had to tell my family and roommate.

My Dad was the only person that I wanted to call in my family. So that was the first person I called. It was a productive conversation as I was having a moment of, I should have's. Like I should have taken her to the Vet earlier that day, or I should have realized something was seriously wrong, or I should have been able to prevent this from happening. My Dad put many of those to rest as I always did everything I could for her. I loved Andora so much and never would have put her unknowingly at risk.

I asked my Dad at the end of the conversation to tell my mom and also call my sister. The reason was that I felt I was not in a place to talk to either of them. Both my mother and sister have the capacity to trigger me especially during moments of vulnerability. So in alignment with my strong beliefs, I asked if my Dad would personally tell both of them. It is important to me that he made the call, as I will further explain.

After discussing many of the topics of the book, I have come across a severe problem we face as a society. Too much, we have come to accept texting as a formal way to communicate, which is sadly delusional. The disconnection that texting creates is possibly the main reason that I highly recommend never texting a death. I repeat and reiterate that you should never text an important person's death to anyone for any reason. It's bad enough most people learn about it through social media, and calls should always be made before you create those posts. People deserve a phone call.

Texting a death is irresponsible, cowardly, and disrespectful to the person who passed. I believe people deserve the call for so many reasons, some of which I won't discuss. The main reason a call should be made is to respect the person in the Beyond. Considering the extensive proof that those people are still with us, it makes sense to appreciate them in life and death. To show them respect and be a respectful human by making the call. It is a respect to show that courage and strength during a time of hardship. People deserve respect in life and death, and please don't forget that.

The second reason why you make the call is for the person you are calling. Simply stated, the person that is getting the phone call deserves to receive the information in a way that is best for them. Merely asking them to sit down, or checking to make sure they are somewhere safe is crucial. Imagine all the places that a text can be received that could create another tragedy. People could be driving or anywhere someone doesn't have the support they need could lead to another tragedy. People deserve to have help during a moment of crisis.

I have several bad examples of this happening to me. While I wish my family had understood that message before Danielle's passing, I think I have made it clear my feelings on the subject, now. I have personally received three death texts from my mother in the past. All texts were horrible in the way they were received, as I will explain in two of the cases.

The first death text I received arrived on my phone four hours after my family had started a wake for my grandmother. I was so upset since my phone at the time was acting up, and text messages were not arriving on time. My family was unaware of this at the moment and didn't have the thought to call me. Sadly at that time, I was sitting at a restaurant depressed because I was a day late to my friend's graduation since I also received that text a day late. So this really hit it home when I didn't get a call from my family.

Only a week later, I would receive a text from my sister about my parents putting my dog Sophie to sleep without me even knowing. The text that told me my dog was dead was, "Sorry to hear about Sophie." Which my response was, "Did mom seriously put my dog to sleep without telling me?" The same Sophie who also appeared to Danielle. It was an interesting time for me because at that time, I started having interesting messages appear.

Over the several days that Sophie was in heaven without my knowledge, I started getting signs. The first was of a polar bear rock that was gifted to me. Then another bear sign in the form of a statue that my friend and I found, and finally, I opened a random book to a page all about bears. It would be shortly after my realizations that Sophie would start to appear to me as a giant white polar bear. It would be Sophie that made contact with Danielle before she passed in the form of an angel. It is far easier to cope, knowing that those that have passed are still with us.

However, I couldn't deny my sadness or anger at the time. I sadly received both of my parent's texts two weeks after they put Sophie to sleep. Those texts only fed my rage towards me not knowing, because they couldn't pick up the phone. The uncertainty of texts and when people receive texts is the main reason I ask for people to make the call. Also, please don't leave a message or text if you don't get through right away. Have that person call you back before dropping the info bomb.

I would learn this lesson the hard way from my own family. I had asked my Dad to call my sister in Thailand to let her know about Danielle's passing. He couldn't reach her initially, so he texted the message. Thankfully, I personally didn't learn this until a year after her passing, as I don't think I would have handled the situation healthily. While I was still upset, I was able to communicate to them just how angry I was. I gave them both my ultimatum about death texts.

I have stated to my family to Never, and I mean Never text me a death. Especially if you want me to attend the funeral of that person. At this point, my own father could pass, but out of respect for him, if I received a death text, I would not attend the funeral. I do that as respect to my father, as I feel it would be disrespectful to create a massive scene about why you don't text a death. It is that important of an issue to me and something I will stand up for, and

I'm not against a sit-out when it comes to a protest. It is a much healthier way to express my anger than to ruin someone's funeral because someone else couldn't respect that person. Make the call. I can't deny the sadness, guilt, and anger that comes with losing those you hold closest. It isn't something many of us deal with regularly, I hope. In those times of crisis, we are tested. We don't need to cause additional hurt and trauma because we can't face our own emotions. Those unable to communicate with others need, and I mean need to find people who are capable of passing the message on to everyone. I use my Dad, and he is excellent despite the past failures. Thankfully I feel my family understands my stance on the topic, and now I hope others can learn from our mistakes.

I was happy that my Dad called my sister when Andora passed. I didn't have the emotional strength to call anyone else except my roommate. She immediately knew what had happened as I was crying profusely. She was sorry that she couldn't be there, but I thanked her for her kind words and prepared for my friend to arrive. I needed emotional support more than ever.

Suddenly losing Andora had dramatically changed my life, and I couldn't deny that. It was a lot to process all at once, but still, processing the feelings helped me cope with the trauma. It hit me hard to realize that I no longer would be traveling all over town with her strapped to my chest. I could already feel the sadness in the city. I would have to say that with everything, the one thing I dreaded the most was having to tell everyone in town—especially Andora's closest friends.

I always used to say that Andora had more friends than I did in Sedona. Mostly because she had a whole collection of friends from her life with Danielle as a dance teacher's dog. Many girls would wave when we would see them, and Andora always made them smile. Andora would make almost everyone smile, and that was something else I couldn't believe was gone.

My temporary roommate at the time arrived home about an hour after my friend had arrived. Thankfully I had settled down by the time both of them came, as I was a big mess for the first 30 minutes after it happened. I couldn't believe what had happened and was still trying to process it through the trauma. It was difficult for me not to see the silver lining in the experience as she passed just after I finished my book, and after I met someone who would help me through the experience. My roommate had even mentioned that miraculous occurrence of someone coming into my life.

It even made me a little less worried about Andora acting out towards any potential romantic partners. I couldn't help but tell my friend about how Andora messed with me when I first started dating Danielle. I was a bit relieved not to have to worry about Andora's jealousy. Even Danielle said that Andora loved me more than her, so I can only imagine the jealousy could have been worse than when I entered the picture. Honestly, it was a huge relief not to have to worry about that future issue.

Now with the book finished, Andora was giving me a vast opportunity also to practice what I preach. Considering my book is all about how death isn't the end, it honestly couldn't have been more synchronistic. That revelation really helped me to see that there was more to this experience than merely Andora dying. It happened after dance nearly one year after Danielle made her presence known at Ecstatic Dance on the Rocks. It felt like it was meant to happen, and there was so much evidence pointing to that.

I would also state for the six months before my book release, about how Andora fixed my PTSD. In fact, I credit her with much of my recovery because of her perfect example. I would always aim to be more Andora like, and that striving made me happier, more loving, and incredibly calm. All things that don't exist when you have severe PTSD. I had thankfully overcome the disorder, and it was Andora who helped bring that new order into my life.

So as much as I loved having Andora in my life, she really had given me all the tools I needed to continue on my path of recovery. Now I would have to face those challenges without her as a physical crutch. However, as much as she wouldn't be a physical presence anymore, I couldn't escape her presence. The messages would be just as profound as the messages Danielle passed on after she went to the Beyond.

Two days after Andora's passing, I was invited to a Quan Yin channeling hosted by one of my close dance friends. A truly magnificent experience like no other. I showed up without Andora, and several people were immediately wondering why she didn't arrive, I initially skirted an answer. I had to gather them as I told them the news. We all shared a beautiful embrace before settling into our seats.

While we were waiting on several more people to arrive, we all started talking about the experience and how it coincided with my book release. My friend informed me another attendee was also writing a book, and her story was just as wild as mine. The woman's son had passed, and now she was in the process of writing a channeled book with him from the Beyond. Which I felt had occurred to some degree with Danielle and writing my book. I still think this book is divinely inspired.

Several minutes after that conversation, the other writer passed on another amazing angel message. She informed me that Danielle and Andora were enjoying dancing in heaven together. I was blown away by the news as I don't think we discussed much about dancing, and that would be the exact thing they would be doing together. It was indeed a powerful confirmation that Andora was doing good.

The channeling session started and continued for nearly two hours, which was a magnificent experience, to say the least. The host was a conduit for Quan Yin and her essence. To say my friend took on an entirely different demeanor would be an understatement, as she started to speak with a brand new vigor and cadence. It didn't feel like my friend anymore, but something more and with messages that still blow my mind.

It was Quan Yin's final message that left the most significant mark. I had made a soft answer on the side to a question she asked, which I had not done throughout the channeling. Now I was soloed out of the group for a message, and Quan Yin made it clear that she had a message specifically for me. She explained to me that there was a little being on her side that was doing really well and wanted to let me know she loved me. It shocked me to my core. Tears of Joy filled my eyes as I felt Andora's presence with me.

After the channeling, I would also discover that my friend, who I had picked up on the side of the road the day she passed, had another experience with Andora. He told me that he was playing frisbee with her during the channeling session. He confirmed another holy trinity of messages from the Beyond. This was one of the few experiences that I can honestly say compares to come of the lessons I have had from Danielle. I felt Danielle needed to pass those previous messages on to me to cement my beliefs. Andora was just making sure I didn't forget those lessons.

The biggest synchronicity that came with finishing my book came with a real opportunity to practice what I preach. The message I took from Quan Yin was not to focus on the negative. I realized how easy it could be to get sucked into the sadness involved in Andora's passing, to discuss the details or how bad I was doing. Most people responded with sincere regret or sadness when I delivered the news. I could tell immediately that it was going to be an uphill battle to focus on the positive. People love to dwell on the negative versus accentuate the positive, creating the opposite was my goal.

Surprisingly, I would show significant success in my new mission. As I delivered the message, I would explain how hard it is to be sad, considering Andora is still with us. I would tell people about the channeling session and restate that she is in a good place with her mother. I personally just have to close my eyes and think of her to have her cheer me up. I've also learned that at least six other people do the same thing, and she appears every time. Although, like her mother Danielle, she seems to do more work in dreams.

I've had many more people explain that Andora visits them in their dreams now. Stating it started happening shortly after her passing. Those joyful visits would confirm to others that she truly is still with us. I had thankfully had those experiences, too, although the first month was weird when I would realize it was just a dream. That part was challenging and uplifting at the same time, considering I don't have much control over my dreams, yet. Dreaming is a skill I am still cultivating.

That first week after her passing was a challenge as I could only handle telling a few people a day. It was a lot to manage my feelings while maintaining the demeanor I desired, and it would take real strength on my part. The strength to not get into the details of her passing, or dwell on the sadness. So many feed off that energy without ever realizing they are just perpetuating those feelings. I didn't want to feel sad every time I talked to someone, and honestly, neither did Andora.

The last thing Andora wanted for me was to be sad about her passing. In fact, every time I tried to be sad, she would appear in my mind to remind me that she was still here. She even talks in the voice I gave her on her book chapter videos, which is even funnier for me. Do you think it is easy to be sad with a helium voice Pomeranian cheering you up? Honestly, it is impossible, and I tried.

Life was still pretty amazing for me as I know "All Dogs Go To Heaven." I now had Andora as my newest guardian angel. She was with her mother, who had passed on other messages that she was also doing great in heaven. They were both doing an outstanding job of looking out for me by passing important messages along. I now felt there was so much to look forward to with the completion of my book. Now that one chapter closed, it meant that another was opening. My life would forever be changed by having Andora in my life, and now I had to face the community.

The first week was also strange because I realized just how much time I spent with Andora. We usually spent an hour minimum everyday taking walks. I usually had to take her out for 2 to 3 ad-

284

ventures with one of those always being a bike ride. Andora loved the bike rides more than anything else in the world and would spin donuts for up to 10 minutes to express her happiness. Now I didn't have to spend all that time getting her ready, and taking her supplies with me.

Andora was as close to having a child a without actually having one. The only nice thing being is that I could leave her alone without being a neglectful parent, but truthfully I rarely did that. So now I found my life to be far more manageable from the standpoint of merely going on errands or taking a short trip. I found Andora to be so much lighter in spirit. Including not having to carry her 15-pound chair up the mountain every Tuesday for Ecstatic Dance on the Rocks. I couldn't deny the ease my new life was providing.

It was hard not to feel guilty about the joy I felt from not having to carry an extra 20 pounds up a mountain. It was even harder to accept that everything that I was planning on doing for the following several months would be easier without her. I had an employee helping me to do two art shows every weekend, starting only two weeks after Andora's passing. It was going to be a massive challenge to do that with Andora coming along for the adventure. However, I also didn't expect for the "Great Pause" to happen after my first double art show weekend.

Although even there, I can't deny that Andora somehow knew that the world was about to hit the fan. It was even more eye-opening as I realized that many of the foods that she liked were in short supply. I can't deny the synchronicity. To top that off, I don't know how I would have been able to take her to Tuesday dance with the lockdown closing the closest trailhead. The new parking location would be an easy hour plus hike at her stop to smell the roses pace. I still swear she knew something was about to happen.

I feel that everything happens for a reason, but sometimes it takes time to see the real reasons. If it was all to get me to write this book, then I feel the universe was successful. Everything that happened from start to finish was one big series of synchronicities. From the moment I met Danielle to the moment, she passed six months and one day after we were married. I can't even imagine the odds of her picking the day we were married as the day she was also diagnosed with cancer. To have Andora pass only four days after the book release, followed by a trinity of messages to confirm everything was okay, made the experience feel otherworldly.

Having a connection to those who are in heaven is mind-blowing, to say the least. The experiences could quickly redefine someone's current reality, as it did for me. If realizing that death is not the end, is the one thing that people walk away with than I feel successful in writing this book. If I can help people to understand that the struggles of life are there to help us grow, I feel doubly fruitful. Everything on the planet has a purpose, and it is up to us to find the purpose through our actions.

I also feel a significant purpose of mine was to expose the criminal for-profit medical industry for the actions taken during my wife's illness. If God wanted cancer gone, he or she definitely pissed the right person off. My mission is technically just beginning as I start to share my experience.

The complete lack of common sense when caring for the health of an individual is pervasive in our medical establishment as I learned. Considering doctors are not required to learn about nutrition, I think that should throw up some red flags for most people. The statistics show less than 5% of doctors are educated in diet, and even the doctors we met showed their complete ignorance.

Instead, I discovered doctors are only pushing dangerous chemicals as cures while denying the failures of those very same treatments. If you doubt me, I recommend doing a little research into vaxxines, as there is a $100,000 reward for anyone that can prove they are safe. All the other failures aside, I believe my wife is one of the medical system's greatest failures and why the system needs to be dismantled, and the people in charge, immediately jailed. It all must end as the worldwide plandemic is also showing everyone how dangerous these people indeed can be.

We can then start by rebuilding a Wholistic Medical Model that includes everything that heals people. No longer will alternative treatments be forbidden from coverage or by doctor ignorance. We would have people who want to inform the public about their health, for sole the purpose of keeping people healthy.

Profits should be removed from healthcare, and I actually believe we should only pay doctors when we are healthy. I feel the incentive to keep us healthy would then be the priority. Subsidize the chronic illnesses that can't be cured, and we would all save billions in health care costs. All I'm trying to say is that there are better ways to do things, and I think we should approach health care differently because people need their rights back.

People should have the option to choose and not be coerced to choose based on what is best for the doctor's pocketbook. Everything our doctors are doing to us is for profit, pushing long term treatments over inexpensive cures. I think I discuss this issue enough in the book, but can't reiterate the importance.

I have personally listened to a dozen "radical" doctors discuss how many of the health problems we face, originate in the gut. Some "radical" doctors are even stating that all health problems arise in the gut. I personally don't know if diet and food are the cause of all issues, but since most doctors aren't even educated on the subject, I would question their knowledge immediately, and trust those who are questioning. I don't know WHO we should listen to about nutrition, but I do know it definitely should not be our politicians or their cohorts.

It is our politicians that pushed most of the regulations on the medical industry in the first place. The fact that there is a law requiring doctors to tell patients that they will die for not choosing to do chemo, radiation, or surgery is both criminal, and through the nocebo effect, killing people every day. Again, if all medications are required to beat the placebo test, then I would expect doctors to understand the power of the nocebo effect. Ignoring the nocebo effect is medical science showing its ultimate ignorance about the ability of our mind to heal or hurt.

Lastly, on a lighter note, if I can inspire people to show proper action when assisting the elderly or dying, then I feel I have accomplished something genuinely magnificent. Even if it is just one person I inspire to get up and completely change the way we do things, then I feel that is possibly the greatest achievement of all. We all have the power to inspire and change the world. Now, who will you inspire?

Thank you, Danielle "Alexandra" Elise Claire and Andora Wells Luxemburg St. Claire Strabala, for inspiring and assisting me in writing and finishing this book.

Acknowledgments

I want to thank Rose and her parents for supporting us in all the ways they did. I will forever be grateful for their generosity. I also want to thank the team of women who stepped up to be there for Danielle when she needed them. I am thankful for everyone else who tried to help us in our endeavor. I want to thank my father for being there for me all my life, because without his support I know I would have had many more challenges to endure. My gratitude goes out to everyone who has helped to make this book a reality through donations and energetic support. Thank you to everyone who continues to share and spread the message. Thank you for all the dance that has manifested in my life. Most of all I thank my Late Wife Danielle Elise Claire for everything she has given me and continues to bless me with. Todah Rabah. הדות

www.ingramcontent.com/pod-product-compliance
Lightning Source LLC
Chambersburg PA
CBHW051856090426
42811CB00003B/357